THE SACRED WEAPON

An Introduction to Pope's Satire

The Sacred Weapon

An Introduction to Pope's Satire

Martin Blocksidge

The Book Guild Ltd.
Sussex, England

The Book Guild Ltd.
25 High Street,
Lewes, Sussex.

First published 1993

Set in Baskerville
Typesetting by Southern Reproductions (Sussex)
East Grinstead, Sussex.
Printed in Great Britain by
Antony Rowe Ltd.
Chippenham, Wiltshire.

A catalogue record for this book is
available from the British Library

ISBN 0 86332 830 X

CONTENTS

ACKNOWLEDGEMENTS

Pope is the most companionable and amusing of poets, but it is his particular tragedy to seem hidden beneath a huge weight of contemporary allusion and obscure literary reference. Equally, his undoubted aggressiveness against his enemies can often be mistaken for gratuitous rancour and bitterness.

It was through trying to rehabilitate Pope for a modern audience that this book came to be written. I have therefore cause to thank my students in Oxfordshire, London and Surrey with whom I have greatly enjoyed reading and discussing Pope over a number of years, and whose needs caused the book to take shape in the mind.

It might well have remained in the mind had it not been for the generosity of two governing bodies. Firstly, I have to thank the Headmaster and Governors of the Royal Grammar School, Guildford, for giving me sabbatical leave during the Summer Term of 1988. I am equally grateful to the Principal and Fellows of Lady Margaret Hall, Oxford, for electing me to a Schoolteacher Studentship for that term and thus providing ideal circumstances for both reading and writing to be carried out as well as much moral support at just the times when it was needed. Additionally, my friend and colleague James Hansford merits an especial debt of gratitude for believing that I ought to write this book, and for repeatedly saying so. No record of my intellectual life over recent years would be complete without acknowledging him.

Pope was the most dutiful of sons and there is a consequent poignancy in the fact that one person who was eagerly awaiting the publication of this book did not live to see it. I dedicate the book to the memory of my mother.

Martin Blocksidge
Guildford, March 1992.

A NOTE ON TEXTS AND SOURCES

All quotations from Pope's poems in the text are taken from the one volume Twickenham edition of 1963, edited by John Butt. This is not only the best, fullest and most authoritative text, it is also an accessible one to students, being available in paperback.

Butt's edition is, however, an abridgement of the original seven volume Twickenham edition (1939-1961) and it is from this edition that all references to editorial material (including Pope's own notes on his poems) are taken.

Pope's correspondence was edited by George Sherburn (five volumes, 1956), but I have, in general, when quoting from the letters, directed readers to the more easily accessible secondary sources where the letters are quoted. A complete bibliography can be found at the end of the book.

1

A WARFARE UPON EARTH

The Life of a Satirist

Pope has always been a controversial figure, liable to arouse strong feelings in his readers. These strong feelings were as much a part of his life as they have been of his reputation since his death. For a man who, in his life, celebrated friendship and was esteemed highly by a range of eminent and discerning people, his posthumous reputation has been defined largely in terms of his apparent enmities and hatreds. He has had many detractors over the centuries, particularly among those readers who enjoy trying to score moral points over authors.[1]

Superficially, it is easy to see why Pope can produce hostility: his satire can be cruel, blunt and unforgiving. It frequently directs itself at individuals who are, as it were, dismembered and left bleeding. Several of Pope's contemporaries have come down to posterity with reputations permanently crippled as a result of Pope's efforts on their behalf. It is difficult not to see the fulminatory nature of some of his writing as excessive and gratuitous, and it is tempting to seek some kind of explanation for his aggression.

A few facts about Pope are well-known and can, by those who choose, be used in easy evidence against him. As a result of a tubercular illness contracted in his boyhood, Pope's growth was severely stunted. He attained a height of little more than four feet. The long-term effects of the illness were severe and inhibiting. They involved curvature of the spine, weakness of the heart and lungs, frequent fevers, and inflammation of the eyes. He was no stranger to pain, exhaustion and the sick room, and was obviously denied many of the pleasures of a 'normal' life, not least as far as mobility and sexual relationships were concerned.[2] Additionally, as the son of two Catholic converts, he was debarred by his religion from the normal processes of education and advancement. Technically Catholicism was illegal and attracted penalties. Although these were often not very systematically enforced, there were perpetual reminders: Catholics were subject to double taxation, and were not allowed to own property. They were associated with political subversion.

Hence, a traditional view goes, Pope had much to be bitter about. He was as twisted psychologically as he was physically. That he wrote satire with such malicious glee was hardly surprising. He was one of nature's outsiders and thus easy prey to rancour and jealousy.

This reading of Pope has always recommended itself to those who take a one plus one attitude to literary biography, and look for easy correspondences between authors' works and their lives. However, to see Pope as the frustrated dwarf venting his spleen on the human race is to ignore the bulk of the known facts about him and to devalue the ease, sociability and sheer busyness of his life. The Pope who emerges from the hands of his biographers is a complex, more rounded and more civilized figure than the caricature who has been appropriated by those who dislike him. Indeed, in examining the facts of Pope's life one is more often struck by its normality and energy than by any kind of pathological bitterness.

It is interesting that many of the least flattering opinions and images of Pope were constructed during his lifetime by his own contemporaries. Where satire was concerned, Pope was much more written about than writing. Think of this, from Edmund Curll in 1728:

> A little scurvy, purblind elf;
> Scarce like a Toad, much less himself
> Deform'd in shape, of Pygmy stature;
> A proud, conceited, peevish, creature
> The stinking venom flows around
> And nauseous slaver hides the ground.[3]

Edmund Curll knew and had reason to dislike Pope: most of those who wrote against him in his own lifetime had never met him. They wrote against him because they were hired for the task. Pope was born into a literary world whose apparent bad manners take some understanding.

He lived from 1688 to 1744. Though Catholic in background, there is little evidence that he himself was particularly devout, but the allegiances of his parents determined much about his early development. In particular, he was denied access to university and received relatively little by way of formal schooling. Like many a literary figure before and since he was blessed with the advantage of a bookish father. Mr Pope senior was a retired linen dealer. The poet had access to Mr Pope's library, and was given every encouragement by him to follow his poetic ambitions. Having left London, the family settled at Binfield in Windsor Forest, where the young Alexander easily took to an isolated, precocious existence. As his older half-sister put it '. . . he did nothing but write and read'. Significantly, in view of the shape his subsequent work was to take, he imitated English poets and translated Latin ones. His father took an interest in his development insisting always on the highest standards of technical accuracy. Pope acquired an assured poetic voice at a very early age.[4]

Like many precocious children before and since Pope found himself more frequently in the company of adults. His first companion was a local landowner and retired diplomat, Sir William Trumbull, with whom he used to ride in Windsor Forest. Trumbull was a man of literary interests too, beguiled by the talented boy. 'The little creature is my darling more and more', he was to say, showing the mixture of pride and patronage with which the older generation soon came to view the strangely gifted little figure from the country.

Trumbull had literary acquaintances in the capital, and soon Pope's fame had spread widely amongst the venerable generation of literateurs to whom the old gentleman had been able to introduce him. Pope was never to forget this early encouragement from the senior members of the literary establishment:

Granville the polite,
And knowing Walsh, would tell me I could write;
Well-natur'd Garth inflam'd with early praise,
And Congreve lov'd, and Swift endur'd my Lays;
The Courtly Talbot, Somers, Sheffield, read,
Ev'n mitred Rochester would nod the head,
And St John's self (great Dryden's friends before)
With open arms receiv'd one Poet more.
(An Epistle to Dr Arbuthnot 135-142)

It is not surprising that Pope became enormously confident of his poetic abilities. He had had blessings and status conferred upon him by some eminent men. He had written a set of four *Pastorals.* They were eventually published in 1709 but had been originally composed when Pope was about sixteen. 'Granville, the polite' was subsequently to write of their author that ' . . . he is not above Seventeen or Eighteen Years of Age, and promises Miracles: If he goes on as he has begun, in the Pastoral way, as Virgil first try'd his Strength, we may hope to see English Poetry vie with the Roman . . .'.[5] The genre of pastoral poetry, with its rather stylized presentation of shepherds and flocks and warbling pipes, may well strike a modern reader as insipid, not to say, derivative. Pope's *Pastorals* are hardly among his most exciting works. But Granville made an important point when he compared Pope with Virgil. Virgil's earliest surviving poetic efforts were in the pastoral vein. In the hierarchy of importance which traditional classical taste attributed to various poetic kinds, pastoral came relatively low. It was the genre with which a poetic career might start. Virgil subsequently became celebrated for a great epic. Hence much was being said about Pope's promise.

The *Pastorals* themselves were printed by Jacob Tonson in one of his *Miscellanies*, which is to say a substantial volume containing work by several poets. Apart from other work by Pope and some by Swift, this edition actually included another set of pastoral poems by Ambrose Philips. There was clearly no reason why the two authors had to become rivals, but rivals they eventually became. Pope's initial response to Philips's work was cordial and appreciative, but when Philips, over the next few years received rather more praise from the literary establishment (he was something of a toady) than Pope himself, it is not surprising that Pope felt hurt. If his pride in his own abilities seems highly developed, we have to admit that Philips's poetic reputation was very soon to sink without trace. Indeed he was to gain, as a result of his writing of pastoral verse, the unflattering nickname of 'Namby Pamby' Philips. It is difficult to take him very seriously as an author, but he clearly had influential friends and a rivalry between the two authors was encouraged. Within a very few years Philips was reported as having described Pope in conversation as '. . . the little crooked bastard . . .'[6] One notices the irrelevance of the criticism and the way in which the man rather than the work is attacked. It was a pattern which was to continue.

In 1711, at the age of twenty-three, Pope published his *Essay on Criticism.* It is a remarkable poem for a young man of not much more than undergraduate age, not simply in terms of its technical accomplishment, but for its assured, assertive voice and its rather reactionary defence of classical values. It partly provides a reading of literary history, and partly a guide as to how literature should be read. Its tone is often advisory, and more than a little omniscient:

> You then whose Judgment the right Course wou'd steer,
> Know well each ANCIENT's proper Character,
> His Fables, Subject, Scope, in ev'ry Page,
> Religion, Country, Genius of his Age:
> Without all these at once before your Eyes,
> Cavil you may, but never Criticise.
> Be Homer's Works your Study and Delight,
> Read them by Day, and meditate by Night
> (118-125)

Chiefly, though, Pope seeks to define the manifold qualities which he thinks the proper critic of poetry should possess. He does not mince his words in talking about the shortcomings of certain contemporary critics:

> Some ne'er advance a Judgment of their own,
> But catch the spreading Notion of the Town;
> They reason and conclude by Precedent,

And own stale Nonsense which they ne'er invent.
Some judge of Author's names, not Works, and then
Nor praise nor blame the Writings but the Men.
(408-13)

A modern reader is free to be exhilarated by this zestfully opinionated poem but it is not surprising that Pope managed to ruffle a few contemporary feathers, in particular those belonging to a prominent literary critic called John Dennis. Dennis's public manner was both grave and choleric. He was much given in conversation to the use of the exclamation 'tremendous'. This finds its way into Pope's poem. Dennis appears under the pseudonym 'Appius':

Twere well, might Criticks still this Freedom take;
But Appius reddens at each word you speak,
And stares Tremendous! with a threatening Eye
Like some fierce tyrant in old tapestry.
(584-7)

It says something for the precarious nature of the literary life of this period, that Dennis the guardian of literary propriety was to fall on hard times and die in destitution. But he enjoyed his power while he had it, and was unamused by this young upstart Pope. He reddened indeed, and went straight into print:

> 'As there is no Creature in Nature so venomous, there is nothing so stupid and so impotent as a hunch-back'd Toad . . .'[7]

And so on. Again, it was the shape of things to come. Pope's reference to Dennis in *The Essay on Criticism* was mischievous and gratuitous. It was teasingly hidden behind a nickname (a character from an unsuccessful tragedy of Dennis's own). Yet it provoked a torrent of immoderate abuse. Part of the pattern of Pope's literary life had been decided. This particular kind of situation was to be replayed numerous times.

'The life of a Wit', Pope was to remark with some world-weariness in the Preface to his 1717 collection of poems 'is a warfare upon earth.' He was then still in his twenties, and the worst was to come, but it certainly seemed as though the precociously gifted and highly assured young poet possessed just the right qualities to irritate other labourers in the field. Pope was never, as a literary figure, quite able to rest comfortably again. There was always controversy in the air, though Pope's response to it was seldom predictable; sometimes he held his fire, other times he found means of counter-attack.

For example he was unable to let the apparent animosities with Philips and Dennis pass. There is no reason to believe that Pope felt any great personal hatred for these men, but he was never too happy when being sniped at by people whose literary abilities he felt to be less than his own. He disdained the kind of rank abuse that he had himself suffered from Dennis, in favour of something more subtle. His responses were strategic, indirect, and involved making himself as invisible as possible. They centre on two particular documents, both of which shed as great a light on the literary habits of the age as they do on Pope himself.

The first of them returned to the question of pastoral poetry and the person of Ambrose Philips. It was perhaps inevitable that Pope, with a growing number of poetic successes to his credit (the first version of *The Rape of the Lock* had appeared in 1712) was going to become uneasy about being bracketed with a man of such obviously inferior talent. Indeed when Pope subsequently came to write his *Peri Bathous or the Art of Sinking in Poetry,* a satirical text book of how not to write, Philips was several times quoted.

Matters came to a head in the early months of 1713 when Richard Steele had published in his periodical *The Guardian,* a series of essays on pastoral poetry. They had, as was customary, appeared anonymously and this made it easy for Pope to submit an additional essay of his own. Whoever had written the preceding essays (probably Thomas Tickell) had shown no great desire to praise Pope. Indeed his own *Pastorals* were scarcely mentioned, though those of Philips frequently were. Pope consequently felt moved to produce one of his characteristically ambivalent pieces, an essay on Pastoral, written in that indulgent tone which the practised reader of Pope inevitably finds suspicious, apparently praising Philips to the skies, and only at the end involving 'Mr Pope . . . whose eclogues . . . are by no means *Pastorals* but *something better.'* They were mentioned alongside those of the best Greek and Roman practitioners.[8]

The second foray of 1713 was directed at Dennis who had rushed into print with some deprecatory comments about Joseph Addison's tragedy *Cato*, then enjoying considerable public success because of its perceived relevance to current political issues. Pope responded with a document which apparently criticized someone else. *The Narrative of Doctor Robert Norris, Concerning the Strange and Deplorable Frenzy of Mr John Dennis.* Norris was an infamous 'quack' psychiatrist, and Pope's pamphlet, in dialogue form, presented a mock examination of Dennis by Norris, in which the former becomes obsessed to the point of gibbering lunacy by 'Cato's' infringement of literary propriety. It has considerable potential as a theatrical sketch and is very close to the world of modern television satire.[9]

The indirectness of both these pamphlets has been already noted: in the first one the satire rests in the skilful manipulation of an apparently inappropriate tone; in the second, the author disappears from the scene completely, leaving his fiction to do the work. Both these strategies were quintessential characteristics of Jonathan Swift whose friendship with Pope had begun about this time. Swift was twenty-one years older than Pope and his relationship with the younger man could partly be seen as an extension of those relationships with literary father figures which Pope had already enjoyed. This relationship, though, rapidly became one between equals and collaborators. Swift was an Irish clergyman who had spent several years in England during the reign of Queen Anne pursuing patronage and involving himself with Tory politics. Indeed, he had hoped to enlist Pope as a political writer for the same cause. Pope's relish of polemic was considerably less well-developed than Swift's, and it was not a role in which he could easily see himself. Swift liked clubs and was the leading light in the foundation of the Scriblerus Club in 1713, to which Pope also belonged in company with John Arbuthnot, John Gay, William Fortescue and Thomas Parnell.

John Arbuthnot (to be especially commemorated in Pope's

Epistle of 1735) was physician to Queen Anne and came from a family loyal to the House of Stuart. This, together with Swift's background in pamphleteering, and Pope's praise of the Queen in his poem *Windsor Forest,* appeared to give the club a political focus but its purposes quickly changed to the collaborative production of satire. The importance of the club to English literary history is out of all proportion to its actual functioning as a club, lasting as it did only a matter of months, before the death of the Queen in 1714 sent Swift, complainingly, back to Ireland, all hopes of advancement lost, and removed Arbuthnot from his official residence at St James's where the meetings were probably held. Various 'Scriblerian' texts, normally the work of diverse hands, have survived, most notably Pope's *The Key to the Lock,* a mock-hostile criticism of his own *Rape of the Lock*; *Three Hours After Marriage,* a farce subsequently performed in 1717; *Peri Bathous* which was published in 1728, and *The Memoirs of Martinus Scriblerus* whose publication Pope was to oversee in 1741. More importantly, Swift's *Gulliver's Travels* and Pope's *Dunciad* were both the ultimate result of Scriblerus Club initiatives, and the genesis of the latter poem, along with its Scriblerian indebtedness is discussed in greater length in Chapter 3.[10]

That Pope and Swift had a stimulating effect on each other cannot be denied. Pope was to remind Swift of all this in his dedication to *The Dunciad.* Likewise, a certain common ground can be discerned between this poem and *Gulliver's Travels* both of which in their own way seek to ridicule 'the works of the unlearned'. Nevertheless, the association was cut short by events, and seminal though Swift's influence on Pope was to be, Pope was not to return to sustained satirical writing for some time, though one small foray in particular is worthy of note, concerning as it does the publisher and bookseller Edmund Curll who has already been referred to.

Curll, perhaps more than anyone else, embodies all those qualities of the contemporary literary world which Pope came most to dislike, and it is largely through Curll's activities that Pope's relationship with that literary world came to be defined. Curll was the very epitome of all that is meant by the term 'Grub Street'. First and foremost, of course, this term denotes a specific location in London. Grub Street, hard by Fleet Ditch and other insalubrious parts of the city was the home of the 'hackney writer', which is to say the writer who wrote for money at a customer's request. His was not a respectable calling. For a start, the income was precarious and the debtors' gaol never far away. Secondly, it was considered professionally demeaning for an author to earn his living by his writing. A gentleman obviously didn't need to, though for the less fortunate the age of private patronage had largely passed. The lowest echelons of the literary world were fast becoming part of a vigorous economy in which a man of Edmund Curll's entrepreneurial confidence and capacity for self-advertisement could do very well, especially if he wasn't afraid of dishonesty and deceit.[11]

Curll had an eventful life: imprisoned three times for his unprincipled publishing activities, occasionally having to go to ground to avoid recriminations, and possibly acting as some kind of informer for Prime Minister Walpole. For all this his business prospered hugely. He 'kept' a number of hackney writers of his own, including at various times John Oldmixon, Charles Gildon and John Breval, all of whom were to find their way eventually into Pope's *Dunciad,* and all of whom were available to write whenever they were asked. There were, of course, many other practitioners of exactly the same sort. In an age in which the concept of copyright hardly existed, they obviously had considerable freedom, which a corrupt bookseller like Curll could exploit to the full.[12]

Basically, Curll specialized in forgeries. These might take one of several forms. He might pass off inferior work by one of his own authors under the name of Swift or Pope or Gay; he particularly specialized in the publication of scandalous biographies or wills and testaments of the recently deceased which, as Arbuthnot quipped, added a new terror to death. Additionally there were 'keys' purporting to explain recently published works, letters by supposedly famous people, and historical treatises on subjects such as flogging or impotence, in which (quite arbitrarily it would appear) historical and contemporary figures were implicated.

Pope and Curll crossed swords for the first time in 1716, over a relatively trivial issue. Curll had published a collection of *Court Poems,* probably written by Lady Mary Wortley Montagu but passed off by Curll as the work of Pope. Pope's initial response to this was non-literary. He asked his publisher Lintot to effect a meeting with Curll, and then administered an emetic to the unsuspecting guest. Even in an age which greatly relished and often practised practical jokes, this was a somewhat childish act, perhaps, but Pope was to make a great deal of capital out of it subsequently, not only by knowing references to the incident in *The Dunciad* and *An Epistle to Dr Arbuthnot,* but also in a pamphlet, published anonymously of course, called *A Full and True Account of a Horrid and Barbarous Revenge by Poison on the Body of Mr Edmund Curll,* in which an exceptionally lurid (and doubtless greatly exaggerated) account of the event was given, rather in the style of *The Narrative of Dr Robert Norris.*

Curll did not have to do very much thinking to identify the author of this piece, and the consequences were obvious. Attacks on Pope became an ever growing part of his publishing business. In particular, Pope's translation of Homer's *Iliad* was beginning to appear and Curll had abundant opportunities to torpedo 'Mr Pope's Popish translation . . .' as best he and his hireling authors could. Pope thus became one of Curll's leading literary butts for the next twenty years. When the first version of *The Dunciad* was published in 1728, Curll was quick to produce a so-called 'Key' to it, which pronounced Pope ' . . . a scoundrel and a blockhead, who has, at one time or another betrayed or abused almost everyone he has conversed with . . . Yet now he kicks and winces because his arrogance and insolence have been exposed . . .' A few years later, Curll was to advertise a *Life of Pope* which would seek to demonstrate and explain '. . . that Natural Spleen which constitutes Mr Pope's temperament . . .'[14]

Again we see the same situation being replayed and replayed just as it had been during the time of Pope's contretemps with Dennis. A cantankerous and irreverent gesture by Pope, who was prepared usually to be amused before he was offended by the works of Grub Street, would provoke an immoderate and abusive response, always quick to attack the person rather than the writing, and to do so in rather predictable ways. Obviously Pope himself was not above employing Grub Street methods against those whom he disliked, but the difference in kind and degree is always noticeable. Pope's contributions are high-spirited and marked by genuine wit. Their targets are clear and their grounds of criticism at root moderate. They keep their distance from gratuitous insult. In literary terms they are invariably more sophisticated than the attacks which he had to suffer himself.

Even so, they highlight a curious contradiction in Pope who, on the one hand held a most exalted view of literature and the poet's calling, yet on the other was prepared to use literature for the most frivolous of purposes. His next major political undertaking was his translation of Homer, a task which could hardly be entered into lightly. It is unlikely that Pope saw himself as 'the English Homer', as his enemies liked to think, but in offering a translation of the classical poet whom he most venerated, Pope was setting himself up as the voice through which Homer might speak to the eighteenth century. He was also, presumably, conscious of the weight of Dryden's translation of Virgil in the previous generation. If the greatest poet of that age could translate Virgil, then, by implication, the greatest poet of the next could translate Homer.

His translation of Homer's *Iliad* was to occupy him for a further six years, the task being finally completed in 1720. After this, he translated the *Odyssey,* which he finished in 1725, the year in which he was also to publish an edition of the works of Shakespeare.

These three ventures accounted for a decade of Pope's creative life. He was, at various times, to complain of the drudgery involved, also to claim that he no longer wished to write poetry. Yet the years which were given to these works of translation and editing were the years in which the pattern of Pope's poetic life became set. In 1717 he took the lease of a villa at Twickenham where he lived with his widowed mother until her death in 1733, and his own eleven years later. A thorough-going programme of building and gardening ensued so that the villa came to embody all Pope's tastes in architecture and landscaping, and indeed was to be something of a showpiece, as well as a symbol of his own poetic eminence. He began to live the life of a wealthy country gentleman. This life was to be largely supported by the considerable fortune which Pope's translations of Homer were to make for him. His relationships with Grub Street were certainly made no easier by this huge commercial success. For one whose enmity towards hackney writers was so acute, his own acquisition of wealth as a result of a literary undertaking has its irony. To the hackney writers, endeavouring to catch as many pennies as they could, it was particularly provoking. And Pope was prepared to be open about the matter, for example in his *Imitation of the Second Epistle of the Second Book of Horace* (1736):

> But (thanks to Homer) since I live and thrive,
> Indebted to no Prince or Peer alive . . .
>
> (68-9)

It is not therefore very surprising that Pope's Homer should have proved one of the most controversial undertakings of his career, for by the time he came to work on it, Grub Street was more than ready to make as much trouble over it as was possible. We have already seen some evidence of Curll's early efforts. Others followed, none more significant than the rival translation by Thomas Tickell which was probably embarked upon with Addison's support and encouragement, and which showed the way in which literary production at this time was influenced by the politics of personalities and factions.

Other criticisms were voiced, too: in particular that Pope in setting himself up as the English Homer was aiming above his station; and that, not having a university education he was not sufficient of a scholar to do the job properly. Indeed the fact that he employed two young poets, William Broome and Elijah Fenton, as assistants seemed to indicate this very point. By the time Pope was working on *The Odyssey,* there was no shortage of Grub Street writing to suggest that Pope's Homer was not his own.

His foray into Shakespearean scholarship was a mistake. Pope was ill-equipped for the task from the start. His knowledge of Elizabethan theatre in general was thin, and his understanding of Shakespeare's language and usage was limited.[15] It was not at all difficult for Lewis Theobald in his pamphlet *Shakespeare Restored: Or A Specimen of the Many Errors As well Committed as Unamended by Mr Pope in his late Edition of this Poet* to point out these shortcomings. Theobald's attack was of a different sort from the ones Pope had been used to receiving. It was a moderate document from a more learned man (who had reputedly read 800 Elizabethan plays) and was less personal in its tone than most attacks from Grub Street had been. Perhaps this was why it irritated Pope so much: its criticisms were sound and would stick. Although it was in the right, more than any of the other attacks hitherto received, it was the one that needed a reply.

The Dunciad appeared in the month of Pope's fortieth birthday, and was perhaps the major literary watershed of his life, for the direction of his writing certainly changed thereafter. By 1728 Pope had a considerable reputation as a poet. This reputation was based on the early *Pastorals, An Essay on Criticism, Windsor Forest,* the rather grandiosely entitled *Works* of 1717, which included the final version of *The Rape of the Lock,* and the Homer translations. With the exception of *The Rape*... all of these undertakings were entirely serious, and none of them had addressed itself in any way to Pope's critics and opponents. Satire had not been the dominant mode of Pope's poetry, indeed his output had been of a rather more lofty kind. Such isolated ripostes as he had chosen to make Grub Street, had been made in pamphlets and in prose. If Pope was to grow tired of being a butt for less refined and capable authors then he was not in a hurry to show it. We know that he kept many of the pamphlets written against him in bound volumes for his own reference, but to see the author (as many of his contemporaries wished to) as perpetually spitting venom against his enemies is a gross simplification. He waited for his moment, and it was the coming together of a number of different considerations which brought out the first version of *The Dunciad* in 1728. The poem, comprehensively savage though it is, is no doggerel. It is multiply allusive and exceptionally wide-ranging using a language dense with literary suggestiveness against a mighty cast of rogues and rabble. Pope, the reader feels, has taken on the whole of Grub Street man by man.

For all its literary sophistication the poem hit its victims hard, and consequently provoked even more of the kind of caterwauling from Grub Street that it had been calculated to stop. Pope was being naive when he wrote to Swift that 'This poem will rid me of those insects.'[16] It didn't. It merely increased hostilities, to the extent that Lord Oxford was to comment to Swift that 'Pope stands by himself *Athanasius contra mundum.'* His half-sister Magdalen reported that Pope never dared to venture out without the company of his Great Dane and with pistols in his pockets.[17]

Yet it was in the years following the publication of *The Dunciad* that Pope began to present himself in his work, not as the literary hostage beseiged by the rabble, but as the man of culture, retired from the fray into an innocent country world reminiscent of the Roman poet Horace's Sabine farm. The picture which it is very easy to construct of Pope in permanent discord with the lesser mortals of the literary world does not quite fit the facts of the next few years, which were certainly Pope's busiest. Much of his writing, it must be said, had a satirical thrust, but the fertility of Pope's mind in the early 1730s meant that he had a great deal of other work on hand too.

The Dunciad was in effect the apotheosis of Pope's Scriblerian satire, which is to say satire directed against the world of writing. He was to return to the poem in 1742 and 1743 in order to extend and adapt it, but with the important exceptions of *An Epistle to Dr Arbuthnot* and parts of *To Augustus,* Pope's work from now on was to concern itself with broader issues and take a much more explicitly moral stance.

Much of the poetry of the first half of the decade takes its colouring from *An Essay on Man,* which was published in instalments in 1733 and 1734. At a time when Pope's every move was the subject of malicious pamphleteering from Grub Street, the anonymously presented *Essay on Man* was a huge success and met with little immediate opposition. It clearly answered to a good many contemporary expectations of what a poem should be. To a modern reader it seems easily the most dated part of Pope's oeuvre. A quasi-philosophical exploration of Man in his relationships with himself, society and God, it owes a great deal to the ideas of Pope's venerated friend Henry St John Bolingbroke. Pope saw it as merely the introductory part of a much larger study of humanity which would encompass treatises on government, education and so forth, and which like many of the larger poetic plans of literary history, never came to fruition. It had off-shoots, though, into the four Epistles which were subsequently entitled *Moral Essays.* Indeed, one of the most striking features of Pope's work in the early 1730s is the way in which his poems take their life from each other. *The Epistle to Cobham,* (published as the first of the *Moral Essays*) was written partly to exemplify certain theories of human behaviour explained in the *Essay on Man,* whilst it is likely that some of Pope's thoughts on education found their way into the *New Dunciad,* the fourth book which Pope added to that poem in 1742. Likewise, the poems which we know collectively as the *Imitations of Horace* were written at various times throughout the 1730s, the earliest of them being contemporary with the *Moral Essays.* The Horatian tone which Pope was seeking was also discernible in parts of *An Epistle to Dr Arbuthnot.*

If the 1730s were Pope's poetically most productive years they were also the most productive years in the pamphlet war against him. 1733 saw at least twelve separate published attacks, all anonymous of course. They were also the years in which the attacks grew more elaborate. Fiction and fantasy tended to replace rank personal abuse. Hence, readers could discover how Pope had supposedly been flogged or tormented or had committed suicide or murdered a woman. There were pictures of him, too, notoriously the engraving which had accompanied the pamphlet *Pope Alexander's Supremacy* of 1729, and which had pictured Pope's head attached to a monkey's body. Pope was to acknowledge the multifarious strategies of his critics in *An Epistle to Dr Arbuthnot*:[18]

> The distant Threats of Vengeance on his head,
> The Blow unfelt, the Tear he never shed;
> The Tale reviv'd, the Lye so oft o'erthrown;
> Th'imputed Trash, and Dulness not his own;
> The Morals blacken'd when the Writings scape;
> The libel'd Person, and the pictur'd Shape;
> Abuse on all he lov'd, or lov'd him spread,
> A friend in Exile, or a Father, dead
>
> (348-55)

Perhaps the most significant charge against Pope, which stuck for a long time, was that in the *Timon's Villa* section of his *Epistle to Burlington,* he had been ungraciously criticizing the Duke of Chandos and his estate at Canons in Berkshire. Pope was thus tarnished with charges of malicious ingratitude and lack of respect to an important figure. It showed the way in which a misrepresentation of Pope's writing could rapidly acquire the characteristics of gospel truth. Indeed when, half a century later, Dr Johnson came to write Pope's life, the myth still held as biographical fact.

It was no doubt partly as a result of the anti-Pope industry that Pope was to proclaim insistently in his later poetry his own independence

> 'Un-plac'd, un-pension'd, no Man's Heir or Slave'
> (*Imitations of Horace Satire II i* 116)

> Let Lands and Houses have what Lords they will,
> Let Us be fix'd, and our own Masters still.
> (*Imitations of Horace Satire II ii* 179-80)

Pope's satire in the 1730s gains greater refinement and applicability. Although Arbuthnot urged Pope to refrain from mentioning actual names in his satirical writing (a point which Pope dramatizes crucially in his *Epistle* . . .), Pope's response was that '. . . general satire in times of general vice has no force . . . it is only by hunting one or two from the herd that any examples can be made.'[19] Pope's satire in the 1730s finds out its own ideology and consequently its own victims with increasing accuracy. Pope becomes more concerned with the lineaments of the 'general vice' which he sees around him, a vice rooted not simply in Grub Street, but in the whole political culture of the age.

Two of his *Moral Essays,* those addressed to Bathurst and Burlington had borne the subtitle *Of the Use of Riches* and whilst it is true that both of these poems attack individuals, they are also evidence of a response to national issues. Pope is beginning to deal not merely with offensive individuals, but with 'society' in general. The economic tone of the age was speculative and expansionist. One of the consequences of this was that whilst huge fortunes were being gained and lost, the Whig nobility were busy constructing huge country houses and gardens for themselves. It was as an offence against order, nature and good taste that Pope saw this environmental profligacy:

You show us Rome was glorious, not profuse
And pompous buildings once were things of Use.
Yet shall (my Lord) your just, your noble rules
Fill half the land with Imitating Fools;
Who random drawings from your sheets shall take,
And of one beauty many blunders make;
Load some vain Church with old Theatric state,
Turn Arcs of triumph to a Garden-gate;
Reverse your Ornaments, and hang them all
On some patch'd dog-hole ek'd with ends of wall
(Epistle to Burlington 22-32)

Burlington, as the passage suggests, was an architectural luminary, and Pope as an ardent disciple in the business of building and landscape gardening was an authoritative source of criticism on these matters of public aesthetics.

The Epistle to Bathurst probes more deeply in its analysis of the age's economic ills. It addresses itself to the Whiggish city gentlemen and financiers who had done so well during the years of Walpole's premiership, yet whose standards of personal morality left much to be desired. Pope sees:

. . . Riches in effect
No grace of Heav'n or token of th'Elect;
Giv'n to the Fool, the Mad, the Vain, the Evil,
To Ward, to Waters, Chartres, and the Devil.
(Epistle to Bathurst 17-20)

Politically, Pope had never been quick publicly to take sides. By reason of his Catholic background and consequent supposed loyalty to the House of Stuart, he was associated with the backward looking and often rather sentimental Toryism whose influence was extinguished with the death of Queen Anne. His friendship with the Tory Swift, and with figures such as Bolingbroke and Atterbury, both of whom were tarred with the brush of Jacobitism, seemed to place him in a definite political camp. Pope was temperamentally much more of an equivocator than he was a partisan, and fought shy of making public statements of position or loyalty:

In Moderation placing all my Glory,
While Tories call me Whig, and Whigs a Tory
(Imitations of Horace, Satire II i 67-8)

Indeed, in the 1720s Pope's relationship with Sir Robert Walpole had been cordial. However, like nearly all contemporary authors, Pope grew increasingly hostile to the corrupt and philistine government that the well-nigh impregnable Walpole sustained on behalf of King George II. Once upon a time the English court had been a nursery of art and artists. George II's indifference to most cultural manifestations was well known, and formed the starting point of Pope's imitation of the First Epistle of Horace's second book, subtitled 'To Augustus'. King George is addressed in the same tones as Horace addressed his patron Augustus (and Augustus, by happy coincidence was George's second name). But where Horace's words were written in sincere appreciation of Augustus, Pope's embody huge ironies:

While You, great Patron of Mankind, sustain
The balanc'd World, and open all the Main;
Your Country, chief, in Arms abroad defend,
At home, with Morals, Arts and Laws amend;
How shall the Muse, from such a Monarch, steal
An hour, and not defraud the Publick Weal?
(To Augustus, 1-6)

Even though Pope was unprepared to claim himself as a political writer, his *Imitations of Horace* certainly take up a political standpoint, and Pope can be seen as writing out of a genuine concern for public virtue rather than out of any kind of personal pique.

Although his attitude to being seen as 'the English Homer' was ambivalent, Pope suffered no such doubts about becoming the English Horace. The development of the Horatian persona is discussed further in Chapter 5. Pope was open about the fact that he found the figure of Horace answerable to his needs of the 1730s. Horace, the man retired from city life, bore obvious resemblances to Pope at Twickenham. Horace was also valued for his spirit of quiet moderation. He wrote satire without bitterness or rancour, he expressed the moral concerns of the reasonable man. Pope, though not so much as Swift, perhaps, had always liked masks. Whether presenting himself as Esdras Barnivelt in *A Key to the Lock,* as Dr Norris in the spoof account of John Dennis's apparent lunacy, or as Martinus Scriblerus in *The Dunciad* notes, he had kept his own identity partly hidden. *The Imitations of Horace* are very characteristic (some would say vintage) Pope, as even a cursory reading of them will show, though the poet clearly enjoys the obliquity inherent in the idea of imitation.

The tone of Horatian urbanity, however, did not serve Pope to the very end. The satirical writings of the final phase of his life are amongst his most urgent. In particular, the huge allegory of the Chariot of Vice at the end of the first part of *Epilogue to the Satires* (1738):

> Lo! at the Wheels of her Triumphal Car,
> Old England's Genius, rough with many a Scar,
> Dragged in the Dust! his Arms hang idly round,
> His Flag inverted trails along the ground!
>
> (151-4)

These two dialogues, Pope was to state, would be his last works. He had decided to publish no more. The 1730s had found him engaged with the exposure of vice and folly, though he had come to find the activity futile. The power against which the later *Imitations* were pitched looked impregnable, and had buttressed itself considerably by introducing censorship in 1737 as a means of vetting all publications for libel against the government. It looked as if the position of the satirist was rapidly becoming marginalized in a self-confidently corrupt age. Pope was prepared to admit defeat, but he did so with characteristic pugnacity:

> Ask you what provocation I have had?
> The strong Antipathy of Good to Bad.
> When Truth or Virtue an Affront endures,
> Th'Affront is mine, my Friend, and should be yours.
>
> (Epilogue to the Satires, Dialogue II, 197-200)

The final years of Pope's life were, in poetic terms, generally quiet ones. This is partly explained by the deterioration in his health. The diverse symptoms which had often plagued him throughout 'this long Disease, my Life' inevitably grew more acute as he grew older, and a prolonged physical decline, horrifying by modern standards, was a source of concern to those close to him. Nevertheless, he continued to visit, as well as to be visited, to enjoy his friendships, and probably to eat and drink too much (a life-long habit). In the company of William Warburton, he worked on revisions of his texts for the collected edition of his works which Warburton was supervising, and which finally appeared in 1751.

But there was one final foray into satire, which was also by way of being a journey into the past. Colley Cibber, an undistinguished comic actor and theatre manager, had contrived, by dint of connections in high places, to be appointed Poet Laureate in 1730. Cibber was in general an unassuming man, presumably being as aware of the incongruity of his appointment as anybody else. Swift had remarked, of the Laureateship, in a letter that the competition for it was '. . . between Concanen or Theobald or some other hero of *The Dunciad*'.[20] He perhaps spoke more than he knew. Cibber had made a fleeting, indirect appearance in the 1728 *Dunciad.* In the revision of the poem which Pope published in 1743, he had chased Theobald from the Dunces' throne completely, and become the hero of the new poem himself. It has been often enough pointed out that, at root, Cibber was a much more obvious candidate for the Kingship of the Dunces than Theobald anyway. He was a man of very little talent who had been elevated far beyond his deserts. What, presumably, had kept his presence in the 1728 version marginal is that he and Pope had had no very profound reason to cross swords. Their relationship had not been without its difficulties, but like so many of Pope's supposed literary animosities, it is difficult to disentangle fact from fiction in the affair, especially when the most crucial document is a pamphlet from Cibber in the best Grub Street vein. Having been hurt by recent references to him in the *New Dunciad,* he decided to retaliate in *A Letter from Mr Cibber to Mr Pope . . .*[21] which ostensibly outlines a whole history of conflict between the two men. It leans on the kind of anecdotal evidence that is very reminiscent of the kind of fantasies about Pope which had circulated widely in the 1730s. It was basically an unexpected and unprovoked attack. Certainly any derogatory comments which Pope had made about Cibber were less offensive than the things which Cibber decided to write about Pope. It was a return to the tone and the tactics of an earlier period of Pope's life, though it did provoke the final version of *The Dunciad* which is the one that has always been most widely read. Cibber kept up occasional sniping against Pope until his death.

The Cibber affair is a neat reminder of the literary world in which Pope was forced to live. Partly as a result of the economics of authorship and of printing, partly as a result of unprecedented political contention, the literary world of the early eighteenth century was not a polite one. Pope was by no means alone in receiving hostile treatment from the gutter press. Certain things about him made him a particularly easy target: his shape and his religion were obvious ones. But there was also his self-conscious assumption of the role of great poet and guardian of traditional literary values. There was his vast wealth, gained from translating Homer, and his retirement to cultured ease at Twickenham. Also there was his espousal of the cause of virtue, moderation and loyalty and his coterie of distinguished friends.

Just as Pope was, literally, the subject of grotesque drawings in his lifetime, so his posthumous reputation has often been reduced to the cartoon-like tiny figure, spattering the world with his malicious couplets. This is, of course, a considerable simplification. Pope's satire (particularly that of his later period) is as much a response to a particular cultural moment as is the recalling of a personal bitterness. Pope was a regular object of satire long before he got into the habit of seeking objects himself. Although he cast many stones, he seldom cast the first, and he was unfortunate to live in an age in which personal abuse was a minor art form in itself. What was unusual about Pope is that his response to such abuse became so important a part of his work. Perhaps the golden boy from Windsor Forest with his prodigious technique and laureate ambitions, could hardly have foreseen the way in which his poetic career was to develop, and that his future fame was to be so closely bound up with his response to ridicule and scorn. It is interesting that the two serious attempts at epic poetry which Pope undertook remained incomplete, whilst *The Rape of the Lock* and *The Dunciad* exist for all to see.

Chapter One: A Warfare Upon Earth

1. James Reeves *The Reputation and Writings of Alexander Pope* (1976) offers a predominantly hostile treatment of Pope's works and his posthumous reputation.
2. See M. Nicholson and G.S. Rousseau: *This Long Disease, My Life: Alexander Pope and the Sciences* (1968).
3. See *Farmer Pope and his Son.* Quoted in J.V. Guerinot: *Pamphlet Attacks on Alexander Pope 1711-1744* (1969) p155.
4. For a more detailed treatment of the events of Pope's early life, see George Sherburn: *The Early Career of Alexander Pope* (1934) Chaps 1 and 2. Also, Maynard Mack: *Alexander Pope: A Life* (1985) Chaps 1 to 8.
5. Quoted by Sherburn p52.
6. Ibid p150.
7. Quoted in Guerinot p3.
8. Reproduced in its entirety in Paul Hammond (Ed) *Selected Prose of Alexander Pope* (1987) pp40-45.
9. Hammond, pp62-73.
10. For the life of Swift see David Nokes: *Jonathan Swift, A Hypocrite Reversed* (1985). The history of the Scriblerus Club is discussed at greater length in Charles Kerby-Miller (Ed) *The Memoirs . . . of Martinus Scriblerus* (1950).
11. For the phenomenon of Grub Street see Pat Rogers: *Grub Street, Studies in a Subculture* (1972).
12. See R. Straus: *The Unspeakable Curil* (1928).
13. See Hammond, pp131-135 for the full text of the pamphlet.
14. The 'Key' is discussed by Guerinot, p114. For the 'Life' see Straus, p156.
15. An account of Pope's contribution to Shakespearean scholarship can be found in Gary Taylor: *Reinventing Shakespeare* (1990), pp81-87.
16. Letter to Swift, quoted by Rogers pp181-2.
17. See Mack *Life* pp489-90.
18. The growth and development of the pamphlet war against Pope is discussed in detail by Guerinot in his introduction to *Pamphlet Attacks.*
19. See Mack *Life* p636.
20. To John Gay, quoted by Kenneth Hopkins *The Poets Laureate* (1954, rev 1973) p73.
21. See Guerinot pp280-294.

2

MODERN LADIES AND ANCIENT POETS

The Rape of the Lock

Relatively little is known about the 'real life' situation which gave rise to *The Rape of the Lock*.[1] What we do know though is that Robert, Lord Petre had cut off a lock of Miss Arabella Fermor's hair, causing considerable concern to her family, and a feud between it and Lord Petre's. It was Pope's friend John Caryll who suggested that the poet might like to write a poem which would 'laugh them together again.' From such fragmentary evidence as there is, it would appear that the poem was, at first at any rate, successful in its aim. Pope reported that the poem was 'well received, and had its effect in the two families', but this statement is probably over-simplified.

Nobody has discovered the time or the place at which the actual 'rape' occurred. Pope locates it in his poem at Hampton Court which is clearly a fiction. Hampton Court was the home of royalty whereas Pope's characters are merely gentry, and Roman Catholic gentry at that, who would perforce at that time have to exist at some distance from the public scene. Thus the *beau monde* elements of the poem, essential though they have come to seem in our understanding of it, are clear elaborations by Pope. Both the families came from Oxfordshire and there is no reason to believe that Pope actually knew them. Although Pope was, in the second edition of the poem, to provide a dedicatory letter and an inscription from the Latin poet Martial addressed to her, it seems unlikely that he knew anything very much about

Arabella Fermor personally, though she had been celebrated in poems by other authors which seems to indicate that she possessed something of a reputation as a 'belle'.

Arabella Fermor, the Belinda of Pope's poem, was in her early twenties at the time *The Rape of the Lock* was composed. Some speculation has inevitably taken place about the nature of the relationship between her and 'the Baron' whose activities led to the 'rape' which the poem records. Certainly, the Baron was not the man she married, as she married a Mr Francis Perkins in 1714. Lord Petre (the Baron) had married in 1711, and died of smallpox the following year, presumably unaware of the dubious immortality which Pope's poem had gained him. Thus it is not absolutely safe to see the man-woman contest as part of a courtship ritual; the poem could, simply, be celebrating a high-spirited prank.

The third 'real life' character in the poem is Sir Plume who was based upon Sir George Browne, a relative of Arabella Fermor's mother. Again there is no evidence that Pope and he were acquainted, though Joseph Spence, Pope's friend and virtually his first biographer, was to claim that the poet had presented 'the very picture of the man' and that the portrait had caused Sir George to threaten Pope with physical violence.

The first version of the poem, Pope tells us, was 'written in a fortnight' and first published in May 1712. This version is considerably shorter than the one which we know today. Pope made important additions to the poem over the next two years, bringing out a new edition of it which was extended from two to five Cantos in 1714. Eventually the poem as we now know it, incorporating an important addition to Canto V, came into being in 1717. This kind of revision and extension was characteristic of Pope: he modified his early *Windsor Forest* written in 1704, for publication in 1713, whilst *The Dunciad* was to exist in no fewer than four different versions during Pope's lifetime.

Speaking generally the 1712 poem provides us with narrative.[2] It is a narrative which any reader of the final version would understand easily enough: Belinda wakes up, makes a river trip to Hampton Court, and taking a cup of coffee during a card game, is deprived of one of her favourite locks of hair by the Baron. Much consternation is caused, Belinda is desolated, the company scandalized and the fated lock ascends to the heavens.

Pope in no way changed this bare-bones narrative in the versions of the poem which follow. He simply added things to it. In 1714 he added what he called the 'machinery' of the poem. This term in Pope's time had quite a specific meaning. It referred to certain features which would commonly be associated with classical epics, where the presence of gods emphasized a supernatural dimension in the context of which the human action took place. Pope offered his own explanation in 1714:

> 'The machinery . . . is a term invented . . . to signify that part which the Deities, Angels or Daemons are made to act in a poem. For the ancient poets are in many respects like many modern ladies; let an action be never so trivial in itself, they always make it appear of the utmost importance.'[3]

In order to invest the actions of his poem with their own particular kind of importance, Pope first of all provided the Sylphs who fulfil a function somewhere between deities and angels. He also invented, in Canto IV, The Cave of Spleen, which echoes the underworld sections of the epics of Homer and Virgil, and thus constitutes Pope's representation of the 'Daemons' in this poem. The 1717 version added the speech of Clarissa to Canto V in order (in Pope's words) 'to open more clearly the moral of the poem.'

One of the ways in which Pope had been entirely consistent, however, was in subtitling *The Rape of the Lock An Heroi-Comical Poem,* in order to draw his contemporary readers' attention to what exactly the poem was. An eighteenth-century reader would be more familiar with the term 'heroi-comical' than we are, and would also be aware of the contradiction inherent in it. *The Rape of the Lock* works by exploiting the incongruity between the 'heroic' (or epic) style and the consciously trivial nature of the events with which it deals. It is by elevating the slight into the grand that Pope enables us to appreciate its very slightness. By judging 'modern ladies' alongside the heroes and heroines of classical epic, there are obviously ways in which the modern characters will seem trivial if not ridiculous.

In Pope's time the classic epics of Homer and Virgil were considerably more accessible than they are today, forming as they did part of the staple literary diet of any educated man. The epic was considered the foremost among the hierarchy of literary forms, standing some distance above tragedy. Milton, twenty or so years before Pope's birth, had produced *Paradise Lost* the most eminent 'classical' epic in English, and had undertaken its composition fully aware of the immense seriousness of the task. Other poets had tried too: Abraham Cowley and William Davenant had both written epics in the seventeenth century, and the worthy Sir Richard Blackmore (later to be one of Pope's satiric butts) had completed no fewer than six of them. They do not tempt the modern reader unduly.

An epic poem is 'heroic' in that its central figure (Homer's *Odysseus* or Virgil's *Aeneas* for example) is a figure of enormous literary size, being both challenged and controlled by the gods, and embodying super-eminent human virtues of an exemplary nature. Homer, Virgil and Milton all provide vast narrative sweeps involving action in Heaven or in the underworld as well as on earth. An epic was nothing if not all-inclusive, and it was thus the very pinnacle of poetic achievement. Pope, who was a consciously ambitious poet, contemplated on at least two occasions during his literary career the composition of an epic, though neither work has survived, which shows us something about the enormously demanding nature of the task. Instead Pope's epic ambitions were channelled into translating, as he worked on Homer's *Iliad* and *Odyssey*. The importance which he attached to Homer is made clear in his *Essay on Criticism:*

> Be Homer's works your study and delight
> Read them by Day, and meditate by night
> Thence form your judgment . . .
>
> (124-6)

The modern equivalent of the term 'Heroi-Comical' is 'mock heroic.' This term points to the fact that *The Rape of the Lock* deals with discrepancy: between human pretension to heroic deeds on the one hand and human pettiness on the other. It emphasizes the gulf between ordinary human activity and the kind of activity which forms the subject matter of the classical epic. It also carries the suggestion that the very epic form itself might be being mocked. On the face of it, given Pope's reverence for the form, this might seem unlikely, but an anonymous piece by Pope, published in the periodical *The Guardian* in 1713 shows the way in which he, although a committed classicist in literary values, can see the absurdity of epic poetry when it enters the wrong hands. His essay is called *A Receit* [ie. Recipe] *to Make an Epic Poem* and it consists of some words of advice to would-be poets:

> Take out of any old poem, history books, romance or legend . . . those parts of the story which afford most scope for long descriptions: put these pieces together, and throw all the adventures you fancy into one tale. Then take a hero, whom you may choose for the sound of his name, and put him into the midst of these adventures; there let him work for twelve books, at the end of which you may take him out, ready prepared to conquer or to marry, it being necessary that the conclusion of an Epic Poem be fortunate.[4]

There is a clear irony in these lines, as the original and most august literary form is comically reduced to a series of stock formulae. Taking the passage out of context one might conclude that Pope saw epic as ridiculous and over-rated but we know this not to be true. Even Virgil himself wrote both epic and mock-epic, and Pope clearly saw no real crime in parodying an extremely serious literary form for comic purposes. If the importance and significance of the epic itself are not granted then the satire fails to work. Pope makes this point in the opening lines of the poem:

> What dire Offence from am'rous Causes springs,
> What mighty Contests rise from trivial Things
>
> (1-2)

The juxtapositon of the 'mighty' with the 'trivial' instantly casts an ironic doubt over the magnitude of the alleged

'Contests'.

Likewise when Pope goes on to ask:

> In Tasks so bold can Little Men engage
> And in soft Bosoms dwells such mighty Rage?
> (10-11)

he is encouraging us in an apparently innocent question to be sceptical about the greatness of the characters he is about to describe. He is distorting the perspective from which we see them, just as his friend Jonathan Swift was to do in the first two parts of *Gulliver's Travels.* Gulliver finds himself cast ashore first of all in the kingdom of Lilliput, where all the natives are much smaller than he is, and then in the kingdom of Brobdingnag, where they are very much larger. Each of these fantasies draws our attention to particular human characteristics which are made the clearer through distortions of size, the Lilliputians representing all that is small in human nature, and the Brobdingnagians all that is large.

A good example of Pope's adjustment of perspective can be found in the description of coffee drinking which forms part of Canto III (105-110):

> For lo! the Board with Cups and Spoons is crown'd
> The Berries crackle, and the Mill turns round.
> In shining Altars of Japan they raise
> The silver Lamp; the fiery Spirits blaze.
> From silver Spouts the grateful Liquors glide
> While China's Earth receives the smoking Tyde.

In one sense it is clear that coffee-drinking is being discussed here. There is enough circumstantial evidence (cups, spoons, beans, a grinder, a pot, a coffee-table). Looked at from another angle, though, the whole process is being rendered in a distinctively unfamiliar way. The word 'coffee' itself has not been mentioned; the tables have become religious and exotic 'Altars of Japan' which are (as if in some royal ceremony) 'crown'd' with cups and spoons. The brazier under the pot is controlled by 'fiery Spirits', as if somehow, it is actually alive. The coffee itself becomes a series of 'grateful

Liquors' and the bottom of the cup is enhanced into 'China's Earth'. In each case the object has been redefined, and indeed changed into something bigger, better, more mysterious than might be commonly expected. This kind of transformation is the first consequence of Pope's 'mock-heroic' writing, and we appreciate its significance: in the world of the poem, coffee drinking is an important act, ritualistic and impressive, taking on qualities akin both to royal and religious observance. It is a manifestation of a highly materialistic culture also, fetishising objects and substances and celebrating such things as china, metal and wood. Pope's mock-epic perspective is ideally suited for encouraging the reader to see commonplace things from different angles. Dr Johnson, writing later in the eighteenth century summed up this aspect best when he observed that in this poem 'New things are made familiar, and familiar things are made new.'[5]

But the question of what, precisely, Pope was satirizing through his manipulation of literary conventions is an important one, even though not absolutely straightforward. Perhaps the first place to look for relevant evidence would be the letter of dedication to Arabella Fermor which has already been mentioned. It was attached to the 1714 and all subsequent editions of the poem. The tone is at first playful and flattering:

> '. . . it was intended only to divert a few young Ladies who have good sense and good humour enough to laugh not only at their sex's little unguarded follies, but at their own . . .'

and likewise in the final paragraph:

> 'If this Poem has as many Graces as there are in Your Person, or in Your Mind, yet I could never hope it should pass thro' the World half so uncensured as You have done . . .'[6]

As we have already seen, it has never been proved that Pope knew Arabella Fermor so these words are probably not being addressed from friend to friend. Pope had no need on a purely personal level, to pay Miss Fermor any compliments at all. It looks rather more likely that Pope was proceeding with caution and attempting to pacify Miss Fermor in advance, in case she felt in any way defamed by what was said about her. Indeed in a letter to John Caryll, Pope wrote:

> '. . . I believe I have managed the dedication so nicely that it can neither hurt the lady or the author. I writ it very lately, and upon great deliberation; the young lady approves of it; and the best advice in the kingdom of the men of sense has been made use of in it . . .'[7]

This seems to suggest a certain unease on Pope's part. On the one hand he wishes to assure Arabella Fermor that there is no offence in the poem, whilst on the other being well aware that there might be. And we are not doing the poem much service if we see it simply as the indulgent and private piece that Pope's dedication would try to have us believe.

In comparison with much of Pope's later satire it is true that *The Rape of the Lock* might seem characterized by good humour. There is an element of fantasy in it; it is free from the feeling that personal scores are being settled and it is insulated from wider political and cultural considerations. Much of the astringency of Pope's later satire is missing. Some critics of the poem have pointed out, for example, the way in which a strong vein of appreciation for Belinda's qualities goes hand in hand with Pope's criticism of them.[8] He grants her genuine beauty and grace. But equally we should remember the pains to which he puts himself in his dedication. Pope could, when it suited him, be devious, and his apparent concern to ensure Arabella Fermor's good reputation seems to suggest that not everything which he has to say can, in the last analysis, be laughed off. Nor is his treatment of the male characters in the poem at all flattering.

We first meet Belinda properly at the end of Canto I. Having roused herself from her slumbers and listened to the warning, though somewhat vague, words of her guardian Sylph, she sits at her dressing table (Pope's word is 'toilet') and begins the elaborate process of making herself up.

And now, unveil'd, the Toilet stands display'd
Each Silver Vase in mystic Order laid.
First, rob'd in White, the Nymph intent adores
With Head uncover'd, the Cosmetic Pow'rs.
A heav'nly Image in the Glass appears,
To that she bends, to that her Eyes, she rears;
Th'inferior Priestess, at her Altar's side,
Trembling, begins the sacred Rites of Pride.
(121-128)

There are obviously features in this passage comparable with those which were found in the description of coffee drinking. Once more commonplace objects transform themselves into larger and more exotic ones. The 'toilet' has, within seven lines also become an 'Altar' (line 127), attended by priestesses. Religious undertones were present from the very beginning, as the very phials on the dressing table are invested with 'mystic order' (line 122). Pope is vague about the nature of the clothes which Belinda is wearing at this point, the only details which emerge about them, again, suggest some kind of exotic initiation (she is 'rob'd', rather than dressed or clothed, and the garment's whiteness carries suggestions of some kind of purification ceremony). The uncovering of the head intimates an act of reverence. Likewise before the image in the glass, Belinda first 'bends' as if in prayer, and then 'rears' her eyes to it, as if in adoration (line 126). The religious parallels are clearly being worked through by Pope with the greatest precision, and undoubtedly what could be presented as a trivial daily task is elaborated into a fascinated study of a special and mysterious process.

It would be easy to see this passage as an end in itself, and forget the essentially satirical force which it has: for example, the very discrepancy which exists between the 'heroic' detail of the description, and the more mundane realities of the action it presents. It might aid Belinda's attractiveness to spend time on her toilette, but the more time she spends in self-beautification the more gratuitously egocentric the activity becomes. Pope deflates Belinda very deftly when he describes her activities as '. . .the sacred Rites of Pride.' There is not much kindness in Pope's reminder that self-worshipping rituals of this particular sort are little better than sacrilege. In a poem written by a catholic, dedicated to a catholic, and about catholics, one can only assume that these suggestions would have their power. Belinda's 'image' in the glass might be 'heav'nly', but she finds it a cause of great satisfaction.

The passage goes on to present Belinda as if she were the centre of the universe:

> Unnumber'd Treasures ope at once, and here
> The various Off'rings of the World appear;
> From each she nicely culls with curious Toil
> And decks the Goddess with the glitt'ring Spoil.
> This Casket India's glowing Gems unlocks,
> And all Arabia breathes from yonder Box.
> The Tortoise here and Elephant unite,
> Transform'd to Combs, the speckled and the white.
> Here files of Pins extend their shining Rows,
> Puffs, Powders, Patches, Bibles, Billet-doux.
> (129-138)

There are some exhilaratingly absurd suggestions in these lines, contained not only in the image of the world spontaneously spreading its 'Unnumbered treasures' before Belinda, but in the more specific implication that such creatures as tortoises and elephants (a particularly grotesque pair) somehow exist especially to be made into Belinda's combs. If all this were mere flattery and no more there would be no necessity for further comment since flattery is based in untruth. However, the fact that the world blatantly does not exist simply to 'deck' Belinda, makes the reader more aware of Belinda's self-absorption and self-deception, and it is a self-deception at which others (and not just 'Th'inferior Priestess') are prepared to connive. These lines with their casual references to India and Arabia testify to a mental world whose boundaries are, in fact, significantly narrowed, and whose priorities are badly ordered. After all, Belinda's 'Bibles' (line 138) are, it would seem, no more important to her than face-powder or love letters. If her making herself up is symbolically a religious activity, Pope is mindful to show us the place of a symbol of genuine spirituality in Belinda's scheme of things.

The next lines have another suggestion to make:

> Now awful Beauty puts on all its Arms;
> The Fair each moment rises in her Charms,
> Repairs her Smiles, awakens ev'ry Grace,
> And calls forth all the Wonders of her Face;
> Sees by Degrees a purer Blush arise,
> And keener Lightnings quicken in her Eyes.
> (139-144)

Belinda's beauty is granted; she emerges from the toilette 'armed' and 'repaired', ready to meet the adoring world. But the passage apart from suggesting in its military image that Belinda's beauty is in a sense a protection against the world, also shows that this beauty is a production: even the blush is artificially contrived. Belinda is a triumph of the 'Cosmetic Pow'rs.' The question whether she is beautiful innately and intrinsically is not asked.

Description of Belinda dominates the opening of Canto II also. If the end of the first Canto shows us Belinda in private, we now see the public persona:

> Fair Nymphs and well-drest Youths around her shone,
> But ev'ry Eye was fix'd on her alone.
> On her White Breast a sparkling Cross she wore,
> Which Jews might kiss, and Infidels adore.
> (5-8)

Predictably enough Belinda's cross is no religious symbol. Indeed there is something rather crude about it. It is worn not simply as a beautiful object (that, perhaps, could have been forgiven) but as a means of advertising Belinda's breasts. Its effect upon the Jews and infidels cheapens both it and her. We find ourselves wondering about Belinda's motives in beautifying herself. She clearly enjoys being the centre of attractions, but in fact she receives a good deal more than she gives:

> Favours to none, to all she Smiles extends,
> Oft she rejects, but never once offends.

> Bright as the Sun, her Eyes the Gazers strike,
> And, like the Sun, they shine on all alike.
>
> (11-14)

Pope was to write in a later poem: 'Most Women have no Characters at all',[9] and it is difficult not to see Belinda proving Pope's point for him here, as she keeps her studied distance from those around her, particularly the men. She becomes an admired object rather than a person, and she clearly calculates this role for herself.

Ariel, her guardian Sylph, provides us with some understanding of the inner life of Belinda. Addressing his cohorts, he presents us with a catalogue of Belinda's mental preoccupations:

> Whether the Nymph shall break Diana's Law
> Or some frail China Jar receive a Flaw,
> Or stain her Honour, or her new Brocade,
> Forget her Pray'rs, or miss a Masquerade,
> Or lose her Heart, or Necklace, at a Ball,
> Or whether Heav'n has doom'd that Shock must fall.
>
> (Canto II, 105-110)

The most hard-worked word in this section is 'or', suggesting as it does, choices and alternatives: alternatives which define the moral parameters of Belinda's existence. Belinda's mental furniture seems of rather flimsy design. It makes no distinction between heart or necklace, prayers or parties. The trivial and the important are neatly paired, Belinda being unable to make any worthwhile discrimination between them. The most interesting juxtaposition is that of breaking 'Diana's Law' (losing her virginity) and 'some frail China Jar' receiving a flaw. Pope equates the frailty of the virginity with a china ornament, thus suggesting, on the one hand, a delicate, easily damaged thing, but on the other something which is apprehended by Belinda entirely in material and physical terms: the flaw is an injury only to the surface of the china jar.

Pope does not let us forget this china jar. After the Baron has deprived Belinda of her lock, we read in Canto III:

Then flash'd the living Lightning from her Eyes,
And Screams of Horror rend th'affrighted Skies.
Not louder Shrieks to pitying Heav'n are cast,
When Husbands or when Lap-dogs breathe their last,
Or when rich China Vessels, fal'n from high,
In glitt'ring Dust and painted Fragments lie!
(155-160)

The force of Belinda's response makes the reaction comic. We do not feel any undue sadness at the thought of the jar in ruins, because the kind of ruin which Belinda herself feels has simply been an attack on her appearance. She is caught up in a drama of over-reaction, highlighting the undiscriminating hysteria which responds in exactly the same way to the death of a husband or of a lap-dog or to the destruction of a household ornament. As Ariel, Belinda's guardian Sylph, has already reminded her, a woman's heart resembles nothing so much as a 'moving Toyshop', (Canto I, line 100), indeed the lock itself, cause of so much trouble, is defined by its very triviality.

This Nymph, to the Destruction of Mankind,
Nourish'd two Locks, which graceful hung behind
In equal Curls, and well conspir'd to deck
With shining Ringlets, the smooth Iv'ry Neck.
Love in these Labyrinths his Slaves detains . . .
(Canto II, 19-23)

It is because this nice aesthetic balance has been broken that Belinda feels so injured by the Baron's 'rape' of her:

For ever curs'd be this detested Day,
Which snatch'd my best, my fav'rite Curl away!
(Canto IV, 147-8)

Indeed the speech which Belinda makes, bemoaning her fate, moves by degrees to the conclusion that to be really raped would be preferable to losing the lock, because the consequences would be so much less visible:

Oh hadst thou, Cruel! been content to seize
Hairs less in sight, or any Hairs but these!
(175-176)

Pope is not afraid of the half-obscene suggestion either here or, for example, when describing the 'underworld' Cave of Spleen a few lines earlier:

Men prove with Child, as pow'rful Fancy works,
And Maids turn'd Bottels, call aloud for Corks.
(53-55)

Indeed it could be argued the poem's very title is suggestive, with the highly serious associations of the word 'Rape' immediately (but not entirely) dissipated by the trivializing word 'Lock'. Pope clearly enjoys the comedy which can be gained from exploiting the overlap between the entirely sham 'dishonour' of a pretended rape, and the commotion which would follow a real one. Thalestris, Belinda's friend and protector, has some harsh things to say about the reputation of a young lady who has been violated:

Methinks already I your Tears survey,
Already hear the horrid things they say,
Already see you a degraded Toast,
And all your Honour in a Whisper lost!
How shall I, then, your helpless Fame defend?
Twill then be Infamy to seem your Friend!
(Canto IV, 107-12)

The beautiful Belinda can soon become damaged goods, and thus an easy outcast. Thalestris is particularly concerned about the waste of effort:

Was it for this you took such constant Care
The Bodkin, Comb and Essence to prepare;
For this your locks in paper durance bound,
For this with tort'ring Irons wreath'd around?
For this with Fillets strain'd your tender Head
And bravely bore the double Loads of Lead?
(97-102)

The Baron's act is a crime as much against cosmetics as against a person. Indeed if Belinda is unable to distinguish between a Bible and a love-letter, the Baron is unable to focus his romantic pretentions on anything so concrete as a real woman:

> Th'Adventurous Baron the bright Locks admir'd
> He saw, he wish'd, and to the Prize aspir'd
> (Canto II, 29-30)

Not surprisingly in this poem, the Baron equates love with things rather than with people. He sees Belinda's locks largely as a prize and again he is prone to make fetishes of his own 'holy' objects. He is bound up in his own peculiar religious rituals, just as Belinda had been:

> . . . ere Phoebus rose, he had implor'd,
> Propitious Heav'n, and ev'ry Pow'r ador'd
> But chiefly Love-to Love an Altar built,
> Of twelve vast French Romances, neatly gilt.
> There lay three Garters, half a Pair of Gloves;
> And all the Trophies of his former Loves.
> With tender Billets-doux he lights the Pyre
> And breathes three am'rous Sighs to raise the Fire.
> Then prostrate falls, and begs with ardent Eyes
> Soon to obtain, and long possess the Prize
> (Canto II, 35-44)

If Belinda's self-regarding performance in front of the mirror was reprehensible, the Baron's performance verges on the silly. His self-imposed religious observances are vapid, pointless and exaggerated ('Then prostrate falls, and begs with ardent Eyes'); it would appear that his knowledge of matters of the heart comes from books ('twelve vast French Romances'); his 'trophies' ('three garters, half a pair of gloves') are images of inadequacy and incompleteness. One wonders that he can find the necessary drive to 'attack' Belinda at all, though as Pope points out, in keeping with the rest of his achievements, this one shows only partial success:

The Pow'rs gave Ear, and granted half his Pray'r,
The rest the Winds dispers'd in empty Air.
(45-6)

Perhaps the fact that he has to be stimulated with coffee (Canto III, 119-20) before brandishing his scissors, shows us what little strength he possesses innately. He is eventually vanquished (Canto V, 80-86) with a pinch of snuff.

It is not too difficult to see why Sir George Browne (characterised as Sir Plume in the poem) was so offended by Pope's portrait of him:

Sir Plume, of Amber Snuff-box justly vain,
And the nice Conduct of a clouded Cane
With earnest Eyes and round unthinking Face,
He first the Snuff-box open'd, then the Case,
And thus broke out –
(Canto IV, 121-5)

Sir Plume also is defined by objects. In his case the snuff-box and the walking stick seem to form his mental boundaries. Playing with his possessions seems almost to have replaced speech. Indeed, when he does open his mouth, he is a fine spectacle of incoherence, Pope cruelly borrowing from contemporary theatrical comedy the current repertoire of phrases which suggest apoplectic spluttering:

. . . 'My Lord, why, what the Devil?
Zounds! damn the lock! Fore Gad, you must be civil;
Plague on't! 'tis past a Jest-nay prithee, Pox!
Give her the Hair' – he spoke and rapp'd his Box.
(127-30)

Although ostensibly a poem about 'modern ladies', Pope seems to reserve his most direct criticisms for the male characters. Apart from equating them with lapdogs and other lower animals ('Men, Monkeys, Lap-dogs, Parrots, perish all!' Canto IV, 120), he ridicules their effete affectations:

A Beau and Witling perish'd in the Throng,
One died in metaphor, and one in Song.
'O cruel Nymph! a living Death I bear'
Cried Dapperwit, and sunk beside his Chair.
A mournful glance Sir Fopling upwards cast,
'Those Eyes are made so killing' was his last
(Canto V, 59-64)

Pope has his last word on this particular subject when he has 'Jove's golden scales' weigh the man's wits against Belinda's lock:

The doubtful Beam long nods from side to side
At length the Wits mount up, the Hairs subside.
(Canto V, 73-4)

In talking of last words, though, it is necessary to give some thought to the content of Clarissa's speech, the very last addition to the poem in 1717, in Pope's phrase, 'to open more clearly the moral of the poem . . .'.[10]

In a poem which relies on the distortions and high spirits of comedy, it might seem incongruous that a 'moral' speech needs to be inserted at all. But it is important to realize that Pope never separated the roles of satirist and moralist. To ridicule is perhaps more fun than to moralize, but for Pope the two activities were indivisible. It is significant, too, that none of the characters in the poem choose to heed Clarissa's wise words:

So spoke the Dame, but no Applause ensu'd;
Belinda frowned, Thalestris call'd her Prude.
(Canto V, 35-6)

These words above all draw our attention to the fact that Pope is encompassing something larger than a description of the 'little unguarded follies' of the fair sex. There are darker hints here and a feeling of things being *sub specie aeternitatis.* Intimations of mortality find their way into the lady's boudoir:

Oh! if to dance all Night, and dress all Day,
Charm'd the Small-pox, or chas'd old Age away;
Who would not scorn what Huswife's Cares produce,
Or who would learn one earthly Thing of Use?
(19-22)

To make a cult of youth is narrow-minded, since of all stages in life it is the most transitory and evanescent:

But since, alas! frail Beauty must decay,
Curl'd or uncurl'd, since Locks will turn to grey,
Since painted, or not painted, all shall fade,
And she who scorns a Man must die a Maid.
(25-8)

Beauty is 'frail', and so are all those things which, in this poem, support it. Belinda's way of life may be entertaining to the beholder, but Pope has other perspectives on it for his readers. Just as the grandeur of mock-epic style and 'machinery' throw into sharp relief the exploits of Pope's 'little men', so Clarissa's words see Belinda's sparkling and brittle world in the perspective of values more durable.

However, this does not prevent Pope from ending his poem with a dazzling flight of fancy. Belinda's raped lock rises to the 'lunar sphere':

A sudden Star, it shot thro' liquid Air,
And drew behind a radiant Trail of Hair.
Not Berenice's Locks first rose so bright,
The Heav'ns bespangling with dishevel'd Light
(127-130)

where, eventually, it will 'midst the Stars inscribe Belinda's Name.'

Clarissa's speech was modelled on the one speech from Homer's *Iliad*, of which Pope had already made a translation.[11] If Homer begins to seem irrelevant amidst the Beaux and Witlings of the final Canto, he is a timely reminder of the poem's mock-epic nature. Indeed it is the almost constant measuring of trivial, particular, material, and utterly modern concerns against the conventions of classical epic which provides the poem with much of its comic dimension, whether it be in the quasi-Homeric description of a sunrise over the Thames (Canto II, 1-4) or in the elevation of a card-game into an equally Homeric battle in Canto III. It is in this latter section that Pope writes most sustainedly in the mock-heroic vein. First of all he turns the very cards themselves into military figures:

> Behold, four Kings in Majesty rever'd,
> With hoary Whiskers and a forky Beard;
> And four fair Queens whose hands sustain a Flow'r
> Th'expressive Emblem of their softer Pow'r;
> Four Knaves in Garbs succinct, a trusty Band,
> Caps on their heads, and Halberds in their hand
> (37-42)

Pope reminded us in a note to this passage that he was alluding to a section of the third book of *The Iliad* here, and that 'This review of the forces is epical in all but length.'[12] He goes on to turn the green baize card table into a field of battle:

> Clubs, Diamonds, Hearts in wild Disorder seen,
> With Throngs promiscuous strow the level Green.
> Thus when dispers'd a routed Army runs,
> Of Asia's troops and Afric's Sable Sons,
> With like Confusion different Nations fly,
> Of various Habit and of various Dye,
> The pierc'd Battalions dis-united fall,
> In Heaps on Heaps; one Fate o'erwhelms them all.
> (79-86)

Pope brings a pseudo-cosmic urgency to this description; the cards not only become elevated into warriors, they represent whole nations, indeed whole continents. Pope resorts to the epic devices not only of listing and enumerating, but of employing large similies for purposes of comparison. This is the same Pope, of course, who was able to gain such eminence as a translator of Homer, and whose style can easily attain to the heroic. However, it would be wrong to see these 'epical' qualities as deployed merely gratuitously. Even though the card-game was an addition to the 1714 version of the poem, it has its own significance in Pope's treatment of Belinda. The game being described is called 'Ombre' (pronounced 'omber'), and the accuracy of Pope's description of it is such that the game can be reconstructed. It was designed to be played by three people:

> Belinda now, whom Thirst of Fame invites,
> Burns to encounter two adventurous Knights,
> At Ombre singly to decide their Doom;
> And swells her Breast with Conquests yet to come.
>
> (25-8)

Thus the battle becomes both an 'encounter' between Belinda and the two men, and also a battle between the two men for victory over Belinda. It is perhaps significant that the word 'ombre' is Spanish for man. Belinda, in this game is almost forced to 'give codille' (ie. concede defeat to the other players) but does, in fact, emerge victorious, showing symbolically the difficulty of a man gaining victory over her on the sexual battlefield. Her triumph is an ironic and short-lived one, though, as almost immediately the Baron plots his 'statagem' for the rape of her lock. Her apparent invulnerability makes this attack seem all the more unexpected and unmannerly.

The attack itself is presented in portentous terms. A small but typical example of this can be found in Pope's unwillingness to use so commonplace a word as 'scissors', essential though it is that we should be aware of the object's presence. Consequently a range of mock-heroic euphemisms is employed:

> Just then Clarissa drew with tempting Grace
> A two-edg'd Weapon from her shining Case
>
> (127-8)

This 'weapon' becomes, variously, 'the little Engine' (132);

'the glitt'ring Forfex' (147); 'the fatal engine' (149); 'the Sheers' (151); and with wonderful epic overstatement, eventually, 'The conqu'ring Force of unresisted Steel' (178).

Another example of the way in which the narrative devices of the traditionsl epic are given an 'Heroi-Comical' flavour, is in Pope's use of the idea of 'the warning' that some dire event is about to take place. Even before Belinda is properly presented to us at the beginning of the poem, her guardian Sylph appears to her in a dream, saying amongst other things:

> I saw, alas! some dread Event impend,
> Ere to the Main this Morning Sun descend.
> But Heav'n reveals not what, or how, or where:
> Warn'd by thy Sylph, oh Pious Maid beware!
> This to disclose is all thy Guardian can.
> Beware of all, but most beware of man!
>
> (Canto I, 109-114)

The joke here is in the warning's vagueness: it is not clear what Belinda should be locking out for, and therefore not surprising that the Baron is able, in due course, to advance upon her, without her appreciating his motives. Although the 'guardian Sylphs' are present in vast numbers at the time, they are rather limited in what they can do, and are restricted again to warning Belinda in the only way they can:

> A thousand Wings, by turns, blow back the Hair,
> And thrice they twitch'd the Diamond in her Ear,
> Thrice she look'd back, and thrice the Foe drew near.
>
> (Canto III, 136-8)

Belinda subsequently make references to warnings and omens too. She partly blames her violated state on having misread the signs:

> 'Twas this, the Morning Omens seem'd to tell!
> Thrice from my trembling hand the Patch-box fell;
> The tott'ring China shook without a Wind,

> Nay, Poll sate mute, and Shock was most Unkind!
> A Sylph too warn'd me of the Threats of Fate,
> In mystic Visions, now believ'd too late!
> (Canto IV, 161-66)

Pope's mock-heroic writing works both ways, of course. We have already seen the way in which he can elaborate the playing of a card game into something resembling a Homeric battle. Here he reduces the epic warnings of gods to heroes to the level of patch-boxes, parrots and lap-dogs.

The most obviously reduced ingredient in the poem, though, is the Sylphs, who constitute that part of the epic 'machinery', as Pope reminds us, normally occupied by gods or angels. Pope's substitution of these august presences with something little better than a band of fairies, also acknowledged a literary precedent. Pope gives us some insight into his thinking on the matter in his dedicatory epistle to Miss Fermor:

> These Machines I determin'd to raise on a very new and odd foundation, the Rosicrucian doctrine of Spirits . . . The Rosicrucians are a people I must bring you acquainted with. The best account of them is a French book called 'Le Comte de Gabalis'.

This book, first published in 1670,[13] had been translated into English more than once. It had been treated as a work of fiction, but, as Pope implies, it had a more philosophical purpose. It consisted chiefly of an imaginary dialogue between a narrator and a Rosicrucian, called The Count of Gabalis. The narrator is sceptical of the Rosicrucian views which the Count expresses, and there is certainly no reason to believe that Pope subscribed to them. He plundered them for their usefulness to his fiction. The Rosicrucians believed that inhabiting the four elements were invisible spirits perceptible only to the initiated. The Sylphs were the creatures of the air and the Nymphs of the seas and rivers. Pope applies the term 'Nymph' to young ladies in general, and the term 'Sylphs' to their guardian spirits. In Belinda's dream at the very opening of Canto I, Ariel describes the purpose of the Sylphs:

Know then, unnumber'd spirits around thee fly,
The light of Militia of the lower Sky;
These, tho' unseen, are ever on the Wing,
Hang o'er the Box, and hover round the Ring.
(41-4)

Pope's response to his Sylphs is ambivalent. On the one hand, they provide a genuine aesthetic enrichment to the text. They show Pope's fascination with their very incorporeality and are the occasion for some of the most delicate description to be found anywhere in his poetry, as we see near the beginning of Canto II:

Transparent Forms, too fine for mortal Sight
Their fluid Bodies half dissolv'd in Light.
Loose to the Wind their airy Garments flew,
Thin glitt'ring Textures of the filmy Dew;
Dipt in the richest Tincture of the Skies,
Where Light disports in ever-mingling Dies
(61-6)

At the same time, though, they provide a comic dimension. For all their fluttering efficiency (Canto II, 111-122), and paramilitary organization (55-8), they are sublimely incompetent when it comes actually to protecting Belinda, and Pope exploits the comic potential of the situation. At the moment of the 'rape' (Canto III, 145-6), Ariel realizes that it is time for a tactical withdrawal:

Amaz'd, confus'd, he found his Pow'r expir'd
Resign'd to Fate, and with a Sigh retir'd.

Likewise a poor Sylph 'too fondly interposed' himself between the Baron's scissors:

Fate urg'd the Sheers, and cut the Sylph in twain
(But Airy Substance soon unites again)
(131-2)

Pope's 'machinery' is an admirably pliable agent of his comedy, though it does not stop with the Sylphs. In *Le Comte de*

Gabalis we are told that the earth is 'filled almost to the centre with Gnomes . . . people of small stature, the guardians of treasures, of mines and of precious stones.' Pope is less interested in developing the Gnomes than he is the Sylphs, but he does, in Canto IV, describe their home to us, the subterranean Cave of Spleen. Both Homer's *Odysseus* and Virgil's *Aeneas* visit, as part of their heroic journeys, the underworld. Equally, Pope was aware of the attention paid to the topography of the Christian Hell by Milton, in *Paradise Lost.* Pope alludes in various ways to all three authors, notably when Pope's visitant to the Cave, a 'sooty' Gnome, carries a parody of Aeneas's golden bough (a kind of token of safe passage):

> Safe past the Gnome thro' this fantastick Band,
> A branch of healing Spleenwort in his hand.
>
> (55-6)

Pope peoples his hell with allegorical figures, characters representing abstractions. (Such allegorization was a prominent feature of Samuel Garth's mock-heroic poem *The Dispensary* which enjoyed considerable popularity and was one of Pope's models for *The Rape of the Lock*.) The word 'Spleen' was applied to any melancholic-hypochondriac illness which women might claim they were suffering from. It enjoyed a certain fashionable status in the early eighteenth century. Spleen is characterized as an ailing Queen:

> Here, in a Grotto, shelter'd close from Air,
> And screen'd in Shades from Day's detested Glare,
> She sighs for ever on her pensive Bed,
> Pain at her Side, and Megrim at her Head.
>
> (21-4)

'Pain' and 'Megrim' (migraine) are turned into allegorical figures too, as are certain other female attributes such as 'Ill-nature' ('like an ancient Maid/Her wrinkled Form in Black and White array'd' (27-8)), and 'Affectation' ('Practis'd to Lisp, and hang the Head aside/Faints into Airs and languishes with Pride' (33-4)). The other inhabitants provide uncomfortably grotesque versions of characters to be found in the upper world:

> Unnumber'd Throngs on ev'ry side are seen
> Of Bodies chang'd to various Forms by Spleen.
> Here living Teapots stand, one Arm held out,
> One bent; the Handle this, and that the Spout:
> A Pipkin there like Homer's Tripod walks;
> Here sighs a Jar, and there a Goose-pye talks
> (47-52)

There is an obviously surreal dimension to the descriptions here, such as Pope was to exhibit in *The Dunciad.* The affected stance ridiculed in 'living teapots' is clear enough to appreciate, and Pope told us in a footnote that the goose-pie referred 'to a real fact; a lady of distinction imagined herself in this condition.' What seems to be described here is the unacceptable face of polite society: the deformed, the diseased and the outcast, banished for ever from the light of day.

It seems unlikely, though, that Pope's original audience took such matters unduly seriously. *The Rape of the Lock* was an astounding success: the 1714 version of the poem sold 3,000 copies in its first four days of publication.[14] Chamber maids were reported as reading it, and before long it was translated into French and Italian. It was frequently illustrated by artists in the eighteenth and nineteenth centuries, and was perhaps the only poem to survive (for all its alleged 'indecency') the Victorian critical reaction against Pope.

Undoubtedly the poem is witty and amusing and the reader is, should he feel inclined, at liberty to dismiss its content as insignificant and inoffensive. This must be one reason why it has often been labelled as good-natured and forgiving, though it is not easily or unarguably so. Apart from the fact that satire by its very nature takes a critical stance, there is in *The Rape of the Lock* a clear-sighted and persistent emphasis upon human folly and pretence. Behind the glitter and the chatter, there is an emergent concern for the moral dimension, and an insistent desire to expose moral and psychological flimsiness. What cools the poet's indignation is the ingenuity of his own invention. On what is really the tiniest of factual promptings, Pope built an elaborate fictional structure of his own. He was distanced by his own detachment from the characters and events which he portrayed. As he wrote in a letter to a Mrs Marriot:

> This whimsical piece of work . . . is at the most a satire, and the most inoffensive of anything of mine . . . 'Tis a sort of writing very like tickling[15] . . .

In saying such Pope acknowledges the strangely painful – yet amusing effect of *The Rape of the Lock,* but fortunately or unfortunately he was never able to be so inoffensive again.

Chapter Two: Modern Ladies and Ancient Poets

1. The standard account of the genesis of the poem is given in the Twickenham Edition Volume II (1940) pp81-102.
2. The 1712 version is printed in Twickenham II pp127-137.
3. Dedicatory epistle *To Mrs Arabella Fermor* Twickenham II pp142-143.
4. A complete version of this is included in *Pope: The Rape of the Lock*: a Casebook Ed. John Dixon Hunt (1968) pp25-30.
5. Samuel Johnson *Lives of the English Poets* World's Classics Edition (1906) Vol II p316.
6. See Twickenham II pp142-143.
7. Quoted in Twickenham II p95.
8. See especially, Cleanth Brooks *The Case of Miss Arabella Fermor* in *The Well Wrought Urn* (1947), Chap 5.
9. *Epistle to a Lady*, line 2. Discussed in Chap 4 below.
10. Twickenham II p195.
11. Pope's translation of Sarpedon's speech to Glaucus from *The Iliad* Book XII, can be found in Twickenham (1963) pp61-62.
12. Twickenham II p169.
13. A translation of *Le Comte de Gabalis* along with other sources and analogues can be found in William Kinsley (Ed.) *The Rape of the Lock: Contexts.* (1979).
14. See Twickenham II pp104-5 for details of the poem's reception, also Robert Halsband, *The Rape of the Lock and its Illustrators 1714-1896* (1980).
15. Correspondence (ed. Sherburn), (1956) Volume I, p211.

3

FLAPPING GILDED BUGS

The First 'Dunciads' and 'An Epistle to Dr Arbuthnot'

Strictly speaking, *The Dunciad* is not one, but four poems. The first version of it, in three books was published in 1728, the second, known as *The Dunciad Variorum,* in 1729. *The New Dunciad,* comprising what we now think of as the fourth book was published in 1742, and a final synthesis of both old and new, modified, extended in places and with a different hero, was published in 1743.

Even allowing for Pope's well-known tendency to revise, polish, and adapt, the growth and development of *The Dunciad* over so many years is remarkable, and is not explicable merely in terms of Pope's perfectionism. *The Dunciad* is a peculiarly, perhaps uniquely, plastic poem, infinitely extendable, as Pope himself noted.[1] It must be the only poem in the English language which, without structural damage, underwent, between editions a complete change of hero, let alone numerous changes in the supporting cast. The poem's malleability is the consequence of its subject matter.

The Odyssey is the story of Odysseus; *The Aeneid* is the story of Aeneas; *The Dunciad* is the story of the Dunces. We have seen in Chapter One the ease by which enemies could be made in the literary world in which Pope existed: it was all but inevitable, and the Dunces, too, were capable of falling out amongst themselves. Pope eventually felt confident enough to identify and then attack the whole tribe.

The word dunce was on its way to acquiring its modern

meaning in Pope's time, but to him it had specific connotations which obviously need to be recovered. In late medieval times the word had been applied to a group of philosophers of whom Duns Scotus was the most prominent. A 'Duns' was a pedant, a hair-splitter or, in terms of ideas, a reactionary. The terms was an abusive one but it did not in its origins simply mean 'fool'. Rather it suggested narrow horizons, and an imperviousness to wider issues. The meaning continued to develop and by the mid-seventeenth century was a term of abuse applicable to any kind of writer. Dryden gave the word currency in his poem *Mackflecknoe,* a satire on the poet and dramatist Thomas Shadwell. In this poem Duncehood acquires richly fictional dimensions. Shadwell is not simply a Dunce, he succeeds to the Kingship of the Dunces. The poem is an elaborate satire on Shadwell's literary shortcomings, best summed up in the lines:

> The rest to some faint meaning make pretence,
> But Shadwell never deviates into sense.
> Some beams of wit on other souls may fall,
> Strike through, and make a lucid interval;
> But Shadwell's genuine night admits no ray,
> His rising fogs prevail upon the day.
>
> (19-24)

The influences on Pope's *Dunciad* are diverse, but the most potent native one is undoubtedly *Mackflecknoe.* Not only does Pope extend Dryden's idea of the kingdom of the Dunces, with its own monarch and corporate mythology, he also develops certain of the associations which Duncehood carried with it in the earlier poem. As the quoted lines show, being a Dunce means not simply being an unsuccessful writer. The Dunce is associated with darkness, fog and night. He is not illuminated by 'wit', and, indeed, comes to be an enemy of it. Dryden's poem goes on to equate literary with economic impoverishment, the Dunce is surrounded by squalor. There is no respectability in his calling.

Dunces are dull. This is to say that the chief quality they represent is 'dullness' (or as Pope spells it, 'Dulness'). Again, the word 'dull' did not mean exactly the same in the eighteenth century as it does now, though its meaning is recognizable. For us the most accurate synonyms for 'dull' are 'tedious', 'uneventful', or 'boring'. For Pope the emphasis was different. To him dullness was a more common, certainly more commonplace, quality. Its connotations were of the humdrum, workaday, fustian, uninspired. This word too stood in opposition to the idea of 'wit'. Where wit implied intelligence, perception and brilliance, dullness was caution, convention, unremarkableness. The word continued to have these meanings throughout the century.

It was a particularly important word in Pope's circle. When the Scriblerus Club had come into existence in 1714 it was essentially against 'dulness' that it pitched itself. If the original purposes of the club had been political, by the time Pope and Gay had joined Arbuthnot and Swift, they were literary and satirical. Pope had hoped to create:

> ' . . . a burlesque monthly periodical in which follies in learning and criticism would be satirised in ironic reviews that depreciated works of merit and cried up the productions of Grub Street.'[2]

Or, as Pope was to put it in another context, he was seeking to bring into existence 'An Account of the works of the unlearned.'[3] Such an account was, of course, satirical in intention, and one of the strangest and most inexplicable features of the Scriblerus group was its fascination with mediocrity, with dulness, hence its apparent support for 'the production of Grub Street.' The group invented its own Dunce, and took its name from him. Martinus Scriblerus was '. . . a man of capacity enough; that had dipped into every art and science, but injudiciously in each.'[4] He was, by diverse hands, provided with a set of fictional *Memoirs,* whose publication Pope eventually masterminded in 1741. There was much of the private joke about Scriblerus club productions. One representative piece was written partly by Pope (Scriblerian satire was usually a corporate activity) about his own poem, *The Rape of the Lock.* Parodying a common Grub Street genre, this piece appeared under the title *A Key to the Lock*. The author was supposedly one 'Esdras Barnivelt, Apothecary', and his serious, pedantic, overblown, utterly dull reading of the poem, is a gleeful demonstration of a sledgehammer trying to crack a nut. It is not surprising that the *Key* comes to wildly inapposite conclusions, seeing *The Rape of the Lock* as a dangerous threat to political, religious and moral stability. The final paragraph runs:

> To sum up my whole Charge against this Author in a few Words: He has ridiculed both the present Ministry and the last; abused great Statesmen and great Generals nay the Treaties of whole Nations have not escaped him, nor has the Royal Dignity itself been omitted in the Progress of his Satyr; and all this he has done just at the Meeting of a new Parliament. I hope a proper Authority may be made use of to bring him to condign punishment . . .[5]

The fact that we do not recognize *The Rape of the Lock* from this description of it is, of course, entirely intentional, though as a satire upon literary critics who 'read too much in' it retains its point. Possibly it has things to hint about the literary pretensions of apothecaries too, but the strangest thing of all about it is its willing identification with a Duncely persona, and the way in which it is directed against a work by its own author. Amusing though the piece is, it possesses all the inherent perversity of the practical joke. It is an odd endeavour for a prominent poet. There is something rather schoolboyish about it.

Scriblerian satire, however, cannot be easily dismissed. There is a little too much of it, and it persisted too long. Perhaps the most crucial influence on the Scriblerus Club was Jonathan Swift. Although there is no reason to associate him closely with *A Key to the Lock,* there is something about the piece's indirection and cantankerousness which is entirely characteristic of him. Swift had published *The Bickerstaffe Papers* in 1708, predicting and eventually announcing the death of John Partridge,[6] the preposterous astrologer whom Pope criticizes briefly at the end of *The Rape of the Lock.*[7] It was widely believed that Partridge had indeed died, despite his issuing assertions to the contrary. Again, there is more than a little of the practical joke in this effort, and, again, it was a pseudonymous work. Bickerstaffe, the supposed author, was a precursor of Scriblerus, Barnivelt and other fictional

Dunces.

Even if the fascination which the Scriblerians had for Dunces was ultimately inexplicable, it was a fascination which led to the making of enemies. Grub Street authors, pedants, editors, writers of Keys were fair game to the authors of *The Rape of the Lock, The Beggar's Opera* or *Gulliver's Travels.* The desire to poke fun at the less gifted did not pass unnoticed, and Pope and Swift in their turns became fair game for Grub Street. If Pope's *Key to the Lock* is an entertaining piece of high-spiritedness, its distortingly pedantic tone is not very different from what had actually been written about the poem by John Dennis, in his own right an established critic. His comments on the opening lines of *The Rape of the Lock* indicate, perhaps, that 'Esdras Barnivelt' contained within him some specific satiric targets:

> '. . . in three Lines there are no less than two Errors in the Sentiments. For, in the first Place, tho' the Author has neither Fable nor general Action, yet he proposes to sing something general, rather than particular Action which is the Subject of his Poem, and he begins as if he design'd to make the Reader expect a Treatise of Love Quarrels . . .'[8]

Pope's objections to pedantry were clearly well-based, the more so since he believed that imperceptive critical writing of this kind threatened to stultify the development of 'real' literature. Dulness was thus a threat to the healthy state of culture, and matters were not helped by the fact that the first generation of 'hireling' writers had colonized Grub Street, with pens at the ready to write anything for anyone (or against anyone) to gain a living pittance.

The history of Pope's relationship with Grub Street has been outlined in Chapter One. *The Dunciad*'s history mirrors it. Although the first version of the poem was not published until 1728, it seems highly likely that its origins lay in the Scriblerian period of more than a decade before. Much miscellaneous unfinished and therefore unpublished writing was done during this period, and went into abeyance with the club in 1715. What resurrected some, at least, of the Scriblerian material were Swift's visits to England in 1726 and

1727, during which period he spent much time with Pope at Twickenham. Swift had for some time planned a journal of the 'travels' of Scriblerus, which he had modified and completed in 1726. Scriblerus had meanwhile become Lemuel Gulliver. One of Pope's embryonic but extant manuscripts was of a poem which he called *The Progress of Dulness,* and it was this work which Swift now urged him to complete. When it is recalled that Swift published *Gulliver* '. . . to vex the world rather then divert it . . .'[9] it is not difficult to see what mood was in the air. Pope was to acknowledge Swift's midwifery when the poem was published. It was printed anonymously but it celebrated Swift (appropriately enough) pseudonymously ('. . . whatever Title please thine ear, Dean, Drapier, Bickerstaffe, or Gulliver!' (16-17)). The collusive, if not collaborative nature of *The Dunciad* also thus marks it as a Scriblerian text.

It is a complex poem partly because it is so many different things at once. Like *The Rape of the Lock* it is mock-heroic in conception, though it relies less consistently than the earlier poem on exploiting the gap between the doings of 'little men' and epic tradition. It is also disconcertingly contemporary: literally hundreds of people are mentioned in it, and the personnel, as we have noted, come and go between versions. It is obstinately Scriblerian too: the 1729 version contained *Notes Variorum* in which Pope in the guise of one of his hated pedants commented with uproarious solemnity on the textual detail of his poem as he went. It is also densely allusive. The debt to Dryden has been mentioned, but Homer, Virgil, Ovid and Milton are present as well. It is as if Pope wants to enlist the whole of Western literary culture against his Dunces. At the same time, particularly in Book Two, he is happily lavatorial.

The earliest stages of its composition tend to indicate that *The Dunciad* was a poem in search of a hero. Pope's conflict with Lewis Theobald over the editing of Shakespeare provided him with one. We have seen that Pope, enjoying a certain scholarly eminence from his Homer translations, set himself to the editing of Shakespeare, and published his work in 1725. Theobald's reply, *'Shakespeare Restored: or a Specimen of the Many Errors . . . Committed . . . by Mr Pope'* appeared the following year. Theobald had scored a palpable hit. His scholarship was greater than Pope's, and he was able to expose the edition as not a great deal more than random guesswork. Pope, needless to say, was not pleased, particularly as Theobald, scholar though he may have been, was otherwise a composer of pantomimes and ephemera in a perfect Grub Street vein. He was not a man to provoke the leading poet of the age with impunity. Pope did, on the whole, hold himself aloof from the Grub Street attacks on him which appeared in such profusion. Satirically, he was much more written about than writing, but where Theobald was concerned, enough was enough. Pope could not respond to Theobald's attack on scholarly grounds, he had to submit to the latter's supremacy in that area, but he was a much better poet, and the arrival of Theobald as material for the poem, concentrated his mind wonderfully. He had already written to Swift:

> 'My spleen is at the little rogues . . . it would vex one more to be knocked on the head with a piss-pot than by a thunderbolt . . . But to be squired to death . . . by apothecaries' apprentices, by the under-strappers of under-secretaries to secretaries who were no secretaries – this would provoke as dull a dog as Philips himself.'[10]

Or as he said in blunter mood: 'This poem will rid me of these insects.'[11] We shall have cause to consider this statement again before very long.

Although the student of the poem is most likely to encounter it in its 'final' four-book version of 1743, it is misleading to do so. *The Dunciad* is very much a poem of Pope's middle period, and certainly influenced the turn which his literary career subsequently took. Also, appealing though it is, it is wrong to see the closing sections of the 1743 version as representing Pope's 'last words'. He reputedly thought this book to be his finest work, but the vision of 'Universal Darkness' with which it ends, is to be found, though in a contextually different mood, at the end of the 1728 version. It is also important to any student of Pope's satire to see the way in which the fluidity of *The Dunciad*'s conception enabled it, over a sixteen year period, to grow and to change. It is in the nature of Duncehood to be ephemeral: some of the 1728-9 Dunces had disappeared by

1743-4, Theobald himself being the most notable example, to be replaced by others and by Colley Cibber as hero. No one can therefore easily say that one version of the poem is 'superior' to the other, though the *New Dunciad*, comprising Book Four, certainly spreads the poem's net wider. The mythology of Duncehood is very much defined by the first version, and to consider the poem as a product of the 1720s obviously leads to a more accurate appreciation of its place in Pope's development.

In a poem which operates simultaneously on so many levels, it is easy to ignore its essentially narrative aspect, but important to appreciate it. Linear narrative, and the rather surreal world which the poem creates are strange bedfellows, though Pope himself was keen to provide us with his own narrative summary, book by book.

Book One deals at its most basic narrative level with the question of succession. Dulness is a variety of things: a mental state, a geographical location, an allegorical personage in the shape of a Goddess, and a mythological kingdom. It is to the kingship of this realm that Lewis Theobald is to succeed. The idea of Dulness as a kingdom originated in Dryden's *Mackflecknoe,* where Shadwell is shown to succeed Flecknoe (an Irish priest with poetic pretensions) on the Duncely throne. In *The Dunciad* Pope presents Theobald as succeeding to the throne vacated by Elkanah Settle, and the festivities occasioned by this succession are paralleled with those occurring on the installation of a Lord Mayor, who, on taking office underwent a progress by land and river of the City of London, moving from East to West and back again.[12]

There are various reasons why the idea of the Lord Mayor's Procession is appropriate. Elkanah Settle (who died in 1724) was the 'City Poet'. This position required him to compose annual poems in celebration of the new Lord Mayor. It required not a great deal more, and even in an age which gave formal poetry a higher priority than more recent times have done, the post hardly needed a towering genius to fill it. Poor Settle was undoubtedly dull, and, as it happens, the last person to hold the post of City Poet before it was abolished. Lord Mayor's processions were important public as well as civic occasions, taking on patriotic and political overtones, and leading to much revelry of a not always sober kind. They were comparable to coronation festivities, and as such formed a worthy image for a poem which, in its opening sections, is dealing with succession to the Kingdom of the Dunces.

Book One begins in celebration of its mock-epic status, with an invocation. Pope tells us something of the nature and surroundings of the goddess Dulness, before introducing us to Theobald (pronounced 'Tibbald') who has been chosen by Dulness to succeed Settle. He is introduced at his lucubrations, and forms a pyre by burning books (an interesting comment on his attitudes to literature), before being taken by the Goddess to her temple and pronounced Settle's successor.

Pope continues the process of mythologizing Dulness which Dryden had started in *Mackflecknoe.* To begin with it is given a political dimension as Pope associates it with the Whig grandees:

> Say great Patricians! (since your selves inspire
> These wond'rous works; so Jove and Fate require)
> Say from what cause, in vain decry'd and curst,
> Still Dunce the second reigns like Dunce the first?
>
> (3-6)

Given the succession of George II to the throne previously occupied by his father George I in 1727, it is difficult not to see a pointed contemporary comment in the last line. Neither king was remotely enlightened about anything cultural, and one wonders what exactly George II made of the copy of *The Dunciad* which Walpole gave him.

Pope presents Dulness as the root of cultural ill, but he clearly enjoys responding to its many-faceted nature, constantly inventing new dimensions to it as he goes: Dulness is a mass of cunningly controlled opposites:

> In eldest time e'er mortals writ or read,
> E'er Pallas issued from the Thund'rer's head,
> Dulness o'er all possess'd her ancient right,
> Daughter of Chaos and eternal Night:
> Fate in their dotage this fair idiot gave,
> Gross as her sire, and as her mother grave,
> Laborious, heavy, busy, bold, and blind,

She rul'd, in native Anarchy, the mind.
(7-14)

The idea of a Goddess being a 'fair idiot' is a typically perplexing one. The word 'idiot' in Pope's time was stronger than it has since become, suggesting not mild, but considerable, almost deforming, stupidity. Calling such an 'idiot' 'fair' is making it even more freakishly unpleasant. The normally complimentary associations of the word have been overturned.

Dulness essentially carries with her attributes which confound normal categorization, being on the one hand 'Gross . . . Laborious . . . heavy . . . ', yet ruling with 'native Anarchy'. Thus it is Dulness's very grossness and inertia, which threaten to overturn order and proportion. The subversive and uncontrollable nature of Dulness is stressed elsewhere. Pope ends both versions of his poem with a reference to Dulness's 'uncreating word': she is presiding over a collective decline into Chaos, her original element. For all the 'solid pudding' which Dulness represents in strictly literary terms, Pope sees something apocalyptic in her power. The poem is urgent in its presentation of upheaval and impending disaster:

Here pleas'd behold her mighty wings out-
spread,
To hatch a new Saturnian age of Lead.
(25-6)

Quite characteristically, the poem weds two different mythologies here. In the Greek tradition, Saturn presided over the first, golden age of the world (rather like the Christian Eden); in alchemical writing Saturn was associated with lead. Dulness possesses the power to hatch the last age (of Lead) to end the world, as the golden age had begun it. An important suggestion too, is that Dulness has the facility to 'hatch', to reproduce profusely smaller versions of herself. There is a misbegotten feel about her progeny, too:

Where wave the tatter'd ensigns of Rag-Fair,
A yawning ruin hangs and nods in air;

Keen hollow winds howl thro' the bleak recess,
Emblem of Music caus'd by Emptiness:
Here in one bed two shiv'ring sisters lye,
The cave of Poverty and Poetry.

(27-32)

Lewis Theobald wrote a poem called *The Cave of Poetry,* so the identification with him is obviously being made in the last line. Pope also seeks to relate literary and economic poverty. Apart from presenting Poverty and Poetry as almost incestuously dependent, he also pins down very specifically the home of literary Dulness in contemporary London. Rag Fair, as its name suggests, was a market for old clothes and rags. It is one of the several downtown venues which mark the purlieus of the Dunces.[13] The romantic, rather glamorous idea of the poet starving in a garret, as critics of *The Dunciad* need to point out from time to time, is a later one which has never quite died. Pope simply sees a starving poet as squalid and debased. Economic poverty means literary poverty. The Dunces occupy the least salubrious parts of town of which Grub Street is merely the best-known and most symbolic.

The image of Dulness as a begetter continues to be emphasized in some of Pope's most surreal writing. That same solid inert Dulness, is also 'ductile', plastic, meandering. The galloping omnipresence of her inventions threatens literary propriety. The works of the Dunces, indeed their very processes of composition, take on a weird, barbarous, riotous energy of their own. Looking around her, Dulness sees:

How Hints, like spawn, scarce quick in embryo lie,
How new-born Nonsense first is taught to cry,
Maggots half-form'd, in rhyme exactly meet,
And learn to crawl upon poetic feet.
Here one poor Word a hundred clenches makes,
And ductile dulness new meanders takes;
There motley Images her fancy strike,
Figures ill'pair'd, and Similes unlike.
She sees a Mob of Metaphors advance,
Pleas'd with the Madness of the mazy dance:
How Tragedy and Comedy embrace;

How Farce and Epic get a jumbled race . . .
(57-68)

In one sense a markedly dynamic process is being described here, with copulations, births, movement, dancing and yet more copulation. But this apparently frenzied literary fervour is, in fact, destructive. Rather than being composed, literature is being unpicked and left as a series of fibres, or component parts. Only verbal freaks and monsters result.

Duncehood is an inner as well as an outer state. What the Goddess sees as she looks through the regions of Chaos which she controls, is an external manifestation of the chaos within the hero's mind:

> Studious he sate, with all his books around,
> Sinking from thought to thought, a vast profound!
> Plung'd for his sense, but found no bottom there;
> Then writ and flounder'd on, in mere despair.
> (111-114)

Pope made an important addition to this passage in 1743, and it is perhaps worth examining it here. Amongst other things it reminds us of the way in which the poet's fascination with Dulness was a growing, developing one. It is as if he found the subject always too big to be finally pinned-down. New dimensions continued to be revealed:

> Round him much Embryo, much Abortion lay,
> Much future Ode, and abdicated Play;
> Nonsense precipitate, like running Lead,
> That slip'd thro' Cracks and Zig-zags of the Head;
> All that on Folly Frenzy could beget,
> Fruits of dull Heat, and Sooterkins of Wit.
> (1743 Text, 121-6)

This passage seems to encapsulate most of the major images which have characterized Pope's response to Dulness so far. The works of Dulness are miscarried and deformed, obstinately remaining as Embryo or Abortion. Likewise the tendency of Dulness to be both solid and ductile at the same time, is underlined in the simile of 'Nonsense . . . like running Lead . . .' The Dunce's head is a disconcerting collection of 'Cracks and Zig-zags', suggesting special mental apparatus of a quite different sort from that possessed by other people.

It has been pointed out more than once that a chief concern of Pope, especially in Book I of the poem, is to emphasize the way in which Duncehood renders literature gross and ponderous.[14] Deprived of any spiritual or intellectual merit, the products of the Dunces are merely physical objects, vast weights of paper and print. Pope has already (line 116) in his description of Theobald shown him surrounded by 'much learned lumber':

> Volumes, whose size the space exactly fill'd
> (117)

A new force is given to the idea of shelves groaning beneath the weight of their contents. The more mediocre the author, the deader the weight:

> Here swells the shelf with Ogilby the great:
> There stamp'd with arms, Newcastle shines compleat
> (121-2)

> De Lyra here a dreadful front extends,
> And there, the groaning shelves Philemon bends.
> (133-4)

The Dunciad protests at the age of lead. It protests more crucially at an age of paper. The ease with which the works of Dulness can be printed is an instant debasing of the literary coinage. The idea can be traced back to *Mackflecknoe,* where Dryden's couplet tells us:

> From dusty shops neglected authors come,
> Martyrs of pies, and relics of the bum.
> (100-1)

The association of literature with consumption and

defecation is not a happy one, but it is a graphic reminder that paper is the common currency of writing, wrapping, and visits to the lavatory.

Pope avoids Dryden's bluntness, and, characteristically, extends the idea. The paper to be found in Theobald's books has managed to ''scape the martyrdom of jakes [ie. lavatory] and fire' (124), avoid being used to wrap spices (131) or made into tapers or pie-wrappings (136). There is a quiet suggestion that paper would perhaps be more useful in these contexts than in helping to propagate the literary abortions of Duncehood. In a mock-religious ceremony, recalling that of the Baron in *The Rape of the Lock,* Theobald makes an offering to the Goddess, Dulness, by burning some of his books:

> . . . A folio Common-place
> Founds the whole pyle, of all his works the base;
> Quarto's, Octavo's, shape the less'ning pyre,
> At last, a little Ajax tips the spire.
>
> (139-42)

He addresses the Goddess at length, in what is really a Dunce's manifesto. Pope is indulging in extended Scriblerian irony here, crying up the works of Grub Street through the mouth of Theobald, who reminds the Goddess of his calling:

> Old puns restore, lost blunders nicely seek,
> And crucify poor Shakespear once a week.
> For thee I dim these eyes, and stuff this head,
> With all such reading as was never read;
> For thee supplying, in the worst of days,
> Notes to dull books and prologues to dull plays;
> For thee explain a thing till all men doubt it,
> And write about it, Goddess, and about it
>
> (165-170)

The original ground of complaint against Theobald was his edition of Shakespeare. Pope's point is that the scholarship which Theobald showed in that edition was little more than nit-picking pedantry which did nothing to illuminate Shakespeare at all. He makes little distinction between the scholar-pedant and the 'bad writer', both are manifestations of the same literary corruption, as Theobald goes on to say:

Not that my quill to Critiques was confin'd
My verse gave ampler lessons to mankind;
So gravest precepts may successless prove,
But sad examples never fail to move.
As forc'd from wind-guns lead itself can fly,
And pond'rous slugs cut swiftly through the sky
(173-8)

Theobald's supplications find favour. Dulness lobs a copy of Ambrose Philips's poem *Thule* onto the fire to quench it instantly by its dead weight, and finally tells her chosen son:

'I see a King! who leads my chosen sons
To lands that flow with clenches and with puns:
'Till each fam'd Theatre my empire own,
'Till Albion, as Hibernia, bless my throne!
I see! I see! –' Then rapt, she spoke no more.
'God save King Tibbald!' Grubstreet alleys road.
(251-256)

A concert of Dunces is a raucous business, and Book I ends amidst the thunder of raised voices:

Loud thunder to its bottom shook the bog,
And the hoarse nations croak'd, God save King Log!
(259-60)

Again there is a mythic dimension to this section. In the fable the frogs desired a king and begged Jupiter for one. He threw them a log. Hence both Theobald, and his Grub Street colleagues have been appropriately characterized.

Two months before *The Dunciad* first appeared, Pope's *Peri Bathous: or the Art of Sinking in Poetry* had been published. This is a Scriblerian text (it is actually signed with the name of Martinus Scriblerus) seeking to prove that, just as the classical literary critics had interested themselves in 'hypsos' or the sublime, it was the business of modern critics to concern themselves with 'bathos', or the profound. With many examples from his lesser contemporaries, Pope went on with Scriblerian mock-seriousness, to illustrate various examples of 'the profound'. Unsurprisingly perhaps, the essay turns out to be an ironic exposure of the mediocrity of much contemporary poetry:

> '. . . Those who have a taste of the sublime [are] . . . Very few, but the Profound strikes universally, and is adapted to every Capacity[15] . . . therefore . . . Mediocrity ought to be allow'd, yea indulged to the good Subjects of England[16] . . . Is there not an Art of Diving as well of flying?[17]

The answer to this last question is provided by the second book of *The Dunciad.* Amongst other things it contains a description of a diving competition. Homer and Virgil had, in their epics, devoted space to the description of heroic games in celebration of funerals or victory. Pope is using a directly 'mock epic' motif here, as he describes the rather different kinds of games which the Dunces play.

There is no better illustration of Pope's multiple allusiveness than the very opening of Book II. Theobald is now installed as King:

> High on a gorgeous seat, that far outshone
> Henley's gilt Tub, or Flecknoe's Irish Throne,
> Or that, where on her Curlls the Public pours
> All-bounteous, fragrant grains, and golden show'rs;
> Great Tibbald sate . . .
>
> (1-5)

This passage begins with a direct parody of the opening of Milton's second book of *Paradise Lost* in which Satan is described as sitting 'High on a throne of royal state, which far/ Outshone the wealth of Ormus and of Ind . . .' Thus the true epic description of Satan is being used mock-epically against Theobald. At the same time, the reader obviously suspects comparisons between Theobald and the Devil, though as

Pope's description is less awesome than Milton's, Theobald becomes a less distinguished devil altogether.

But this is not all. A 'tub' such as that described in the second line (a bathetic enough object in itself) was used by dissenting preachers, like the dubious 'Orator' Henley[18] when performing in the open air. Flecknoe, the Irish priest, we have already met through Dryden's poem. The place next described, '. . . where . . . the Public pours/All-bounteous, fragrant grains . . .' is the public pillory in which Edmund Curll was condemned to stand for publishing obscene material (though he never in fact served the punishment). One wonders what the 'fragrant grains and golden show'rs' might actually have consisted of. In its own way, this passage tells us an enormous amount about Pope's ways of working in *The Dunciad.* It also shows why the poem can so often be so disconcerting to the reader. On the one hand, there is a vein of parody and allusion to other works of Western literature. At the same time, there are private jokes, emerging from the most topical of references. It is by veering between the highly literary and the scabrously contemporary that Pope is able to render so many of his Dunces so grotesque.

The first of the games described is a running race, and the prize is 'A poet's form', in fact a model of a poet. The model turns out to be identified as James More (later known as Moore Smythe), who had offended Pope by his plagiaries. Pope's own note to this section points out the appropriateness of presenting More as a model, since in literary terms as a plagiarist he could hardly be said to have any 'real' existence of his own. As the property of booksellers, though, he has his attractions, and the race becomes a competition between Curll and Lintot (described throughout by his christian name of Bernard) to see which one can possess him as an author for publication. The race is closely run:

> So lab'ring on, with shoulders, hands, and head,
> Wide as a windmill all his figure spread,
> With legs expanded Bernard urg'd the race,
> And seem'd to emulate great Jacob's pace.
>
> (61-4)

However, there is mischief afoot.

Full in the middle way there stood a lake,
Which Curl's Corinna chanc'd that morn to make,
(Such was her wont, at early dawn to drop
Her evening cates before his neighbour's shop,)
Here fortun'd Curl to slide; loud shout the band,
And Bernard! Bernard! rings thro' all the Strand.
Obscene with filth the Miscreant lies bewray'd
Fall'n in the plash his wickedness had lay'd
(65-72)

Even this passage can be taken at different levels. At the first level, it represents Curll slipping on a pool of human excrement ('Renew'd by ordure's sympathetic force' (95), he goes on to win the race). But Pope is not simply being lavatorial for the sake of it. He seems especially keen to explain how this filthy 'lake' came into existence.

One of Edmund Curll's earliest skirmishes with Pope involved the unauthorized publication of some youthful letters of the poet to his friend Henry Cromwell. These letters were published under the pseudonym 'Corinna' by a Mrs Elizabeth Thomas, who claimed to have 'found' them. The idea that one of Curll's authors should be in the habit of defecating before his shop (67-8), is quickly susceptible of metaphorical interpretation. The productions of the Dunces are equated with excreta and filth. Unpleasant and extreme though this idea may be, it is not new to Pope. He can be seen experimenting with it in *The Art of Sinking in Poetry*:

> '. . . Poetry is a natural or morbid Secretion from the Brain. As I would not suddenly stop a Cold in the Head or dry up my neighbour's Issue I would as little hinder him from necessary Writing . . . there is hardly any human Creature past Childhood, but at one time or other has had some Poetical Evacuation and no doubt was much better for it in his Health.'[19]

One can see the association of ideas: poetry is a secretion, by extension an excretion. The works of Dulness are produced by exercise of the bowels as much as of the brain. Or for that matter of the bladder. The next game is a urinating competition:

> Chetwood and Curl accept the glorious strife,
> (Tho' one his son dissuades, and one his wife)
> This on his manly confidence relies,
> That on his vigor and superior size.
> First Chetwood lean'd against his letter'd post;
> It rose, and labour'd to a curve at most
> (159-64)

> Not so from shameless Curl: Impetuous spread
> The stream, and smoaking, flourish'd o'er his head . . .

> Thro' half the heav'ns he pours th'exalted urn;
> His rapid waters in their passage burn.
> (171-2; 175-6)

A possible criticism of these lines would be on the grounds of their childishness. The kind of jokes which Pope is obviously enjoying here are not the sort which one normally associates with a grown man, especially one whose poem is about the sad decline in contemporary literary culture. But we should remember that these descriptions are being used to ridicule his Dunces. Pope is showing them in gross and undignified physical postures, enjoying childish pleasures. They are, too, assigned to their proper sphere. Curll and Chetwood, Pope reminds us, are virtuosi in a pissing competition, but possess few qualifications as publishers of worthwhile literature.

Recent criticism of *The Dunciad* has tended to stress the indulgent tone which underlines Pope's descriptions of his Dunces in Book II. Perhaps the best summing-up of this position is that by Emrys Jones:

> 'These dunces are . . . like unabashed small children . . . The world they inhabit is, like that of early infancy, wholly given to feeling and sensation, and so all the activities are of a simple nature: they run races, have urinating, tickling, shouting and diving

competitions, and finally vie with each other in keeping awake until "the soft gifts of Sleep conclude the day" . . .'[20]

Certainly the tickling and noise-making competitions are gleeful occurrences, though they also underline the rowdy, insurrectionary qualities which Pope associates with Grub Street. If the Dunces are children, they are extremely noisy ones:

> Now thousand tongues are heard in one loud din:
> The Monkey-mimicks rush discordant in.
> 'Twas chtt'ring, grinning, mouthing, jabb'ring all,
> And Noise and Norton, Brangling and Breval
> Dennis and Dissonance: and captious Art,
> And Snip-snap short, and Interruption smart.
> (227-32)

There is an inseparability between the authors and the noise they make, Breval becomes synonymous with brangling, Dennis with dissonance, and so forth. Duncehood is a blatant rather than an obscure state tending always to self-advertisement and exaggeration.

It is precisely this perception of grossness which underlines the mud-diving competition. The arts of poetic sinking are easy ones for the Dunces:

> Not Welsted so: drawn endlong by his scull,
> Furious he sinks; precipitately dull.
> Whirlpools and storms his circling arm invest,
> With all the Might of gravitation blest.
> (293-6)

Both symbolically and topographically, the mud-diving contest is perhaps the most important section of Book II. It is, for example, closely defined in terms of place:

> This labour past, by Bridewell all descend
> (As morning pray'r and flagellation end.)
> To where Fleet-ditch with disemboguing streams

Rolls the large tribute of dead dogs to Thames,
The King of Dykes! than whom, no sluice of mud,
With deeper sable blots the silver flood.

(257-62)

If it is easy to find Pope vulgar in Book II of *The Dunciad*, he must be allowed a certain euphemism here. 'The King of Dykes' was in reality a large open sewer disgorging into the Thames from the north. Its relative closeness to Grub Street renders it an appropriate Duncely location in a geographical sense. The fact that, in practice, it is not simply a dyke or ditch, make it symbolically fitting also. Its contents are more than simply mud, or even dead dogs, and the diving in it which the Dunces do, is thus entirely in keeping with the faecal associations that Pope has already made. Dulness makes the rules:

'Here strip my children! Here at once leap in!
Here prove who best can dash thro' thick and thin,
And who the most in love of dirt excel,
Of dark dexterity of groping well'

(263-6)

At this point Pope is perhaps able to embarrass his Dunces the most, showing them up in the least dignified poses possible:

In naked majesty great Dennis stands,
And Milo-like, surveys his arms and hands

(271-2)

Likewise, Jonathan Smedley, Irish clergyman, enemy of Swift and supporter of Walpole:

Next Smedley div'd; slow circles dimpled o'er
The quaking mud, that clos'd and ope'd no more
All look, all sigh, and call on Smedley lost;
Smedley in vain resounds thro' all the coast.

(279-82)

The thought of the name of 'Smedley' resounding through the air, as the name is called out on all sides, is a particularly grotesque one, especially as the lines are a direct parody of Virgil's description of the Argonauts wailing for the dead Hylas on the shore.[21] Smedley, however, is to return:

> Sudden, a burst of thunder shook the flood.
> Lo Smedley rose, in majesty of mud!
> Shaking the horrors of his ample brows,
> And each ferocious feature grim with ooze . . .
>
> First he relates, how sinking to the chin,
> Smit with his mien, the Mud-nymphs suck'd him in:
> How young Lutetia, softer than the down,
> Nigrina black, and Merdamante brown,
> Vy'd for his love in jetty bow'rs below;
> As Hylas fair was ravish'd long ago.
> (301-4; 307-12)

Between the two references to Smedley, it seems that he has indeed disappeared for good. There is clear comedy as he re-emerges ('grim with ooze') with his tale of mud-laden fantasy. It is one of the most surreal-seeming moments in the poem, mainly because of Pope's exploitation of the incongruity between the gently mythological world of sea-nymphs on the one hand, and the palpable realities of Fleet Ditch on the other. One senses too, the wishful thinking involved in consigning an enemy, however temporarily, to deepest darkness.

Once more the reader is made particularly aware of the poem's densely topical nature. Pope's note on Smedley makes clear the reasons why the poet should dislike him, but his sheer unimportance to literary history means that he has in a quite different metaphorical sense, sunk without trace. A sceptical student of the poem, might well feel inclined to ask why Pope finds it necessary to treat such obvious nonentities so elaborately.

An answer to this question is partly provided by another observation which has been made about *The Dunciad:* that Pope in fact helped to preserve those very reputations which he wished to destroy.[22] Dennis, Smedley, Blackmore, and other notorious Dunces, actually owe most of the posthumous fame they possess to the almost mythological status which Pope's imagination creates for them. There is a sense in which he is flattering them by admitting their presence in his poem. Although an eminent literary figure in his time, most modern students know of John Dennis primarily as an enemy of Pope, rather than through reading his works. It is also arguable that Pope is genuinely concerned by the sheer power of Dulness. In a poem which frequently makes use of imagery of procession, crowds and assemblies, one cannot but be aware of the massing of numbers. If, for example, the Scriblerians as a group numbered five, this was a small mustering of genius against the concentrated mediocrity of the Grub Street hordes. Indeed when mediocrity is so easy to find, it must certainly be rampant, and Pope's mythologizing of it continually reminds us of the incongruity betwen the ultimate literary insignificance of *The Dunciad*'s cast and the enormity of its works and actions.

As we have already seen, Book II closes with that appropriate Duncely activity, general sleep:

> While others timely, to the neighbouring Fleet
> (Haunt of the Muses) made their safe retreat.
>
> (395-6)

In comparison with the broad humour of Book II, the third book of *The Dunciad* seems considerably more serious, and 'epical', recalling not only the underworld locations of Homer and Virgil but those scenes in both classical and modern epic in which the work's hero is presented with a survey of present, past and future happenings. This book finds Theobald, first of all, asleep in the lap of Dulness in her temple. Later he is met by the ghost of Elkanah Settle, who, taking him to a mountain top, shows him a vast conspectus of the works of Dulness. In particular he is shown how Dulness has particularly marked out Great Britain as a place to extend her empire. A procession of the works of Dulness is then presented, before a prophecy that all these things will eventually 'return in their original Chaos.'

Pope's review of the history of Dulness is wide-ranging and, to begin with, serious. We are a very long way from Fleet Ditch when, for example, Pope begins his survey with a reference to Emperor Chi Ho-am-ti:

> He, whose long Wall the wand'ring Tartar bounds.
> Heav'ns! what a pyle! whole ages perish there:
> And one bright blaze turns Learning into air.
>
> (68-70)

The qualifications of this particular Emperor for Duncehood lie less in his construction of the Great Wall of China than in his destruction of all learned writings, so that a new age of learning could be seen to start in his reign. Likewise the destructiveness of the Egyptian Caliph who caused the Ptolomean library to be burnt:

> From shelves to shelves see greedy Vulcan roll,
> And lick up all their physick of the Soul.
>
> (73-4)

Such activities easily lead on to a treatment of the Goths and Huns whose cultural depredations are imaged in a passage of Miltonic grandeur:

> The North by myriads pours her mighty sons,
> Great nurse of Goths, of Alans, and of Huns.
> See Alaric's stern port, the martial frame
> Of Genseric! and Attila's dread name!
>
> (81-4)

The natural consequence of a description of such activity is a lament for the death of ancient Rome, and regret over subsequent developments in her history, in which she unfortunately came to represent the very embodiment of cultural darkness:

> Lo Rome herself, proud mistress now no more
> Of arts, but thund'ring against Heathen lore;
> Her grey-hair'd Synods damning books unread,
> And Bacon trembling for his brazen head:
> Padua with sighs beholds her Livy burn:

And ev'n th'Antipodes Vigilius mourn.
(93-8)

There is no more graphic representation of the scale of *The Dunciad* than the transformation which takes place from China, Egypt and Rome on the one hand to Grub Street on the other. It is to this location that the history of Dulness is hastening:

Not with less glory mighty Duchess crown'd,
Shall take thro' Grubstreet her triumphant round
(127-8)

The reader can be excused for thinking that he is now back where he started. Pope has returned the poem to its own ground. Fictionally, Settle is showing Theobald a conspectus of London's literary Dullards and again the reader is witnessing a procession ('. . . first . . . Cibber . . . And . . . Durfey, Ward . . . next . . . Haywood, Centlivre . . . Horneck . . . sneering Goode . . .') and so forth. This section is perhaps the most obscurely contemporary in the whole poem, and it is significant, of course, that it was with the Dunces of Book III that Pope did a fair amount of reshuffling in his 1743 version: so transiently insignificant are some of these Dunces (' . . . ev'ry nameless name . . .' (151)) that, fifteen years later, they have needed replacing with others ('The Pindars and the Miltons, of a Curl' (158)):

Sense, speech, and measure, living tongues and dead,
Let all give way – and Durgen may be read.
(161-2)

The modern reader's ignorance vindicates Pope's choice of examples here. Grammatically, we might feel inclined to read 'Durgen' as the name of yet another insignificant author. It was in fact, the name of of an attack on Pope by Ned Ward. The fact that author and work are now indistinguishable is the final testament to literary perishability.

The last major subject of Pope's satire in this Book, is of contemporary theatrical developments. Pope had himself no puritanical hatred of the theatre, but he saw the kind of gratuitous stage spectacle encouraged by John Rich (line 257) in the Lincoln's Inn Fields Theatre as debasing the drama, and making it merely a series of elaborately contrived thrills:

> All sudden, Gorgons hiss, and Dragons glare,
> And ten-horn'd fiends and Giants rush to war.
> Hell rises, Heav'n descends, and dance on Earth,
> Gods, imps and monsters, music, rage, and mirth,
> A fire, a jig, a battle, and a ball,
> Till one wide Conflagration swallows all.
>
> (231-6)

The sham apocalypse of contemporary stage machinery, eventually gives way to an apocalyptic vision of a more personal and compelling nature:

> This, this is He, foretold by ancient rhymes,
> Th'Augustus born to bring Saturnian times:
> Beneath his reign, shall Eusden wear the bays,
> Cibber preside Lord-Chancellor of Plays,
> B[enson] sole Judge of Architecture sit,
> And Namby Pamby be prefer'd for Wit!
>
> (317-22)

Poetry, architecture and drama are moving towards their final decline, and this decline in its turn is the sign of a greater dissolution:

> Signs following signs lead on the Mighty year;
> See! the dull starts roll round and re-appear.
> She comes! and Cloud-compelling Pow'r behold!
> With Night Primaeval, and with Chaos old.
> Lo! the great Anarch's ancient reign restor'd,
> Light dies before her uncreating word
>
> (335-40)

These are portentous lines by any standards. In a poem which has been mischievous, scatological, topical, bursting with private jokes and personal animus, these last lines strike an undeniably serious note. They form an even more decisive conclusion to the 1743 poem, which at least one contemporary report says Pope could not recite without tears. The vision of Chaos come again, a return to 'Night Primaeval' and '. . . the great Anarch's ancient reign . . .' are all extensions of the mythology which the poem has created from the beginning, but the mythology has now been rendered challenging, real and unanswerable. If it is the vanity of the cultured person to see around him cultural degeneration (just as the moralist sees moral degeneration) then it is difficult to think of any passage of English literature which voices this fear so clearly or movingly. As Emrys Jones writes of the lines:

> 'The conclusion to *The Dunciad* is uninterruptedly solemn and sublime: indeed its sublimity may be felt to be somewhat disconcertingly absolute . . .'[23]

However, there is a particularly important difference between the conclusion of the early and late version. In 1728-9, Pope's final lines are:

> Thy hand great Dulness! lets the curtain fall,
> And universal Darkness covers all.'
> 'Enough! enough!' the raptur'd Monarch cries;
> And thro' the Ivory Gate the Vision flies.
>
> (355-8)

In the *New Dunciad,* the portentousness of the closing lines is increased:

> Lo! thy dread Empire, Chaos! is restor'd
> Light dies before thy uncreating word:
> Thy hand, great Anarch! lets the curtain fall;
> And Universal Darkness buries All.
>
> (1743 Text, Book IV, 653-6)

Apart from the obvious intensification of the last line (Darkness now buries, rather than merely covers) and the more explicit connection betwen Dulness and anarchy, the later version separates the closing lines from any fictional speaker (in 1728-9 they form the conclusion of Settle's speech to Theobald), rendering them resolutely the poet's own. Most importantly, though, the last two lines of the earlier version render its conclusion a degree more light-hearted, and indeed less conclusive. There is an abruptness in the hasty departure of Settle's ghost which makes the ending uncertain in tone and somewhat provisional, lacking the monumental finality of the later version. In one sense this is not surprising as it points to something inherent in Pope's own view of the first *Dunciad.* His final words in the synopsis which he provided of the 1729 Book III were:

> A scene, of which the present Action of the Dunciad is but a Type or Foretaste, giving a Glimpse or Pisgah-sight of the promis'd Fulness of her glory; the Accomplishment whereof will, in all probability, hereafter be the Theme of many other and greater Dunciads.[24]

We have already considered the view that there is something essentially extendable about this poem, and Pope is clearly drawing attention to it himself here. It is tempting to contemplate the degree to which he realized the prophetic nature of his words: there was, after all, to be another and greater *Dunciad*, and it is indeed possible (though not ultimately provable) that parts of it were already in existence. They required only fit occasion in order to see the light of day.

The response to the publication of the first version of the poem was overwhelming. The Twickenham editor reports the testimony of Richard Savage:

> On the day the Book was first vended, a crowd of Authors beseig'd the Shop; Entreaties, Advices, Threats of Law, and Battery, nay cries of Treason were all employ'd, to hinder the coming out of the 'Dunciad': On the other Side, the Booksellers and Hawkers made as great Efforts to procure it . . .[25]

The Dunces' behaviour, clamorous and turbulent, was true to form, as was that of John Dennis:

> . . . But what Probability is there . . . in the Games which take up a third Part of the Piece. Is it not monstrous to imagine any Thing like that in the Master Street of a populous city?[26]

Dennis's view, almost more than anything else which could be quoted, tells us why the poem needed to be written.

Even so, Maynard Mack thinks that there was much folly in what Pope did:

> '. . . its victims and their sympathizers . . . pursued him implacably from then on with a few damaging truths and a host of slanders and lies . . .'[27]

Pope's half-sister was to report that from this time Pope did not find it safe to go about without carrying a stick, nor without the company of his great dane. In a purely strategic sense the first *Dunciad* was not a success at all. The insects of which Pope wished to be rid, remained and continued to sting.

This is partly at any rate why the 1728 version of the poem was a commencement rather than a termination of its own particular brand of hostilities. Edmund Curll was quick to provide *A Compleat Key*[28] to the poem, but Pope, again urged on by Swift, decided to produce his own. It is worth remembering that the poem had been published anonymously. In itself this was not a particularly unusual practice so it is not quite fair to accuse Pope of cowardice. People were able to spot the style and the man easily enough. Scriblerian jokiness was probably a part of Pope's strategy: it made the poems' reception more fun and left the way open for the greater mischief of the poem's second edition of 1729. Pope had written to Swift the previous summer:

> 'The Dunciad is going to be printed in all pomp . . . It will be attended with Proeme, Prolegomena, Testimonia Scriptorum, Index Authorum and Notes Variorum . . .'[29]

In other words Pope was going further to mock the Dunces by creating himself some specimens of the 'learned lumber' which he had condemned in the poem. Not only was he going to be his own annotator, he was going to satirize the whole process of annotation. Swift had done this as early as 1704 in his *A Tale of a Tub* in which the reader has to pick his way through a vast acreage of introductions, dedicatory epistles, commendations, letters from the bookseller and so forth, all in satiric imitation of the elaborate paraphernalia which often surrounded the publication of the flimsiest and dullest of works. Pope, in his 'Variorum' edition, apart from inviting Swift to assist him, also assumed Swiftian pseudonymity and published his notes under the name of Martinus Scriblerus. Pope continued to take as much delight in imitating a Dunce as in denouncing him. Once again the effect is of a tortuously sustained private joke.

A 'Variorum' edition is one which presents the text accompanied by notes amassed from several commentators. It is as *The Dunciad Variorum* that the 1729 *Dunciad* has come to be known, though the spoof Variorum notes which Pope, and possibly Swift, provide, are only part of the richly elaborate 'Key' to the poem which Pope invents, as any reader of the poem in the Twickenham edition will see. The text threatens to sink completely beneath long drawn out introductory matter, commendations, dedications and so on.

Except that in *The Dunciad Variorum* these notes are a text as well. There is little point in surveying them in detail (rather like Dr Johnson's dictionary, much casual entertainment can be found by judicious dipping), but it is always necessary to remember that the notes are as satirical as the poem. Quite apart from the opportunity which they provide for additional well-honed malice, Pope is clearly enjoying the whole business of exploiting his anonymity. Thus we find a reference to Susanna Centlivre (Book II, line 379), relatively innocent in itself, but providing the deliciously deadpan note: '. . .She writ many Plays, and a song . . . before she was seven years old. She also writ a Ballad against Mr Pope's Homer before he begun it'. Likewise the comment on Ned Ward's *Durgen* which we have already encountered. (Book III, line 162), where 'Durgen' is glossed as 'A ridiculous thing of Ward's.' A Durgen was a dwarf; hence its insulting nature to Pope, whom it attacked. Needless to say, the more monumental enemies, such as Curll and Dennis, receive much more prominent treatment. The note to Book I, line 104, where Dennis first appears, is an outburst of Duncely apoplexy, damning Dennis by giving him many paragraphs' worth of his own treatment.

Clearly *The Dunciad* is an elaborate work. The present discussion of it has inevitably been synoptic and selective. The experience of working on the poem at any length can best be imaged in terms of encountering mist and darkness, and penetrating unknown territory step by step. To a modern reader, its very subject matter is obscurity and an obscurity which Pope's mythology merely serves to intensify. Its range of reference, allusion and illustration is enormous, in keeping with the poem's epic assumptions. It certainly bears, indeed requires, repeated readings. A text which consistently defamiliarizes its subject matter, it challenges its reader's expectations of order, coherence and even decorum. It flies completely in the face of the Neo-Victorian tradition of Pope criticism which sees Pope as ordered, restrained, and fatally prosaic.[30] Pope could as well write the anarchic *Dunciad* as he could the philosophical *Essay on Man,* but it is in the former poem that he was, for better or for worse, quintessentially himself.

An Epistle to Dr Arbuthnot

If we are applying the neatest of categorizations to Pope's poetry we might choose to separate a treatment of *The Dunciad* from that of *An Epistle to Dr Arbuthnot,* rather than discussing them together. *The Dunciad* is the great Scriblerian text, which though first published in 1728 looks backwards over the literary animosities of the previous fifteen years or so. *An Epistle to Dr Arbuthnot* leans more towards Pope's Horatian tone of the 1730s. It seeks judicious independence and detached urbanity. Indeed, by the time that it was published three of Pope's *Imitations of Horace* had already been written.

There is also the question of the authorial stance. *An Epistle to Dr Arbuthnot* is much more a poem about Pope than *The Dunciad* is. The mythologizing nature of the latter poem and Pope's use of pseudonyms and allusions in it, not to mention his conscious hiding behind the Scriblerian persona tend, in intention at least, to conceal the author. In *An Epistle . . .*, Pope claims to be speaking in his own voice and for himself. There may be some fictionalizing of that self, but the poem is a personal document rooted in immediate experience in a way which *The Dunciad* could only very indirectly be.

There are consistencies though. Both poems are poems about the state of literature, and about Pope's literary opponents. Duncehood remains present in the epistle, both as an entity and a target. We are not allowed to forget its misbegotten profusion:

> The Bard whom pilf'red Pastorals renown,
> Who turns a Persian Tale for half a crown,
> Just writes to make his barrenness appear,
> And strains from hard-bound brains eight lines a-year:
> He, who still wanting tho' he lives on theft,
> Steals much, spends little, yet has nothing left:
> And he, who now to sense, now nonsense leaning,
> Means not, but blunders round about a meaning:
> And he, whose Fustian's so sublimely bad,
> It is not Poetry, but Prose run mad . . .,
>
> (179-188)

There are some familiar Duncely associations in this passage. Writing is associated with theft, with subsistence economy: the half-crown payment for the 'pilfer'd pastoral' was also the standard fee given to the prostitute, though the author is associated with barrenness rather than with promiscuity. The 'straining from hard-bound brains' suggests constipation, and the equation of Grub Street writings with evacuation rather than with inspiration. There is the suggestion too, that such writing, in its anarchic and subversive mediocrity, will inevitably 'run mad.'

Also *An Epistle to Dr Arbuthnot* is as much a compilation as a composition. Although it specifically emerged as a tribute to Arbuthnot, as he lay dying, it, too, is a backward-glancing poem. Pope pointed out in his own preface that the poem '. . . was begun many years since, and drawn up by snatches, as the several Occasions offer'd . . .'[31] The portrait of Addison (Atticus) (193-214) had been in existence for almost twenty years, for example. So there is an overlap between its contents, and the concerns of *The Dunciad,* despite the superficial differences of style and method.

Both poems also, are in the nature of ripostes. *The Dunciad* was immediately provoked by Theobald's criticisms of Pope's Shakespeare (though Pope was able to include attacks on a good many other literary adversities as well); *An Epistle to Dr Arbuthnot* was a response to recent developments in the pamphlet war against Pope. In particular, his erstwhile friend Lady Mary Wortley Montagu had joined the battle against him (it seems unlikely that we shall ever know for certain the grounds of their quarrel), and had joined forces with the equally witty and malicious John, Lord Hervey, George II's Vice-Chamberlain. They had almost certainly been writing anonymously against Pope since 1728.

In an age protected by libel laws it can be difficult to imagine the ease with which, in the early eighteenth century, writers were able to insult and abuse each other. Although, theoretically, libel was illegal, there was no systematic enforcement of any statutory sanction. The production of pamphlets was quick and cheap, and to be the author of one provided an easy pittance for a starving Grub Street hack. Hence, many of the printed attacks on Pope came from people who did not know him personally, nor had any axe to grind against him. They came from indigent members of the literary underworld who knew a bandwaggon when they saw one. So the sheer irrelevance of many of the attacks is hardly surprising, provocative though they were:

> The distant Threats of Vengeance on his head,
> The Blow unfelt, the Tear he never shed;
> The Tale reviv'd, the Lye so oft o'erthrown;
> Th'imputed Trash, and Dulness not his own;
> The Morals blacken'd when the Writings scape;
> The libel'd person and the pictur'd Shape;
> Abuse on all he lov'd or lov'd him spread,
> A Friend in Exile, or a Father, dead . . .
>
> (348-55)

Between 1728 and 1734 there are nearly seventy extant published pamphlet attacks[32] on Pope which have survived, and they were the followers in a tradition which John Dennis had started as early as 1711.

So, despite the malice which frequently surfaces in it, *An Epistle to Dr Arbuthnot* is not a hot-headed poem. It was not Pope's habit to rush into print to defend himself against the unwarranted attacks which were made upon him, as he has cause to remind us several times. ('Full ten years slander'd, did he once reply?' (373); 'I never answer'd, I was not in debt' (154); 'I kept, like Asian Monarchs, from their sight' (220); 'He stood the furious Foe, the timid Friend' (343)).

Even so it is difficult not to hear the tones of self-justification and self-righteousness in these statements, and any account of *The Epistle to Dr Arbuthnot* has to try to overcome an initial temptation to take sides. It is very easy to see the poem in simple terms of rights and wrongs, and to point out that the Pope who strongly protests against his victimization by Grub Street, also offers a variety of malicious salvos, some scarcely surpassed in the history of abuse. A reader who wishes to conclude from this Epistle that Pope was a thoroughly unpleasant (not to say hypocritical) man is free to do so, but when the poem is set in any kind of biographical and literary context it becomes less easy (and indeed less relevant) to read the poem in such a morally simple way.

Pope's attitude to the published attacks upon him was a complex one. He took considerable care to preserve them, and indeed had them bound together in special volumes. This argues both a patience and a fascination with his attackers, not to say a certain stoical resignation to the situation. One is also reminded of his relish of, and indeed personal identification with, the works of Dulness to which the Scriblerians were so tenaciously opposed. There was certainly a way in which Pope found the experience of opposition and controversy stimulating. *The Epistle to Dr Arbuthnot* may be the work of a proud and combative man, but it is not the work of a bitter one, and the poem's rhetorical cut and thrust is grounded in wider concerns about the nature of writing and the public position of the poet, as he attempts to '. . . maintain a poet's dignity and ease' (263) amidst the chaos of a literary world which threatens the values for which he believes himself to stand.

Hence follows another difficulty. Just as it is disabling to read the poem exclusively as presenting a moral conflict between right and wrong, so it is misguided to look for much unity in it. Pope himself took pains to point out the piecemeal nature of the epistle's composition, and the reader soon notes that in addition to a diversity in the subject matter of the poem, there is a comparable diversity of the tones of voice employed in it. There is both attack and defence; praise of friends and family; complaint about the economics of writing; concern for cultural standards. The poem is about Pope to an extent, it is also about the literary culture in which Pope found himself, and it inevitably makes efforts to define Pope's relationship with that culture. None of those concerns though, are ends in themselves, and none is pursued singly to its own conclusion. Pope speaks bluntly, complainingly and comically, by turns. In places there is a tendency to tease. In places, too, a tendency to mythologize his own position as a poet. In many ways *An Epistle to Dr Arbuthnot* is the most cornucopian of Pope's poems, and if one were to select one text which above all others characterizes him, it would perhaps be this one, for it is the often contradictory character of Pope himself which binds the poem's diversities together.

Pope especially enjoys manipulating personae, as we can see at the very opening of the poem, a celebrated and arresting piece of comic writing, joyfully complaining about the pains of literary fame:

> Shut, shut the door, good John! fatigu'd I said,
> Tye up the knocker, say I'm sick, I'm dead,
> The Dog-star rages! nay 'tis past a doubt
> All Bedlam or Parnassus, is let out;
> Fire in each eye, and Papers in each hand,
> They rave, recite, and madden round the land.
> What walls can guard me, or what Shades can hide?
> They pierce my Thickets, thro' my Grot they glide,
> By land, by water, they renew the charge,
> They stop the Chariot, and they board the Barge,
> No place is sacred . . .
>
> (1-11)

To take this passage too literally is to miss its point. There is a conscious absurdity in Pope's presentation of himself as in a state of seige, though as the poem runs on we witness a sly importation of real people:

> Is there a Parson, much be-mus'd in Beer,
> A maudlin Poetess, a ryming Peer,
> A Clerk, foredoom'd his Father's soul to cross,
> Who pens a Stanza when he should engross?
> Is there, who lock'd from Ink and Paper, scrawls
> With desp'rate Charcoal round his darken'd walls?
> All fly to Twit'nam, and in humble strain
> Apply to me, to keep them mad or vain.
> Arthur, whose giddy Son neglects the Laws,
> Imputes to me and my damn'd works the cause:
> (15-23)

Some of these people turn out to be Pope's enemies rather than seekers of his favours. For example, Laurence Eusden (punningly 'be-mus'd in beer') and James Moore Smythe (the 'giddy Son') have both figured in *The Dunciad.* Comparably there is the wretched and composite Dunce whose poverty reduces him to infantile wall-scrawling. The fact that his Charcoal is 'desp'rate', extends the comparison between poetry and lunacy ('Bedlam or Parnassus') which is insisted upon at the very beginning of the epistle. We recognize the lineaments of Duncehood once more: these 'scribblers' threaten the temple of 'real literature' ('No place is sacred . . .') by their self-important urgency, their works manifesting nothing but madness and folly.

Pope is keen to define his own position in the literary world when he says that these people 'pierce my Thickets, thro' my Grot they glide'. Pope's garden and grotto were his two chief indulgences. The elaborate programmes of building and cultivation from which they resulted were the chief fruits of Pope's literary and economic success, hence they become symbolic of his poetic position. Again, there is no way in which these places would be literally penetrated by importunate Dunces, but Pope makes reference to them in order to highlight the way in which true and deserved literary eminence is being affronted by the mediocre hordes.

Yet Pope is happy to indulge in self-mockery too:

> Poor Cornus sees his frantic wife elope,
> And curses Wit, and Poetry and Pope.
>
> (25-6)

Although he subsequently reminds us that he has been hurt by those published attacks which insulted his deformities, he disarms his enemies in *The Epistle* . . . by making light of them:

> There are, who to my Person pay their court,
> I cough like Horace, and tho' lean, am short,
> Ammon's great Son, one shoulder had too high,
> Such Ovid's nose, and 'Sir! you have an Eye . . .'
> Go on, obliging Creatures, make me see
> All that disgrac'd my Betters met in me . . .
>
> (115-120)

Backhandedly, of course, Pope is aligning himself with the great figures of the Classical past (just as he did indirectly in *The Dunciad,* and was to do more explicitly in the *Imitations of Horace*). Also, in his reference to Alexander the Great ('Ammon's great Son') he is reminding us about those pamphleteers who could happily play with his name in an attack such as 'Pope Alexander's Supremacy'.[33]

Pope is as conscious of his position amongst the moderns as he is of his relationship to the ancients:

> But why then publish? Granville the polite,
> And knowing Walsh, would tell me I could write;
> Well-natur'd Garth inflam'd with early praise,
> And Congreve lov'd, and Swift endur'd my Lays;
> The Courtly Talbot, Somers, Sheffield read,
> Ev'n mitred Rochester would nod the head,
> And St John's self (great Dryden's friends before)
> With open arms receiv'd one Poet more.
>
> (135-142)

Pope is keen to provide a meticulous catalogue of those

individuals whose early encouragement constituted a conferral of poetic status upon him to the extent where it is easy to accuse him of gratuitous name-dropping. In particular he is keen to remind us that these men were 'great Dryden's friends before', and that thus he stands in some kind of apostolic succession to the most revered English poet of the previous generation.

However, the passage does more than merely suggest that Pope has a niche in a native tradition of literary greatness. Certainly Garth and Congreve were among the literary luminaries of the period of Pope's boyhood and youth, but he imports other firgures whose claims to fame rest on different grounds. Francis Atterbury, Bishop of Rochester, and Henry St John Bolingbroke were both Tory political figures tarred with the brush of treason and Jacobitism: both had been forced to suffer exile and neither was exactly a 'safe' friend to admit to having. Pope is thus making clear the nature of his enduring loyalties and looking backwards to a literary and political culture sustained by men of learning and stature. It is a comment on the tawdriness of the times that:

> From these the world will judge of Men and Books,
> Not from the Burnets, Oldmixons and Cooks.
> (145-6)

It is easy to see Pope as arrogantly claiming for himself an exalted literary position and those readers who find the poem objectionable often stop there. Blatant immodesty is seldom appealing and can often prove a sticking point to sympathy. But Pope is looking much more closely than this at his own position. If he is able to see himself as Dryden's successor, basking in the favours of the cognoscenti, he is also aware of the pains of this favoured position and *The Epistle to Dr Arbuthnot* asks some important questions about it which are not easy to answer. They remain questions:

> Heav'ns! was I Born for nothing but to write?
> Has life no joys for me? or (to be grave)
> Have I no Friend to serve, no Soul to save?
> (272-4)

'Why did I write? . . .' (125)

'But why then publish?' (135)

Pope attempts an explanation:

As yet a Child, nor yet a Fool to Fame,
I lisp'd in Numbers, for the Numbers came.
I left no Calling for this idle trade,
Nor Duty broke, no Father dis-obey'd
The Muse but serv'd to ease some Friend, not Wife,
To help me through this long Disease, my Life
(126-131)

Pope is mindful of two quite contradictory aspects of his poetic status. On the one hand there is the justified acclaim from the literary establishment (' . . . knowing Walsh, would tell me I could write . . .') on the other, an awareness that genius is an incubus which cannot be shuffled off, and over which the individual has relatively little control. There is a negative emphasis in the passage quoted: Pope wrote poetry, it seems, because he had little option but to do so, and, in consequence, he became the immediate prey of ignorant and unscrupulous critics:

Soft were my Numbers, who could take offence
While pure Description held the place of Sense?
Like gentle Fanny's was my flow'ry Theme,
A painted Mistress, or a purling Stream.
Yet then did Gildon draw his venal quill;
I wish'd the man a dinner, and sate still;
Yet then did Dennis rave in furious fret;
I never answer'd, I was not in debt
(147-154)

Pope seeks to assert his own innocence. Attacks upon his writing dated from the publication of his pastorals as early as 1709, and he is accurate enough in his analysis of the provenance of those attacks: Gildon and Dennis were both mercenaries. Hence Pope is the victim of the venal as well as the unsophisticated, and Dennis's 'furious fret' becomes both absurd and trivial.

Pope is keen to emphasize his separateness from the rest of the literary world. He sees his public position as largely of other people's making rather than his own:

> What tho' my Name stood rubric on the walls?
> Or plaister'd posts with Claps in capitals?
> Or smoaking forth, a hundred Hawkers load,
> I sought no homage from the Race that write;
> I kept, like Asian monarchs, from their sight
>
> (215-220)

Pope seeks to dissociate himself from the promotional activities of booksellers and tradespeople.

The plea for privacy with which *An Epistle to Dr Arbuthnot* opens is thus reiterated in several places. Pope wishes to be left alone by Grub Street, and by those readers who would seek in any way to misinterpret or misrepresent him. It is almost as though Pope wishes to rid himself of an audience entirely, in favour of the cultured detachment which he sees as being appropriate to the condition of a poet:

> Oh let me live my own! and die so too!
> ('To live and die is all I have to do:')
> Maintain a Poet's Dignity and Ease,
> And see what friends, and read what books I please.
> Above a Petron, tho' I condescend
> Sometimes to call a Minister my Friend:
> I was not born for Courts or great Affairs,
> I pay my Debts, believe, and say my Pray'rs
> Can sleep without a Poem in my head,
> Nor know if Dennis be alive or dead.
>
> (261-270)

Pope presents a passive and innocent portrait of the poet's position, one indeed which almost defines him out of existence. The retired self-sufficiency (in both economic and spiritual senses), conducive to 'Dignity and Ease' is worlds apart from, for example, Wordsworth's view of the poet as a man with an important message for his fellow men or

Shelley's belief that poetry could change the world.[34] Pope makes the poet into a cultural mandarin.

Yet the poet is not dissociated from moral concern. Pope is careful to remind us:

> Curst be the Verse, how well soe'er it flow,
> That tends to make one worthy Man my for,
> Give virtue scandal, Innocence a fear,
> Or from the soft-ey'd Virgin steal a tear!
>
> (283-6)

> A Lash like mine no honest man shall dread,
> But all such babling blockheads in his stead.
>
> (303-4)

For all the poetic detachment which Pope seems to require, the last couplet shows just how much anger lurks beneath the surface, and the exposure of this anger is a recurrent feature in the poem. In the first line Pope speaks as a moralist who prefers a position above the fray but in the second line one feels that the blood-pressure is rising in contemplation of the corps of 'babling blockheads' who are, to a large extent, the poem's *raison d'etre*:

> 'But why insult the Poor, affront the Great?'
> A Knave's a Knave to me, in ev'ry State
>
> (360-1)

As we know, the Knaves will not go away. In all the passages which we have been examining even when Pope appears to be at his most defensive and confessional there is a niggling aggressiveness which undercuts the more urbane tone and shows him consistently seeking out enemies. It is the distance between the desired 'Dignity and ease' and the more squalid realities of daily literary life which provides the tension from which much of the poem springs.

The passages which have already been discussed offer examples of this tension. Pope's appreciation of Granville, Garth, Congreve and the other friends of his youth is balanced by a swiftly contemptuous dismissal of the likes of Burnet, Oldmixon and Cooke. His account of his early poetic career contains the statement 'Like gentle Fanny's was my flow'ry Theme' (149). Fanny was Pope's pseudonym for the hated Lord Hervey, and the one word, judiciously placed, imports an insidious aggressiveness. Likewise at the very moment when Pope draws attention to his own blamelessness ('I pay my Debts, believe, and say my Pray'rs' (268)) he cannot resist a gratuitous tilt at an old enemy ('Can sleep without a Poem in my head/Nor know if Dennis be alive or dead.' (269-70)).

The complementary strategies of attack and defence never quite attain an equilibrium in the poem, though Pope acknowledges this state of affairs by projecting it onto his enemies:

> A dire Dilemma! either way I'm sped,
> If Foes they write, if Friends they read me dead
>
> (31-2)

Equally, Pope accepts the likely futility of so many of his attacks. Castigating folly and vice might seem imperative to a lover of virtue, particularly to one with a number of scores to settle, but Pope reminds us that folly is a state impervious to suggestion and criticism: 'No creature smarts so little as a Fool' (84).

> Whom have I hurt? has Poet yet, or Peer,
> Lost the arch'd eye-brow, or Parnassian sneer?
> And has not Colly still his Lord and Whore?
> His Butchers Henley, his Free-Masons Moor?
>
> (95-8)

In such a context as this, Pope reminds us, his satire can but seem moderate and harmless, for all the caution that he makes a putative Arbuthnot urge upon him: ('Good friend forbear! you deal in dang'rous things (75); 'No Names-be calm-learn Prudence . . .' (102)). Warburton's edition of the poem in 1751 printed it in dialogue form, and subsequent editors have often preserved this feature. To do so reminds us of the ongoing but friendly difference of opinion which Pope and Arbuthnot had. Arbuthnot was always rather queasy about Pope's naming of names in his satire, necessary though he thought the satire was in itself. Pope's rejoinder that folly and vice will go on despite his attacks is not a comforting one, though it echoes Juvenal's assertion that it is difficult *not* to write satire. Nor did it stop Pope from being openly aggressive when it suited him. Many readers must inevitably be struck by the power of the unambiguously direct attacks which Pope mounts on certain named individuals. His dissatisfaction with the economics of the literary market-place is as clear in this poem as it is in *The Dunciad.* Publishers do not get a good press. At the same time, Pope is critical of the practice of private patronage which is what commercial bookselling largely superseded. Pope's picture of a literary patron is a picture of a self-regarding cypher who has no taste at all. Pope calls his character Bufo (in Latin the word means a toad) and decks him out with features that form a composite protrait of two contemporary characters, Bubb Doddington and the Earl of Halifax:

> Proud as Apollo on his forked hill,
> Sate full-blown Bufo puff'd by ev'ry quill;
> Fed with soft Dedication all day long,
> Horace and he went hand in hand in song.
> His Library, (where Busts of Poets dead
> And a true Pindar stood without a head)
> Received of Wits an undistinguish'd race,
> Who first his judgment ask'd and then a Place
> (231-8)

There is a heavy and self-deluding pomposity about the patron. In practice his literary taste can really only comprehend the derivative flattery of himself which his 'admirers' serve up. His pitiful absence of taste and culture is best symbolized by the headless bust of Pindar. Bufo is harbouring a half-destroyed piece of unrecognizable statuary, just as he harbours his 'undistinguish'd race' of wits. He is in the last analysis as philistine as Edmund Curll for all his affectation of cultural grandeur.

But even genuine literary eminence can fare badly under Pope. His portrait of Joseph Addison is also critical of a man who set himself up as a cult figure. The history of Pope's relationship with Addison is complex. There seems little doubt that in his youth Pope had been friendly with Addison and had received some encouragement from him. He had even provided a prologue to Addison's tragedy *Cato* in 1713. The original version of what we now think of as the 'Atticus' passage in *An Epistle to Dr Arbuthnot* dated from 1715, and explicitly carried Addison's own name. There is evidence that Addison saw the passage and was not unduly offended by it, though in the years before his death in 1719 there was a certain amount of mutual suspicion between himself and Pope, particularly as Pope believed that Addison had encouraged Thomas Tickell's rival translation of Homer.[35]

The passage runs to just over twenty lines, and its effect is slow and cumulative:

> Peace to all such! but were there One whose fires
> True Genius kindles, and fair Fame inspires,
> Blest with each Talent and each Art to please,
> And born to write, converse, and live with ease
> (193-96)

There is no irony in these lines. Pope begins by being genuinely appreciative of the man. What he objects to is the insidious way in which Addison entraps others. It was Addison's self-cultivated position of literary lion which Pope disliked:

> Shou'd such a man, too fond to rule alone,
> Bear, like the Turk, no brother near the throne,
> View him with scornful, yet with jealous eyes,
> And hate for Arts that caus'd himself to rise;
> Damn with faint praise, assent with civil leer,
> And without sneering, teach the rest to sneer
> (197-202)

Like Bufo, Atticus was surrounded by smaller-scale models of himself:

> Like Cato, give his little Senate laws,
> And sit attentive to his own applause,
> While Wits and Templers ev'ry sentence raise,
> And wonder with a foolish face of praise.
> (209-212)

This portrait is concentrated and sustained. The characteristic movement of *An Epistle to Dr Arbuthnot* is an unpredictable, darting one, and this degree of concentration on one target is rare, though it is worthy of note that the portrait occurs at the very central point in the poem and thus constitutes something of a minor climax. Obviously having died fifteen years before the epistle was published, Addison can hardly be seen as an immediate enemy of Pope, nor does the measured, analytical pace of the description (in its own way mirroring Addisonian gravitas) betoken anger or bitterness. Also, the judiciously restrained tone of the passage counterpoints the savageness of the subsequent attack on Lord Hervey.

But there are some uncomfortable likenesses between Atticus and Pope. Pope could not easily respect the heavy decorum which surrounded Addison. Yet the side of him which aspired to '. . . maintain a poet's Dignity and Ease . . .' and desired to keep 'like Asian monarchs' from the sight of those he felt unworthy of him, links Pope at least in part with aspects of Addison he had been keen to condemn. Dustin Griffin has seen both this and the Lord Hervey passage as containing elements of self-portraiture, as if Pope were trying to exorcise certain features of himself by projecting them onto others.[36] Attractive though this theory is, it tends to oversimplify the history of Pope's relationship with Addison. His objection to Addison's consciously cultivated literary persona went back a good many years and pre-dated his own desire for a dignified position above the fray. What Pope seems to be objecting to is not the concept of the literary mandarin but Addison's abuse of it. Addison has debased those talents which should characterize the distinguished man of letters. His eminence manifests itself by sneering and leering.

The portrait of Lord Hervey (Sporus) is not a self-portrait. It is a redirection against his own victim of many of the terms of abuse which Pope had himself received. If the measured stateliness of the Atticus passage underlines the public position of Addison, the descent to more vulgar tactics subverts that of Hervey.

Many of the published attacks on Pope himself were far from being subtle. As long as twenty years before the publication of this poem, John Dennis had written *à propos* Pope:

> As there is no creature in Nature so venomous, there is nothing so stupid and so impotent as a hunch-back'd Toad.[37]

In 1731 John ('Orator') Henley had managed this:

> The mind that inhabits his little glass case is like ASSA FOETIDA in a thumb-bottle, or flat vinegar in a broken cruet; ill within and worse without doors; it gnaws and preys upon his body . . . a public WORM by his own private one; his life is a corrosive that eats first on itself, then on other people . . . he lives on scandal like a maggot on putrefaction, or a fly on excrement: he is a small hand-grenado charg'd with feathers that burst, fly about, give offence and DO NO HARM whatsoever is intended.[38]

Even Edmund Curll had been provoked into verse in 1728:

> A little scurvy, purblind elf;
> Scarce like a Toad, much less himself
> Deform'd in shape, of Pigmy stature:
> A proud, conceited, peevish creature
> The stinking venom flows around
> And nauseous slaver hides the ground[39]

These extracts are valuable evidence for a number of reasons. Clearly they illustrate the context of open abuse in which Pope lived. There is more gratuitous malice in these passages than there is intelligent thought and it is scarcely creditable to modern taste that more or less self-respecting literary figures could indulge in such guttersnipe tactics. In particular the constant association of Pope with various kinds of lower animal begins to seem merely derivative.

Yet, in his attack on Lord Hervey, it is the association with lower animals which Pope chooses particularly to exploit. The toad reappears, the muck-loving insect is there too, and so is the spitting venom. Likewise the passage plays, as do the Henley and Curll extracts, with the contradiction that, though the behaviour and person of Hervey are highly offensive, at the same time he is impotent, harmless and negligible:

> Yet let me flap this bug with gilded wings,
> This painted Child of Dirt that stinks and stings;
> Whose Buzz the Witty and the Fair annoys,
> Yet Wit ne'er tastes, and Beauty ne'er enjoys,
> So well-bred Spaniels civilly delight
> In mumbling of the Game they dare not bite
> (309-14)

Pope had spoken of *The Dunciad* as the means by which he would rid himself of 'these insects' of the literary world. It is interesting that the metaphor re-surfaces here. This passage becomes Pope's most definitive personal attack, perhaps the most completely destructive one which he ever made, but whilst one can hear vituperative frenzy in it, one must also note its analytical precision. These lines tell us a great deal about Lord Hervey, or at least about Pope's perception of him. There is an offensive malice in Hervey, exploited in the extended insect metaphor: he stinks, stings, buzzes, but then suddenly turns into a fawning spaniel with no teeth. Indeed the freakishly contradictory and inconstant nature of Hervey is emphasized in all sorts of ways: he is a bug yet his wings are made of gold; he is a 'child of dirt' yet he is painted, suggesting both a fair but deceptive outward appearance. It is not surprising that the inherent contradictions which Pope is keen to find in Hervey seem to be explained by the latter's sexual ambiguity:

> Whether in florid Impotence he speaks,
> And, as the Prompter breathes, the Puppet squeaks;
> (317-8)

> His Wit all see-saw between that and this,
> Now high, now low, now Master up, now Miss,
> And he himself one vile Antithesis.
> Amphibious Thing! that acting either Part,

The trifling Head, or the corrupted Heart!
Fop at the Toilet, Flatt'rer at the Board,
Now trips a Lady, and now struts a Lord

(323-9)

As in Pope's almost contemporaneous portrait of the Duke of Wharton in his *Epistle to Cobham*, inconstancy and changeableness in a character are seen as marks of corruption. These traits stand opposed to the more solid strengths of virtue, and Hervey's moral shortcomings are made abundantly clear:

Or at the ear of Eve, familiar Toad,
Half Froth, half Venom, spits himself abroad,
In Puns or Politics, or Tales, or Lyes,
Or Spite, or Smut, or Rhymes, or Blasphemies

(319-22)

Whilst one may wonder whatever Hervey could have done to provoke Pope to such a degree, one also notices the circumstantial accuracy with which Pope makes his case. Hervey's sins are sins against, on the one hand, literary decorum, and on the other political morality. As George II's Vice-Chamberlain, he was Walpole's man in the palace, and was in particular a confidant of Queen Caroline, herself the centre of an 'alternative' court. Hence the emphasis on Hervey's busyness in this passage, he is trying hard to be so many things to so many people: ('Now high, now low, now Master up, now Miss'). Yet he can never quite manage to become human:

Eve's Tempter thus the Rabbins have exprest,
A Cherub's face, a Reptile all the rest

(330-1)

It will inevitably be that some readers will find the rhetorical verve of this passage exhilarating whilst others will find it offensive. Anyone looking at this passage alone and out of context would be forced to conclude that Pope possessed little ability to turn the other cheek (though he was conscious himself of this accusation and, as we have seen, has a defence against the charge). Likewise the very proximity of its tone and imagery to that used so frequently against Pope by the gutter press can be troubling. We shall never know precisely why Pope was so injured by Hervey as to require to injure him so much in return, though it has been considerably more difficult for Hervey's reputation to withstand this one attack than for Pope's to withstand the hundreds made on him. If Pope was consciously (as it seems likely he was) employing the same language of abuse from which he himself suffered, the very intricate nature of the passage and the fecundity with which it is able to represent Hervey's shortcomings, prevents the aggressiveness within it from ever becoming merely gratuitous and derivative. The piece after all is not hack-work. Pope is not simply following a pattern of abuse laid down as a kind of *lingua franca,* as many of his own critics did. He is substantially, and definitely recreating Hervey in such a way as to reveal the most fundamentally offensive roots of his nature.

It is entirely characteristic of this poem that, well within a hundred lines, as Pope begins to draw to his conclusion, his tone changes completely. For all the abuse and pent-up violence of the Hervey portrait, the ending of the poem reminds us 'That an *Epistle to Dr Arbuthnot'* is essentially grounded in friendship, loyalty and love. Pope was a most loyal friend, and a conspicuously dutiful son. He concludes his poem with a tribute to his parents, first his father:

> Born to no Pride, inheriting no Strife,
> Nor marrying Discord in a Noble Wife,
> Stranger to Civil and Religious Rage,
> The good Man walk'd innoxious thro' his Age.
> Nor Courts he saw, no Suits would ever try,
> Nor dar'd an Oath, nor hazarded a Lye:
> Un-learn'd, he knew no Schoolman's subtle Art,
> No Language, but the Language of the Heart
> (392-9)

Initially it is the reverent simplicity which strikes in this passage. Pope's father is the very opposite of the arrogant, aggressive, tawdry and fickle characters with whom the poem has hitherto been largely concerned. Pope is also describing someone near to him, and we encounter, as we have encountered before in the poem, an unexpected baring of the heart. The analytical care with which his father is described is parallel to that with which Hervey is attacked, yet, superficially at least, there seems little that is exaggerated here, with only the smallest compromise with rhetorical effect. The very ordinariness of Pope's father is striking too: he stands outside all those tensions and problems which beset his son. He is completely removed from influences which corrupt or debase. He is a model of inoffensive mediocrity, and it is odd that Pope should wish to emulate him: ('Oh grant me thus to live and thus to die' (404)).

The fact that Pope does wish to emulate his father represents at least a partial rejection of his own literary position, and is the culmination of all those complaints about fame and success which have characterized much of the poem's discourse.

Two other features of this passage are worthy of note. Firstly, Pope is keen to emphasize the fact of his parents' noble birth:

> Of gentle Blood (part shed in Honour's Cause,
> While yet in Britain Honour had Applause)
> Each Parent sprung – 'What Fortune, pray?' – Their own.
> And better got than Bestia's from the Throne.
> (388-391)

Given the frequent suggestions about Pope's humble origins which his pamphlet attackers made, it is not perhaps surprising that Pope was defensive about his background. In the note on this section which he himself attaches to the poem, he remarks that his father was '. . . of a Gentleman's Family in Oxfordshire, the Head of which was the Earl of Downe . . .'. Pope was quite wrong in this: his grandfather had been a clergyman in Andover, which is where his family originated.[40] Likewise the side-swipe at Bestia (the Duke of Marlborough) makes a comparison which seems designed to latter his own family just as much as to criticize Marlborough.

Secondly, there is the Horatian echo. The sixth of Horace's

first book of satires contains a fulsome tribute to his father.[41] Given the increasingly Horatian cast of Pope's thinking in the early 1730s, it is difficult not to see an influence. Horace is keen to stress the efforts which his father, a humble man, took to ensure a proper education and upbringing for his son. To read the passage in Horace's poem is to become aware of how passive a presence Pope's father is in *An Epistle* . . . He seems strangely distanced: no hint of relationship or reciprocity between father and son is suggested, and the man's life and work is constantly defined by negatives, as though he was shut out from participation in the world in which other people lived. (. . .'no Pride' . . .'no Strife. . .' '. . . Nor marrying Discord . . .' '. . . innoxious . . .' '. . . Nor Courts . . .' '. . . no Suits . . .' '. . . Nor dar'd . . . nor hazarded . . .' '. . . Un-learn'd . . .' etc.) It is, in the end, a strangely distancing portrait: apparently warm in tone yet ultimately elusive.

Pope's treatment of his mother is shorter but more immediate:

> Me, let the tender Office long engage
> To rock the Cradle of reposing Age,
> With lenient Arts extend a Mother's breath,
> Make Languor smile, and smooth the Bed of death.
> (408-411)

There can be few poets who were as attentive to their parents as Pope, whose care for his mother was a principal concern until only about a decade before his own death. The picture of the poet's vigil at his mother's bedside is thus an appropriate one. The lines date from 1731, and Pope's mother died in 1733, so that by the time the poem was published the dutiful vigil was past, and the forward-looking impulse of the lines outdated. There is a subtle play of frankness and fiction about Pope's treatment of his parents.

Given the twistings of facts and conditions which these closing lines contain, it is inevitable that we should consider their effect and appropriateness as a conclusion to a peom whose concerns have seemed, on the whole, so very different. In one sense they form, in Johnsonian phrase, a 'conclusion, in which nothing is concluded.' The 'dire dilemma' of Pope's relationship with the literary world, with his enemies, and with his vocation is ultimately shelved in favour of a portrait of an exemplary 'innoxious' man, and a presentation of Pope, as dutiful son, attentive to the cradle of reposing age. That the poet was meant to emerge favourably from the latter portrait need not, perhaps, be questioned. His final 'placing' as devoted son presents him in as different a light as possible from that favoured by his literary enemies. In that respect there is something about these closing lines which seems calculated to disarm further criticism.

But there is another aspect to them. Pope's final benediction is not to his mother but to John Arbuthnot himself:

> Preserve him social, chearful, and serene,
> And just as rich as when he serv'd a QUEEN!
> Whether that Blessing be deny'd or giv'n,
> Thus far was right, the rest belongs to Heav'n.
>
> (416-9)

Pope's parents were dead, Dr Arbuthnot was dying. Pope's tribute to Arbuthnot is backward looking. Pope is asking for good health for Arbuthnot but it is a knowingly desperate request. There is a feeling of developing isolation about these final lines. Pope is not usually thought of as sentimental but one is aware in this poem that his backward-lookingness is not simply to injuries and enmities. His recalling of youthful days in the company of Garth, Congreve, Bolingbroke and others, alongside the wistfulness of these final lines, reminds us that insofar as the poem offers any alternative to its complaints about the present, those alternatives are fixed intangibly in the past.

Pope's imagination always had a mythologizing tendency. In this poem he presents himself in a variety of half-fictionalized postures; he builds his parents into embodiments of 'noble blood'; he recreates the warmth of past times when he first came before the literary world as a marvellous boy. It is the tension between the here and now on the one hand, and the mythologized past on the other, which is also productive of much of the poem's power, and it is a tension which is never resolved.

As we have already noted, *An Epistle to Dr Arbuthnot* is a piecemeal poem, one which takes up different postures and speaks in different tones of voice. Ultimately it is impossible to discriminate between these voices, to say that one is or is not the true voice of Pope, or to say that one of Pope's postures is more right or wrong than another. The poem was described by Pat Rogers as 'A Drama of Mixed Feelings'[42], and it is the ultimate witness to the multifariousness of these feelings that they remain mixed. *An Epistle to Dr Arbuthnot* deals with the complexities of Pope's life, and the issues which it encounters are beyond the power of poetry to solve.

Chapter Three: Flapping Gilded Bugs

1. Pope's *Argument to Book the Third,* Twickenham V (1953) pp55-56. The point is also made by Ian Jack *Augustan Satire* (1952) p120; Emrys Jones *Pope and Dulness* (Proceedings of the British Academy 1968) p238; David Nokes *Raillery and Rage: A Study of Eighteenth Century Satire* (1987) pp56-60.
2. Letter quoted by Charles Kerby-Miller (Ed) *The Memoirs of . . . Martinus Scriblerus* (1950) p14.
3. Letter to *The Spectator* (1712) quoted by Kerby-Miller p15.
4. Ibid p30.
5. The complete *Key to the Lock* can be found in John Dixon Hunt (Ed) *The Rape of the Lock: A Casebook* (1968) pp33-48.
6. For further details see David Nokes *Jonathan Swift, A Hypocrite Revers'd* (1985) pp79-83.
7. *The Rape of the Lock* Canto V line 137.
8. See Hunt, *Casebook* pp59-60.
9. Letter to Pope 29 September 1725 reprinted in *Jonathan Swift* (Oxford Authors) Ed. Angus Ross and David Woolley (1984) p470.
10. See Introduction to Twickenham V Introduction pp x and xi.
11. Twickenham V, Introduction p xi.
12. See Aubrey Williams *Pope's Dunciad, A Study of its Meaning* (1955) pp30-34.
13. See Pat Rogers *Grub Street, Studies in a Subculture* (1972) Introduction and Chapter 1.
14. See Jones, pp247-8; also Howard Erskine-Hill *Pope: The Dunciad* (1972) p44.
15. *Peri Bathous or . . . The Art of Sinking in Poetry* in Hammond (Ed.) *Selected Prose of Alexander Pope* p173.
16. Ibid p174.
17. Ibid p175.
18. A freelance preacher and lecturer whose sermons were frequently and gratuitously abusive of Pope. He is the subject of a biography by Graham Midgley (1973).
19. Hammond p174.
20. Jones p253.
21. Virgil Eclogue VI. Trans. C. Day Lewis 1963 p26.
22. Jones p235.
23. Ibid p259.
24. See 1 above.
25. Twickenham V Introduction, p xxii.
26. See *Pope: The Critical Heritage* Ed. John Barnard 1973 p226.
27. Mack *Life* p473.

28. See Guerinot *Pamphlet Attacks* pp110-114.
29. Quoted in Twickenham V, Introduction p xxiv.
30. The most notable exponent of this view was Matthew Arnold *Essays in Criticism, Second Series* (1888).
31. Pope's *Advertisement* to the poem Twickenham IV p95.
32. See the chronological list in Guerinot *Pamphlet Attacks.*
33. Guerinot p166.
34. See Wordsworth *Preface* to *The Lyrical Ballads* (1800) Shelley *A Defence of Poetry* (1840).
35. For a detailed treatment of Pope's relations with Addison see Mack *Life* pp272-282.
36. Dustin Griffin *Alexander Pope: The Poet in the Poems* (1978) pp173-190.
37. See above Chap 1 Note 7.
38. Graham Midgley *The Life of Orator Henley* (1973) pp173-4.
39. See above Chap 1 Note 3.
40. For Pope's family background see Mack *Life* pp3-12.
41. See Penguin Classics edition Ed. and Trans. by Niall Rudd (1979) p69.
42. *The Use of English,* Vol 25, No 2 (1973) pp142-146.

4

VIRTUE'S FRIENDS

Epistles to Several Persons

Following the furore which surrounded the publication of *The Dunciad*, Pope thought it prudent to preserve anonymity in his next major undertaking. *An Essay on Man* was published in four parts (called Epistles) between February 1733 and January 1734. The work gained instant success and was widely read. On this occasion it seems Pope was not suspected as the author and the poem even went down well in Grub Street whose inhabitants refrained from hostilities.[1]

An Essay on Man has been considerably less popular in more modern times when tastes in poetry have not favoured the philosophic and didactic. The philosophical 'scheme' of which *An Essay on Man* is only a small part was nothing if not ambitious. The poem itself considers man in his relationship to the created universe, governed by 'A universal Cause', more or less equated with a beneficent God. The *Essay*, though complete of itself was, in Pope's mind, merely the starting point for a huge undertaking which he came to call his *Opus Magnum.*[2] Pope described the *Essay* as being '. . . what a scale is to a book of maps':[3] it was to be followed by further books on arts, sciences, learning, politics, religion and morality, along with a treatment of the 'Orders, Professions and Stations of human life'.[4] Part of the plan was to have comprised an epic poem, illustrating the role of man 'in his Social, Political and Religious capacity.'

It is not surprising that this 'system of ethics', as Pope called the work in a letter to Swift, remained incomplete.

Wordsworth, in due course, was to contemplate a similarly complex and all-embracing philosophical poem, and that too failed to be finished: the epic-length *Prelude* was merely the autobiographical introduction.

One part of the poem which Pope did develop was the section of the *Opus Magnum* which was to be devoted to 'private Ethics or practical morality'.[5] He had already, in 1731, written and published the first version of an epistle to Lord Burlington, dealing with the question of taste in architecture and gardening. Between 1731 and 1735 three more epistles followed: to Lord Bathurst (1733); to Lord Cobham (1734); to Martha Blount (1735). The epistles to Burlington and Bathurst both subsequently acquired the subtitle *Of the Use of Riches*; that to Cobham became *Of the Knowledge and Characters of Men*, and that to Martha Blount: *To a Lady, Of the Characters of Women.* Thus it would appear that Pope was seeking to demonstrate in practical and local terms aspects of human behaviour consonant with his wider, more all-embracing theories of man.

The verse 'Epistle' was an acceptable form during Pope's lifetime. It had impeccable classical credentials (Horace was a noted exponent) and consequently would aim, with the occasional backward glance to ancient Rome, to combine observation of the contemporary scene with a certain amount of criticism of it. The epistle's field of interest would inevitably be calculated to appeal to the taste of the addressee. *The Essay on Man* itself had had an epistolary structure, the whole poem being addressed to Pope's 'Guide, Philosopher and Friend', Henry St John Bolingbroke, whose influence lay behind much of the poem's thinking. Bolingbroke, Burlington and Bathurst were among Pope's oldest and closest friends, and in addressing himself to them he was providing an opportunity to express freely his points of view on a number of subjects. It is perhaps unfortunate that William Warburton, Pope's first editor, chose to title these works *Moral Essays*, which is what, on the whole, they are still known as. The title makes them seem graver than they are. Pope was, in places, keen to illustrate points which he had made in *An Essay on Man*, and certainly none of the poems have the sheerly provocative mischief of *The Dunciad.* Pope wrote to Swift in 1737:

> 'You call your satires libels. I would rather call my satires epistles. They will consist more of morality than of wit, and grow graver, which you will call duller.'[6]

However, there is no need to feel intimidated by these professions of gravity on Pope's part: the poems contain plenty of wit and a characteristically bracing refusal to spare his victims' blushes. Alienated from the values of Sir Robert Walpole's all but impregnable Whig government, both by birth and inclination, Pope was genuinely concerned about what he took to be various public ills. He was to engage more directly in political satire in his *Imitations of Horace,* but the concerns of, for example, the Epistle to Bathurst, took him further into the public domain than he had yet ventured. Whereas in *TheDunciad*, Pope's subject had been the muddy underside of the literary world, in the epistles to Bathurst and to Burlington he leaves *Poverty and Poetry* for a consideration of the abuses of wealth.

The Epistle 'To Allen, Lord Bathurst'

Allen, Lord Bathurst[7] had been raised to the peerage in 1712. He was a life-long Tory, and a long-serving MP for Cirencester, immediately to the west of which stood his ancestral home, Oakley Grove. Although Pope had known him for many years, he was on the face of it the very last man it seems likely that the poet would find much in common with. Bathurst was vigorous, volatile, hard-drinking, and an inveterate womanizer. He was, in fact, very much the caricature of the eighteenth-century landowner: a more august version of Fielding's Squire Western. He and Pope, however, had one great binding interest: landscape gardening and 'improvement'. Pope had been a frequent summer guest at Oakley Grove, and while Bathurst offered Pope hospitality and encouragement with his translation of Homer, Pope offered Bathurst advice and encouragement in the cultivation of his large estate.

Although the 'landscape garden' as we understand it was a development which took place after Pope's lifetime, he had been instrumental in creating the climate of opinion out of which the landscape garden movement grew. His own garden at Twickenham enjoyed an international reputation so it is not perhaps surprising that Pope's aristocratic friends, though possessing much more land than he did, were happy to seek his advice on planting and design. Questions of gardening and architecture are more strictly relevant to Pope's Epistle to Burlington, but they are relevant considerations in the Bathurst epistle too. Much of the thrust of this epistle is grounded in Pope's respect for Bathurst as a model of the socially responsible landowner. The fact that Bathurst was a great planter of trees is seen by Pope as a manifestation of considerable social responsibility:

> To balance Fortune by a just expence,
> Join with Oeconomy, Magnificence;
> With Splendour, Charity; with Plenty, Health;
> Oh teach us, BATHURST! yet unspoil'd by wealth!
> That secret rare, between th'extremes to move
> Of mad Good-nature, and of mean Self-love.
>
> (223-8)

The epistle presents us with numerous examples of contemporaries who had not moved between such extremes, and whose acquisition and abuse of wealth offered nothing at all to the public good.

> 'John Ward of Hackney, Esq.; Member of Parliament, being prosecuted by the Duchess of Buckingham, and convicted of Forgery, was first expelled the House, and then stood in the Pillory . . . He was suspected of joining in a conveyance with Sir John Blunt to secrete fifty thousand pounds of that Director's Estate forfeited to the South Sea Company by Act of Parliament . . . Ward was imprisoned, and hazarded the forfeiture of his life by not giving in his effects till the last day, which was that of his examination. During his confinement, his amusement was to give poison to dogs and cats and see them expire by slower or quicker torments . . .'[8]

So reads Pope's footnote to line 20 of the poem. It points to several of the work's characteristic features: its anecdotal and parable-like nature; its concern with public vice and fraud; its interest in the individual career, and in the rise and fall of those who had become rich through ruthless speculation.

Pope took his *Epistle to Bathurst* very seriously, referring to it in his correspondence as *The Moral Book,* and telling Swift, 'I never took more care in my life of any poem.'[9] The extraordinarily circumstantial note on the activities of John Ward is in itself a testimony that Pope's targets were real and at hand. Some of the portraits which he paints in the epistle are composites, but all contain detail drawn from contemporary behaviour. It is clear that there was abundant evidence of the perils of financial corruption and of the morally questionable consequences of growing rich from the 'new money' which abounded in the early years of the eighteenth century.

The financial climate of this period was revolutionary and expansionist.[10] The preceding decades had created most of the nation's financial institutions as we now understand them, in particular the Bank of England and 'Exchange Alley' (or the Stock Exchange). The latter organization had come into existence as a result of the growth of Joint-Stock companies, financed by investors or shareholders. Thus 'the City' as we know it (in both its geographical and economic senses) had come into existence, and was typified by the development of the South Sea Company. This company very soon outgrew its original trading functions, and, particularly under the directorship of John (later Sir John) Blunt, saw itself as a possible alternative to the Bank of England and a means of solving the national debt. The company had received royal patronage from George I, and Blunt genuinely believed that investment in it was in the nation's interest. Consequently stocks rose sharply in the years before 1730 and Pope himself invested £500. He was one of the many who suffered losses, when, in 1720, the South Sea 'bubble' burst, and the value of the Company's stocks plummeted. The whole affair took on the proportions of a national scandal, and Walpole's involvement with the company almost led to the fall of his government. It thus became and has remained a symbol for the financial malpractice of the age. It is not surprising that details of it find their way into Pope's poem.

Another notoriously scandalous concern was the Charitable Corporation, which ostensibly existed to help the poor by making them loans upon security. Its affairs eventually had to be investigated by parliament, and the three Directors (all MPs) were expelled from the House of Commons. Needless to say, none of the Directors evinced any sympathy at all for the plight of the poor, and one of them, Denis Bond, was quoted as saying: 'Damn the poor, let us go into the City, where we may get money.'[11]

So there was clearly no shortage of ready raw material for Pope's poem and it is not surprising that Sir John Blunt comes in for some attack. He was a promising subject, for his interest did not simply extend to his South Sea Company dealings. Pope mocks Blunt's (quite genuine) moral earnestness; his belief that he had a genuine mission to save his country, and his wrapping of his financial chicaneries in pious clothing. In another footnote, Pope reminds us that Blunt '. . . was a Dissenter of a most religious deportment, and profess'd to be a great believer.'[12] Pope was sensitive, as modern social and economic historians have been, to the close relationship between the new 'moneyed men' of the city and low-church protestantism of a neo-Puritan kind. This not only renders a character such as Blunt the more morally monstrous, but also, potentially, the more grotesque. Pope's description of him begins almost indulgently:

> Much injur'd Blunt! why bears he Britain's hate?
> A wizard told him in these words our fate:
> 'At length Corruption, like a gen'ral flood,
> '(So long by watchful ministers withstood)
> 'Shall deluge all; and Av'rice creeping on,
> 'Spread like a low-Born mist, and blot the Sun'
> (135-140)

Pope almost makes Blunt seem like a friend, unjustly punished, and suffering unaccountably, persecuted as a prophet in his own country. His divinely-inspired prescience in the face of 'a gen'ral flood' makes him sound almost like a second Noah.

Unfortunately, Blunt's promptings come from nothing more than 'A Wizard', and we begin to hear irony in Pope's voice. The apparent friendliness in the tone is deceptive: Pope is looking at Blunt's career with embarrassing thoroughness, as he goes on to outline the consequences of ruthless speculation:

> 'Statesman and Patriot ply alike the stocks,
> 'Peeress and Butler share alike the Box,
> 'And Judges job, and Bishops bite the town,
> 'And mighty Dukes pack cards for half a crown.
> 'See Britain sunk in lucre's sordid charms,
> 'And France reveng'd of ANNE's and EDWARD's arms.'
>
> (141-146)

Avarice, Pope has already told us is 'low born' and 'creeps'. There is something insidiously vulgar about it, as it covers everything around it like a mist. Its social consequences are unnatural and levelling, fusing both government and opposition ('Statesman and Patriot') in the same corruption, and causing a *nouveau riche* servant to oust a Duchess from her time-honoured seat in the theatre. It makes Britain a laughing stock in Europe too.

Thus the kind of corruption represented by Blunt cannot easily be localized. It is in its very nature to spread and do damage. Blunt has initiated more than he realizes, because, as Pope goes on to show, there is something illogical about the immense power which this one man can have.

> 'Twas no Court-badge, great Scriv'ner, fir'd thy brain
> Nor lordly Luxury, nor City Gain.
>
> (147-8)

Pope exploits most of the incongruities which Blunt's character represents. To call him a 'great Scriv'ner' is a most revealing contradiction in terms. Scriveners were not a popular breed, and they had been getting above themselves. They were, essentially, writers and conveyancers of legal documents, and sometimes indulged in money-lending. Both Blunt and Peter Walker had made vast fortunes as 'middle men', when essentially they were not much more than glorified clerks. Hence, to find 'greatness' in a Scrivener would in practice be grotesque. The new makers of money were obscure by origin and profession. It seems highly unlikely also, that Blunt's financial dealings were as disinterested as he liked to make out. Although he claimed that he required no position for himself, Pope is inevitably sceptical:

> Whether he did really credit the prophecy [that referred to on line 136] . . . is not certain, but . . . constantly . . . he declaimed against the corruption and luxury of the age . . .[13]

The key image in Pope's description of Blunt is the 'gen'ral flood' of corruption. Imagery of inundation, of things spreading, growing, becoming disproportionate and uncontrollable, are important in the poem, and are obviously the terms in which Pope views the remorselessly expansionist financial world. They inform the more general discussion with which the poem begins, where Pope presents an imagined dialogue between himself and Bathurst. After reviewing the differences between the two men's views of human nature, Pope finds that the issue of wealth provides common ground:

> Both fairly owning, Riches in effect,
> No grace of Heav'n or token of th'Elect;
> Giv'n to the Fool, the Mad, the Vain, the Evil,
> To Ward, to Waters, Chartres, and the Devil.
> (17-20)

It is only the corrupt, such as Blunt, who see wealth as God-given, and who, by implication, therefore worship it. The galloping list of types and individuals in the last two lines shows just how uncontrollable the spread of this attitude is.

Pope allows himself a fantasy about payment (or bribery) in kind:

> Could France or Rome divert our brave designs
> With all their brandies or with all their wines?

What could they more than Knights or Squires confound
Or water all the Quorum ten miles round?
A Statesman's slumbers how this speech would spoil!
'Sir, Spain has sent a thousand jars of oil;
'Huge bales of British cloth blockade the door;
'A hundred oxen at your levee roar.'
(39-46)

He stresses the sheer gross bulk of wealth. If bribery was done in kind, then the sheer scale of it would render the whole process unmanageable. If money did not exist then we would have to invent it, which is in a sense precisely what a contemporary of Pope's did. John Law was a Scottish economist who had persuaded the French king to revolutionize the nation's monetary system by replacing coin with paper notes. Thus the modern monetary system, divorced from associations with land of physical objects was developing. It too, rapidly became the currency of corruption:

Blest paper-credit! last and best supply!
That lends Corruption lighter wings to fly!
Gold imp'd with thee, can compass hardest things,
Can pocket States, can fetch or carry Kings;
(69-72)

Not only is corruption like a flood, it can now also fly. The word 'imp'd' is used of birds when their feathers have been cut to facilitate flight. Pope stresses the two opposite qualities of paper money: its insubstantiability on the one hand, and its power on the other:

A single leaf shall waft an Army o'er,
Or ship off Senates to a distant Shore;
A leaf, like Sibyl's, scatter to and fro
Our fates and fortunes, as the wind shall blow:
Pregnant with thousands flits the Scrap unseen,

And silent sells a King or buys a Queen.
(72-77)

Paper money flies high, based as it is on insubstantial scraps, as if being wafted about in the wind. Yet it is active and influential. The passage is full of verbs which underline paper money's power. It can 'compass', 'pocket', 'fetch', 'carry', 'waft' and 'ship'. Likewise the sheer subtlety of its power is emphasized in the line 'Pregnant with thousands flits the scrap unsees', where the heavy corporeality implicit in 'pregnant', is instantly contrasted with the 'flitting' of the scrap.

The passage is not without factual basis. Pope reminds us in his notes that kingdoms had indeed been traded like commodities; that ministers had been forced to flee, and that the whole of Louis XV's parliament had been expelled from Paris for its opposition to John Law's reforms.[14] The last line of the passage refers to Queen Caroline (wife of George II), who had accepted large cash payments from the South Sea Company.

Just as Pope exposes the connection between the lightness of paper currency and the heaviness of the corruption which it enables, so too he is aware of the interrelatedness of wealth and poverty. The Charitable Corporation, whose activities have already been mentioned embody quite the opposite of a charitable concern for the poor:

Perhaps you think the poor may have their part?
Bond damns the poor and hates them from his heart:
The grave Sir Gilbert holds it for a rule
That 'every man in want is knave or fool':
'God cannot love' (says Blunt, with tearless eyes)
'The wretch he starves' - and piously denies:
But the Bishop, with a meeker air,
Admits, and leaves them Providence's care.
(101-108)

What is particularly offensive about the points of view which Pope is attacking is not the absence of compassion or the belief that poverty was a sin (such a belief was common enough for centuries), but the way in which the beliefs have been appropriated by those who claim to be embodying the highest standards of public morality. Blunt presumes to speak ('piously') on God's behalf, and in so doing says that 'God cannot love . . .' with splendidly unchristian frankness, and without tears. Morally equal with this attitude is that of the Bishop who, without any further thought on the matter, '. . . leaves . . .' the poor to the care of providence. Pope's conclusion is:

> . . . to be just to these poor men of pelf,
> Each does but hate his neighbour as himself.
> (109-10)

Again, we hear that apparently condoning ironic voice ('Yet to be just . . .'), whilst at the same time being made to see that, in any worthwhile terms, these are indeed 'poor men'. The word 'pelf' means riches, so in the phrase 'poor men of pelf', Pope has not for the last time in the poem shown the contradiction inherent in those who are materially wealthy yet morally impoverished, though the alliterative link between the two words seems to insist upon a necessary and unavoidable connection between the two states.

The idea that riches are but another form of poverty is implicit in the two (probably fictional) portraits which Pope goes on to give us of the two Cottas, father and son. The question of whether Pope had specific people in mind in his descriptions has been much discussed, but to treat them as fiction does not cause them to lose their point:

> Old Cotta sham'd his fortune and his birth
> (179)

and he did so through parsimony. Pope's accusation against the elder Cotta is twofold. First there is his own, personal impoverishment:

> His court with nettles, moats with cresses stor'd
> With soups unbought and sallads blest his board.
> (183-4)

The practice of vegetarianism and plain-living need not, in themselves, offend the reader, particularly as Pope is prepared to acknowledge the religious and spiritual imperatives which have often determined such abstinence:

> If Cotta liv'd on pulse, it was no more
> Than Bramins, Saints and Sages did before.
>
> (185-6)

Unfortunately Cotta's self-denial comes not from any spiritual source but from a desire to keep himself rich by keeping himself poor. His wealth shows itself not in prodigality but in denial.

This denial is not confined to Cotta himself. Pope's second accusation against him is that, as a wealthy landowner, he is failing in his public duty. Traditionally the country landowner was responsible for his tenants and for the well-being of the local community. The 'big house' was, ideally, the centre of philanthropy and hospitality. Ben Jonson's poem *To Penshurst* is an excellent illustration of the point. Cotta's influence is quite different:

> Like some lone Chartreux stands the good old Hall,
> Silence without, and Fasts within the wall;
> No rafter'd roofs with dance and tabor sound,
> No noontide-bell invites the country round;
> Tenants with sighs the smoakless tow'rs survey,
> And turn th'unwilling steeds another way.
>
> (189-94)

All in this section is absence and dereliction, loneliness and isolation. There is absolutely nothing warm or welcoming about Cotta's hall. His self-denial has become, by extension, a misanthropy which extends beyond himself and out into the larger community.

We might hope for something better from Cotta junior:

> Not so his Son, he mark'd this oversight
> And then mistook reverse of wrong for right.
>
> (199-200)

In the biblical parable of the prodigal son the son learns the errors of his ways and is pardoned by his father. Young Cotta experiences neither of these privileges. His prodigality leads to thoughtless destruction, environmental as well as personal. The greater the status his wealth confers upon him, the lower in Pope's estimation he sinks. First of all he reverses his father's inhospitable habits:

> What slaughter'd hecatombs, what floods of wine,
> Fill the capacious Squire and deep Divine!
>
> (203-4)

We are with inundation and profusion again; Cotta's hospitality is mere grossness, as Pope's punning adjectives remind us. The Squire is 'capacious' in position and the clergyman 'deep' in learning and spirituality, but in both cases the adjectives turn against the characters and simply suggest insatiable appetites. Ironically, we see the development of the 'right' political sentiments in Cotta:

> 'Tis GEORGE and LIBERTY that crowns the cup,
> And Zeal for that great House which eats him up.
>
> (207-8)

Such politics are, Pope tells us, naturally acquired by the prodigal and the reckless. Cotta's zeal is less for 'Liberty' than for his own self-advancement: the Whig party pledged to the support of the House of Hanover was very much the party of men on the make, Walpole's power being very much supported by 'new money'.

However, it is the onward move to self-destruction that Pope responds to in the younger Cotta. First of all he pillages the local landscape for his own profit:

> The woods recede around the naked seat,
> The Sylvans groan – no matter – for the Fleet:
> Next goes his Wool – to clothe our valiant bands,
> Last, for his Country's love, he sells his Lands.
>
> (209-212)

Cotta rapes the environment in order to profit from the sale of his produce. A similarity which he shares with his father is the selfish abuse of his social responsibilities as a landowner. He prefers to become one of the new City men instead, and his degeneration is seen as much in ideological terms as economic ones:

> To town he comes, completes the nation's hope,
> And heads the bold Train-bands, and burns a Pope.
> (213-4)

The 'completion' of Cotta's career, coincides of course, with the final stage of his progress to bankruptcy. His espousing of good City causes, like law and order (a Train-band was a kind of special constabulary), and anti-Jacobitism (burning an effigy of the Pope) is but the ideological equivalent of the financial ruin which awaits him:

> In vain at Court the Bankrupt pleads his cause,
> His thankless Country leaves him to her laws.
> (217-8)

Amidst ruthless and competitive capitalism, the Bankrupt cannot of course expect sympathy. He simply goes to the wall.

In the two Cottas Pope has given us two opposing illustrations of the destructive effects of wealth, by parsimony on the one hand, and prodigality on the other. The second half of the poem makes much use of exemplary portraits, and operates on the whole, through contrast and comparison, balancing one character against another. Having explored the shortcomings of the Cottas, Pope offers us John Kyrle, 'The Man of Ross'.

This portrait is a remarkable one, if only for the substantially accurate treatment which Kyrle receives on the basis of largely hearsay evidence. Although a considerable local benefactor, Kyrle was essentially an obscure man, living in the small provincial town of Ross on Wye, in Herefordshire.[15] It seems that Pope discovered most of what he knew about Kyrle from information provided by Herefordshire friends. Such anecdotal information adds up to a circumstantially very coherent portrait.

John Kyrle lived from 1637 to 1724. Although from a landowning background, and educated at Oxford and the Middle Temple, he was never himself a particularly wealthy man. He did not practise the law for any great length of time, and settled in a modest house in the market place at Ross. He was not a landowner in the conventional sense, having no estates, though he did own parcels of lands and woods scattered here and there in the neighbourhood. His public-spiritedness was legendary and well-documented and he was known as 'The Man of Ross' in his lifetime (even, Pope suggests, by 'each lisping babe').

> Of Debts, and Taxes, Wife and Children clear,
> This man possessed – five hundred pounds a year.
> (279-280)

This is not a wealth of the Cotta order, but John Kyrle's contribution to the public good is greater by many degrees. Firstly, his public-spiritedness is shown by his improvements to the local environment. Kyrle's improvements are both beautiful and useful:

> Who hung with woods yon mountain's sultry brow?
> From the dry rock who bade the waters flow?
> Not to the skies in useless columns tost,
> Or in proud falls magnificently lost,
> But clear and artless, pouring thro' the plain
> Health to the sick, and solace to the swain.
> (253-258)

Where the younger Cotta sold trees for personal gain, Kyrle plants them for the public good. Pope's rather biblical question (line 254) reminds us that Kyrle paid for a 'waterworks' to provide the town of Ross with water from the River Wye. He was also responsible for providing funds for the rebuilding of the Parish Church ('Who taught that heav'n-directed spire to rise?' (261)), and for giving alms to the poor:

Him portion'd maids, apprentic'd orphans blest,
The young who labour, and the old who rest
Is any sick? the MAN of ROSS relieves,
Prescribes, attends, the med'cine makes and gives.
(267-270)

Pope's description of Kyrle provides a centrally placed positive in the poem. It shows us that it is possible to find a man who loves rather than hates his neighbour, and who sees money as best being put to use in helping the community. It is significant, though, that Pope has to search so hard to find such a paragon. John Kyrle was in no sense a national figure but an obscure provincial, and Pope therefore seems to be making the almost Dickensian point that large-scale public corruption can only be challenged by acts of private charity.

If the description of John Kyrle emphasizes the moral aspect of this epistle, and concerns itself somewhat earnestly with homely, decent values, the three remaining portraits show Pope at his most obviously satirical, exposing the consequences of human perversity. The first two portraits deal with actual figures, the final one is a composite.

The portraits of Villiers, Duke of Buckingham[16] and Sir John Cutler[17] again rehearse a pattern of contrast. Both portraits consider ends, and they explore both meanings of the word: ends as terminations, and ends as purposes. What is the end of wealth? Again spendthrift (Buckingham) is opposed to miser (Cutler - thought by some critics to have been the original for Old Cotta). Both portraits are images of destruction.

In the worst inn's worst room, with mat half-hung,
The floors of plaster, and the walls of dung,
On once a flock-bed, but repair'd with straw
With tape-ty'd curtains, never meant to draw,
The George and Garter dangling from that bed
Where tawdry yellow strove with dirty red
Great Villiers lies . . .
(299-305)

Pope withholds the name for some time, making the last line at once both climax and anti-climax. We hear eventually the mention of the 'great' name, the name of one who ought to be lying and dying in state. Instead the word 'Great' with the insidious irony so characteristc of this poem is actually turned against Buckingham as Pope shows into what insubstantial 'tawdry' objects the symbols of his position have been so easily transformed. One detail of degradation gives way to another, it is '. . . the worst inn's worst room . . .', the substances which surround him are plaster rather than wood; dung rather than plaster; straw rather than feathers; even the curtains are denied their own function ('never meant to draw'). All those surroundings which Buckingham might expect have gone. Even his Order of the Garter ribbon has been defamiliarized into a piece of gaudy cloth.

This is an important passage in the poem, even though Pope's details are to an extent fictional. Although Villiers did die in obscurity he was not surrounded by as much squalor as Pope would like to think. Pope provides the detail to form a clear contrast with Sir John Cutler's 'end' which follows. Cutler had been a prominent and public-spirited London merchant in the time of Charles II. Like Villiers he had become something of a legendary figure by the time that Pope was writing about him. Hence again, some of the details about his death are drawn from popular rumour rather than from impeccably scholarly sources (Pope, for example, is inaccurate about the number of daughters Cutler had).

> Cutler saw tenants break, and houses fall
> For very want: he could not build a wall.
> His only daughter in a stranger's pow'r,
> For very want; he could not pay a dow'r.
> A few grey hairs his rev'rend temples crown'd,
> 'Twas very want that sold them for two pound.
> (323-8)

The phrase which Pope repeats in this passage is 'very want'. Again, he plays with two different and apparently contrasting meanings of the word: to want, in its modern sense, is to desire, and in its more traditional sense, to lack. What Cutler desires, he also lacks, in that his desire to keep his great fortunes unspent causes him to lack just about everything else. In having (and keeping) so much, Cutler has nothing, and the munificence of the Man of Ross, imaged in terms of building, constructing and irrigating, is the precise opposite of the crumbling walls and collapsing houses with which Cutler is surrounded.

> Say, for such worth are other worlds prepar'd?
> Or are they both in this their own reward?
> A knotty point! to which we now proceed.
> But you are tir'd – I'll tell a tale. 'Agreed'.
>
> (335-9)

Just at the moment when we might expect some kind of moral conclusion from Pope, such as we find in his other epistles, he breaks off and decides to tell us a story instead, bringing his 'moral book' to a Hell for leather ending with his story of Sir Balaam. The effect on the reader is rather like seeing a film suddenly speeded up, for this is (and for good reason) a spectacularly breathless narrative, though it does contain a deft summing up of a good many of the points which Pope has been making about wealth throughout the poem.

The biblical Balaam was a man of principle, and the recipient of visionary admonition from Heaven. Pope's Balaam is dull, pliable, and open to temptation. He is compared also with Job, from whom, likewise, he differs:

> The Dev'l was piqu'd such saintship to behold,
> And long'd to tempt him like good Job of old:
> But Satan now is wiser than of yore,
> And tempts by making rich, not making poor.
>
> (349-52)

Pope is condescending and patronizing in his treatment of Sir Balaam. His tone implies that he feels a certain pity for the man's folly. There is a strange mixture of innocence and corruption within him, as if he is in a world which he is scarcely able to understand. He sounds morally naive rather than morally monstrous, as the rather 'Once upon a time' nature of his narrative seems to suggest.

There dwelt a citizen of sober fame,
A plain, good, man and Balaam was his name;
Religious, punctual, frugal and so forth,
His word would pass for more than he was worth . . .
(341-4)

Constant at Church and Change; his gains were sure,
His givings rare, save farthings to the poor.
(347-8)

Pope is discussing a type rather than an individual in these lines. 'Constant at Church and Change', Sir Balaam is a City merchant through and through: low church, dissenting, hard-working, acquisitive, 'Church and Change' seem almost parts of the same institution. He seems safe, predictable, bourgeois.

He also becomes wealthier:

'I'll now give sixpence where I gave a groat,
'Where once I went to church, I'll now go twice –
'And am so clear, too, of all other vice.'
(366-8)

Balaam seems to treat church-going as an essential investment too, which is perhaps why he is blind to the fact that his financial success is all the work of 'The Tempter', who convinces Balaam that he has outgrown his reliance on God's providence now:

Things change their titles as our manners turn:
His Compting house employ'd the Sunday morn;
Seldom at Church ('twas such a busy life)
But duly sent his family and wife.
(379-82)

For all the appreciable moral decline which Pope is charting, he still indulges Balaam's dedication and conscientiousness and the reckless economic rise continues. Balaam 'leaves the dull Cits' and uses his new money to hoist himself onto the coat tails of the aristocracy, as wealthy city merchants were tending to do:

> His daughter flaunts a Viscount's tawdry wife;
> She bears a Coronet and P-x for life.
> In Britain's Senate he a seat obtains . . .
>
> (391-3)

Part of Pope's joke against Sir Balaam, as the reader cannot fail to see, is that he reaches the climax of his career a mere eight lines before the end of the poem. Destruction comes upon him almost instantly:

> My lady falls to play; so bad her chance,
> He must repair it; takes a bribe from France;
> The House impeach him; Coningsby harangues;
> The Court forsake him, and Sir Balaam hangs
>
> (395-8)

Sir Balaam's bubble reputation is easily pricked, and Pope enjoys contemplating the end of his worldly prosperity:

> The Devil and the King divide the prize,
> And sad Sir Balaam curses God and dies.
>
> (401-2)

End of poem. Pope concludes with a smirk, and feels no inclination at all to add anything by way of moral gloss: the parable is self-sufficient. Avoiding 'knotty points', Pope's anecdotal review of Balaam's career concludes the sermon on avarice with an unblushingly satirical thrust and reminds us in brief of all the ills of ungoverned wealth. It is an abrupt but sufficient conclusion to the epistle.

Epistle 'To Richard Boyle, Earl of Burlington'

Commentators on Pope's *Epistle to Bathurst* have pointed to its darkness and pessimism. The tone of the *Epistle to Burlington* is considerably lighter. Where Pope referred to the Bathurst poem as his 'Moral Book', the Burlington epistle was an extension of his 'gardening poem'. Where the text of *To . . .*

Bathurst seems conscious of bearing the sins of the world, *To . . . Burlington* verges on being a *jeu d'esprit.* It allows Pope to talk about two of his favourite subjects, gardening and architecture.

These might seem rather trivial matters for a lengthy poem but both to Pope and to Burlington they were fraught with significance. Important changes in taste were afoot:

> You show us, Rome was glorious, not profuse,
> And pompous buildings once were things of Use.
> Yet shall (my Lord) your just, your noble rules
> Fill half the land with imitating Fools
>
> (23-6)

If *To . . . Bathurst* deals with corruption, *To . . . Burlington* deals with folly. The former poem reminds us of the economic consequences of an expansionist age, whilst the Burlington epistle deals with the cultural ones. It was addressed to one of the most cultured men of the age.

Richard Boyle, the third Earl of Burlington[18], was born in 1694. From his first grand tour (to Italy in 1714) he brought home a large collection of paintings and *objets d'art.* He was also a friend and patron of the young Handel, and a sponsor of the Royal Academy of Music. He is cheifly remembered for his consuming interest in architecture. This was largely brought about by the publication, in 1715, of a volume entitled *Vitruvius Britannicus* by a young Scottish architect called Colen Campbell. This volume consisted of plans and architectural drawings which paid tribute to 'antique simplicity', a quality found in England in the work of Inigo Jones whose imitation of Roman models possessed the classical virtues of order, proportion and restraint. In the same year also, appeared an extended study of the works of the Italian architect Antonio Palladio. These two publications affected Burlington profoundly, and much of the rest of his life was spent in propogating the 'palladian' style of architecture. He remodelled Burlington House (which still stands, home of the Royal Academy) in London's Piccadilly, before turning his attention to his estate in Chiswick, where he built a strict, rather academic villa, which can also still be seen.

Pope was much influenced by Burlington's new and uncompromising views and he, too, set to work on Palladian 'improvements' at his villa in Twickenham, with the assistance of James Gibbs and William Kent, perhaps the two most prominent figures of the age in building and garden design.

The Palladian movement posed both an aesthetic and a political challenge to prevailing architectual styles, which explains why it became something of an artistic crusade to its adherents. Arguably, all European architectural styles have looked back in their own way to classical sources. Even the design of a gothic church is based on that of a Roman basilica. The predominant late seventeenth-century baroque buildings of Wren and Vanbrugh find their origins in Roman arches, pillars and domes. The 'Greek revival' of the turn of the nineteenth century went back to the square, straight lines of the Parthenon. Palladian architecture looked backwards in search of harmony and purity. It found Wren's baroque showy, vulgar and uncomfortable. Pope equates it with prodigal expense:

> At Timon's Villa let us pass a day
> Where all cry out, 'What sums are thrown away!'
>
> (99-100)

The new Palladianism is associated with discretion and responsibility, also with retirement. Rather oddly, it was, on the whole, a Whig architecture, much favoured by the newly wealthy whose prosperity contributed to a country house building boom in the early eighteenth century. Pope consequently feels it important to warn the landlords, less of their responsibilities to their tenants, as of the responsibility for maintaining good standards of taste. He issues stirring exhortations to Burlington at the end of the poem:

> You too proceed! make falling Arts your care,
> Erect new wonders, and the old repair,
> Jones and Palladio to themselves restore,
> And be whate'er Vitruvius was before . . .
>
> (191-4)

Bid harbours open, public ways extend,
Bid Temples, worthier of the God, ascend;
Bid the broad Arch the dang'rous Flood contain
The Mole projected break the roaring Main;
Back to his bounds their subject Sea command,
And roll obedient rivers thro' the Land:
These Honours, Peace to happy Britain brings,
These are Imperial Works, and worthy Kings.
(197-204)

The almost boundless visions which Pope conjures up at the end of the poem show us the faith which the Palladians had in their cause, and when we discover that Burlington had gone so far as to submit plans for a new palace of Whitehall and Houses of Parliament, we appreciate the seriousness with which the new style was taking itself.

One of Pope's early subtitles for this poem was *Of False Taste*, and it is perhaps not surprising that he spends much of the poem condemning those with more wealth than discretion. It was easy to find the same kind of injurious activity amongst competitively 'imitating fools' as could be found among the City speculators criticized in the *Epistle to . . . Bathurst.* There is little point in building when 'just . . . noble . . . rules' of art are mangled by those who have no taste:

For what has Virro painted, built and planted?
Only to show, how many tastes he wanted.
What brought Sir Visto's ill got wealth to waste?
Some Daemon whisper'd, 'Visto! have a Taste.'
Heav'n visits with a Taste the wealthy fool
And needs no Rod, but Ripley with a Rule.
(12-17)

Thomas Ripley[19] was Walpole's pet architect, and Pope's line suggests that Ripley's talents extend only to measuring. Virro and Visto are clearly composite portraits. Burlington is the exact opposite of them:

Oft have you hinted to your brother peer,
A certain truth, which many buy too dear;
Something there is more needful than Expence,

> And something previous ev'n to Taste – 'tis sense
> (39-42)

This gives Pope the opportunity to lay down before the sympathetic ear of his addressee, his own views on building and planting. The building of houses and the design of gardens were seen as related, as indeed inseparable, activities. Burlington's protégé William Kent was active as both gardener and architect. Thus it is artificial, in a discussion of the poem, to treat building and gardening as separate entities, but it makes analysis easier to do so.

The centrally placed 'set piece' of the poem is the description of Timon's Villa, which embodies in dazzling profusion a satirical catalogue of all the things about building and design that Pope and Burlington hated. It seems first of all, as if we are to be taken on a guided tour:

> At Timon's Villa let us pass a day,

but the innocence of the invitation is swept aside by the devastating:

> Where all cry out, 'What sums are thrown away!'

and it soon becomes clear that Pope does not approve at all:

> So proud, so grand, of that stupendous air,
> Soft and Agreeable come never there.
> Greatness with Timon, dwells in such a draught
> As brings all Brobdingnag before your thought.
> (100-103)

The words 'stupendous' and 'Greatness' are being used pejoratively, of course. This passage is deeply hostile to gratuitous magnificence. Pope is concerned with size and proportion:

> To compass this, his building is a Town,
> His pond an Ocean, his parterre a Down:
> Who but must laugh, the Master when he sees,

A puny insect shiv'ring at a breeze!
Lo what huge heaps of littleness around!
The whole a labour'd Quarry above ground!
(105-111)

Homes, even stately ones, are meant to be lived in by people, and Pope's reference to the 'puny insect', apart from drawing attention to the moral negligibility of its subject, underlines the way in which human nature has been ignored amidst the splendidly paradoxical '. . . huge heaps of littleness . . .'. The last two lines of this passage bear a verbal resemblance to some comments made by Pope about Blenheim Palace, the house built for the Duke of Marlborough near Oxford, by Sir John Vanbrugh. A visitor to Blenheim can still judge for himself the accuracy of Pope's description.

If the outside of Timon's Villa is a repository of architectural disaster, the inside is also a catalogue of errors:

My Lord advances with majestic mien,
Smit with the mighty pleasure, to be seen:
But soft – by regular approach – not yet –
First thro' the length of yon hot Terrace sweat,
And when up ten steep slopes you've dragged your thighs,
Just at his Study-door he'll bless your eyes.
(127-132)

Pope conducts us by turn to the study, chapel and dining room. Evidence of ill-taste is all around. The study, for example, contains 'Books, not Authors'. Timon was presumably not the first and certainly not the last man to buy books because they looked good rather than because he wanted to read them:

To all their dated Backs he turns you round,
These Aldus printed, those Du Sueil has bound.
Lo some are Vellom, and the rest as good
For all his Lordship knows, but they are Wood.
(135-138)

A comparable poverty is to be found in the chapel. If Timon denies the true purpose of books, by collecting them for their bindings, his chapel denies the true purpose of worship:

> And now the Chapel's silver bell you hear,
> That summons you to all the Pride of Pray'r:
> Light quirks of Musick, broken and uneven,
> Make the soul dance upon a Jig to Heaven.
>
> (141-44)

The house is inappropriate as a home; the study is merely there for show; the chapel is hardly a spiritual retreat (its atmosphere embodying at least one of the seven deadly sins). The crime of Timon's Villa is that all its features are disproportionate, incongruous and unrestrained. There is an intellectual vacuity at the centre of it. Nor is the owner redeemed by the nature of his hospitality. It is again, above all else, calculated to impress. Timon's entertainment hovers between being a religious festival and a military campaign, and it is enacted in front of *objets d'art* of frightening tawdriness:

> The rich Buffet well-colour'd Serpents grace,
> And gaping Tritons spew to wash your face.
> Is this a dinner? this a Genial room?
> No, 'tis a Temple, and a Hecatomb.
> A solemn Sacrifice, perform'd in state,
> You drink by measure, and to minutes eat.
>
> (153-8)

A hecatomb was an ancient Greek religious ritual for which vast numbers of oxen were slaughtered. Pope uses religious imagery in this passage in much the same apparently inappropriate way as he did in *The Rape of the Lock,* as a means of pointing up the misplaced importance attached to trivial or mundane objects by those bent upon being impressive at all costs. Pope, once more, is employing his satirical strategy of playing with scale and perspective:

> Treated, caress'd, and tir'd, I take my leave,
> Sick of his civil Pride, from Morn to Eve;

I curse such lavish cost, and little skill
And swear no Day was ever past so ill.

(166-9)

Pope's tone sounds ungrateful and pusillanimous, as he presents himself cursing and swearing at his host's generosity. To sneer at the tastelessness of Timon's architecture is one thing, to criticize, as a guest, his hospitality is another. It adds what might seem a querulously personal touch to the discussion, as if some sort of score is being settled. It is perhaps, therefore, not surprising that the Timon's Villa section of the poem became something of a minor scandal in Pope's life. We do not know precisely who first circulated the rumour that Pope was here describing the Duke of Chandos's house at Cannons, but the rumour spread quickly and rapidly took on the status of established fact (Dr Johnson, in his life of Pope, certainly treated it as such[20]). Pope issued disclaimers that he had in any way defamed the Duke, but these were ignored. His own feelings towards the Duke were perfectly cordial and he makes a flattering reference to him in the epistle to Cobham. The matter all goes to show the climate in which Pope worked, in which the denizens of Grub Street were prepared to make instant scandal and controversy out of his writing. It also shows the drawback of preserving the discreet secrecy over his targets which Pope sometimes favoured. If naming names brought out into the open certain personal animosities, it at least prevented Pope from being publicly misrepresented.

Perhaps the ultimate point of the passage in question was to show the way in which styles of building could reflect certain moral qualities. Timon ransacks the landscape for his '. . . labour'd Quarry above ground . . .' and flies in the face of nature in constructing monuments to his own self-importance. Timon is, after all, no more than '. . . a puny insect . . .'.

A rather curious passage follows, which Pope tells us contains 'the Moral of the whole'[21]:

Yet hence the Poor are cloath'd, the Hungry fed;
Health to himself, and to his Infants bread
The Lab'rer bears: What his hard Heart denies,

His charitable Vanity supplies.

(169-72)

His suggestion is that Timon's extravagance presents certain, rather backhanded, advantages to the local community. The landlord's vanity is charitable in that it enables the labourer at least to gain an honest living out of supplying his wants. It is a grudgingly optimistic conclusion to the destructiveness of the previous passage, though it is important in underlining one of the main concerns of the poem, which is the relationship between the works of man and the workings of nature. Burlington combined an enthusiasm for building with an enthusiasm for gardening, and Pope's own place in the history of English gardening is an important one.

As with architecture, gardening in Pope's lifetime was caught up in a conflict of styles. Although Pope speaks with approval of Le Notre in this poem, he was reacting in his own designs at Twickenham against the highly geometrical gardens which Le Notre planned at Versailles. As the eighteenth century progressed there emerged a recognizable 'landscape garden' movement, whose chief practical exponent was 'Capability' Brown. Although Pope's preferences in gardens were different from those favoured later in the century, the landscape garden movement could certainly claim Pope as a founding father and the movement was certainly literary in origin, taking many of its prescriptions for garden design, rather freely, from Horace.

The basis of Pope's gardening reforms was a respect for 'nature': formal seventeenth-century gardens tended to be rectangular, symmetrical, and enclosed by high walls. These features all served to emphasize the difference between the garden and the wild nature growing beyond it. Pope's own garden made use of symmetry and artifice, with its mounds, obelisks and Grotto, but his belief that 'all gardening is landscape painting'[22] indicates that Pope saw gardens as a manifestation of natural growth, rather than as an opposition to it. Pope's ideal country house garden would preserve the formality of parterres (terraces) and flower beds near to the house, but would, by degrees, give way to 'artful wildness' (line 116). This was best encompassed in the building of 'parks' (small forests) such as Bathurst had undertaken at

Oakley Grove. The park provided a 'natural' boundary, always to be preferred to high stone walls, which were also replaced by 'ha-has' or sunken fences, which did not spoil the 'prospect' from the house.

Pope stresses the relatedness of building and planting:

To build, to plant, whatever you intend,
To rear the Column or the Arch to bend,
To swell the Terras, or to sink the Grot;
In all, let Nature never be forgot.

(47-50)

These are busy lines, suggestive of purposeful activity: 'build . . . plant . . . rear . . . bend . . . swell . . . sink . . .' underline the dynamism of that nature which both gardeners and architects are urged to consult. If it seems relatively obvious that a gardener should work with, rather than against, nature, Pope is happy to provide us with a cautionary tale or two on the matter. Benjamin Styles (lines 75-6) at his country seat in Hertfordshire, vandalized the landscape by cutting a hole between two hills to improve the view (the damage can still be seen at Moor Park)[23], only to discover that in so doing his house and gardens were placed straight in the path of the north winds. Pope also relates (fictionally, probably,) how Sabinus plants woods, only to have them destroyed in the next generation by his son who prefers an open view (lines 89-98). Pope believes in planting and building according to the 'Genius' (ie. spirit) of the surroundings:

Consult the Genius of the Place in all;
That tells the Waters or to rise, or fall,
Or helps th'ambitious Hill the heav'ns to scale,
Or scoops in circling theatres the Vale,
Calls in the country, catches opening glades,
Joins willing woods and varies shades from shades.

(57-62)

Nature is seen as, of itself, ordering and controlling, and again the reader is struck by the judicious profusion of Pope's verbs: 'tells . . . helps . . . scoops . . . calls . . . catches . . . joins . . .'. Nature has its own harmony and balance, which produces a scene which can be discussed in terms equally appropriate to landscape painting:

> Still follow Sense, of ev'ry Art the Soul,
> Parts answ'ring parts shall slide into a whole,
> Spontaneous beauties all around advance,
> Start ev'n from Difficulty, strike from Chance:
> Nature shall join you, Time shall make it grow,
> A Work to wonder at – perhaps a STOW.
>
> (65-70)

The gardens of Timon's Villa are an affront to this picture of nature as spontaneous yet balanced. Perhaps the greatest enjoyment Pope shows in the Timon passage is in comprehensively listing the shortcomings of the garden:

> His Gardens next your admiration call
> On ev'ry side you look, behold the Wall!
> No pleasing Intricacies intervene,
> No artful wildness to perplex the scene;
> Grove nods at grove, each Alley has a brother,
> And half the platform just reflects the other.
>
> (113-8)

Nature has been routed in Timon's garden, kept at bay by the omnipresent wall. As Pope sums up:

> The suff'ring eye inverted Nature sees,
> Trees cut to statues, Statues thick as trees.
>
> (119-120)

As trees and statues change places, we see the complete confusion in Timon's mind betwen nature and art.

Pope believes that things will improve, though. As we have already noted, the end of this epistle is resolutely optimistic:

> Another age shall see the golden Ear
> Imbrown the Slope and nod on the Parterre,
> Deep Harvests bury all his pride has plann'd
> And laughing Ceres re-assume the land.
>
> (173-6)

Pope is comforted that there are men like Bathurst and Burlington to encourage the reformation of taste, and remind the world that: ''Tis Use alone that sanctifies Expence . . .' (179).

The poem ends on a note of triumphant conviction: Pope finds a great deal more to be sanguine about in this poem than he does in the *Epistle to . . . Bathurst*. On the surface the concerns which he has discussed at such length may seem entirely private, personal and minor ones, and it is certainly true that viewed from the perspective of two centuries or more Burlington is considerably less important a figure than Pope, in the poem's peroration, seems to think. Burlington was an influential part of a contemporarty revolution in taste, but he never achieved the distinction which Pope hopes for, of transforming the buildings of the land. At the same time, though, architecture was a live and indeed a political issue: architects could be patronized by the Whig grandees just as authors could. The philistine and mercantile influences which supported Pope's political opponents, were showing off their new wealth with even grander, indeed almost megalomaniac, building schemes.[24] These could be disruptive of the rural economy, as well as being an affront to aethetic standards. Pope had some particular enemies in mind, too. If Timon, Villario, Sabinus and the rest are pseudonyms, there are also more explicit and specific references to people and events in the poem. The Duke of Chandos furore showed that Pope was living at least slightly dangerously, but his assertion to the ever-conciliatory Arbuthnot showed the uncompromising position that he was coming to hold:

> '. . . general satire in times of general vice has no force . . . it is only by hunting one or two from the herd that any examples can be made.'[25]

Pope was clearly becoming more certain of his moral ground as he grew older.

Epistle 'To Richard Temple, Viscount Cobham'

Although a direct friend of Pope's riper years (the earliest account of their meeting is 1725), Sir Richard Temple, Viscount Cobham, was the embodiment of many of the virtues of taste which Pope had praised in the epistle to Burlington.[26] Cobham had followed a military career in his youth, gaining the rank of Lieutenant General during the War of the Spanish Succession. He had been a staunch Whig until 1733, when he went into opposition against Walpole. Pope had come to know him as a gardener and builder. He had praised Cobham's house at Stowe ('A Work to Wonder At') in the epistle to Burlington. Pope regularly made summer visits there, and said of it in a letter of 1731: 'If anything under Paradise could set me beyond all Earthly cogitations, Stowe might do it.' Cobham was an excellent host and it is clear that Pope enjoyed the conviviality of life at the house, as well as fully appreciating the gardens. Not only did these comprise woods and prospects, but also obelisks, temples, pavilions, grottoes and pyramids. In the grandiose 'Temple of British Worthies', a bust of Pope was placed and Cobham greatly appreciated the attention which Pope had given him in the poem. He subsequently thanked Pope for 'the public testimony of your esteem and affection.' After Cobham's death his wife had the closing lines of the epistle inscribed on a memorial tablet at Stowe.

This epistle is probably the most formal of the four. About half of it is taken up with a theoretical discussion about the characters of men. This discussion owes much to *An Essay on Man* where Pope's theory of the 'Ruling Passion' originated. Pope is sceptical of general or reductive theories of human behaviour:

> There's some Peculiar in each leaf and grain,
> Some unmark'd fibre, or some varying vein:
> Shall only Man be taken in the gross?
> Grant but as many sorts of Mind as Moss.
>
> (15-18)

He sees a dynamism in the characters of men: they are ever-changing and whirlpool-like:

> Our depths who fathoms, or our shallows finds
> Quick whirls, and shifting eddies, of our minds?

Life's stream for Observation will not stay
It hurries all too fast to mark their way.

(29-32)

Oft in the Passions' wild rotation tost,
Our spring of action to ourselves is lost

(41-2)

Man is too various to be easily generalized about; each individual is a special case, containing even within himself opposing and contradictory qualities:

See the same man, in vigour, in the gout;
Alone, in company; in place, or out;
Early at Bus'ness, and at Hazard late;
Mad at a Fox-chace, wise at a Debate;
Drunk at a Borough, civil at a Ball,
Friendly in Hackney, faithless at Whitehall.

(130-5)

We can begin to feel the satirical edge to Pope's voice: his choice of illustrative examples is far from innocent. In Hackney, MPs for Middlesex were selected, and Pope seems to suggest that this giddy collection of attitudes when concentrated in one man, can ultimately lead to his betrayal of others ('faithless at Whitehall').

Pope's desire to convince us that such contradictions are intrinsic to the human condition requires reference to his theory of the Ruling Passion:

Search then the Ruling Passion: There alone,
The Wild are constant, and the Cunning known;
The Fool consistent, and the False sincere;
Priests, Princes, Women, no dissemblers here.

(174-7)

He does not offer us a clear or discrete definition of the Ruling Passion in this particular passage, but he speaks about it at greater length in the second Epistle of *An Essay on Man.* Talking of pleasures, Pope says:

All spread their charms, but charm not all alike;
On diff'rent senses diff'rent objects strike:
Hence different Passions more or less inflame,
As strong or weak, the organs of the frame;
And hence one master Passion in the breast,
Like Aaron's serpent, swallows up the rest.
(*Essay on Man,* II, 127-32)

Pope is not suggesting that each man is motivated by one passion, but rather that there is a predominant one which 'swallows up the rest', and gives the other varied and contrary 'passions' a kind of solving consistency. Pope did not believe that the Ruling Passion was easy to find (hence the injunction to 'Search' it), he saw it as inevitably hidden behind a mass of surface complexities. His discussion of the topic in *An Essay on Man* is theoretical and general. In the epistle to Cobham, Pope proceeds by means of concrete example. As usual, there is one to hand:

This clue once found, unravels all the rest,
The prospect clears, and Wharton stands confest.
(178-9)

The Duke of Wharton had had a somewhat unusual political life.[27] Born to a Whig family, he found himself attracted to the Stuart cause, and visited the Old Pretender in France. This was just about the most extreme change of political views imaginable, but it was only a beginning. Wharton subsequently became a Roman Catholic, sided with Spain in the war against England, and was officially outlawed by parliament. There is no clear reason for Pope's animosity towards Wharton: no grounds for personal enmity have been discovered. Pope amasses a considerable case against him, though: his disapproval of the Duke is more than just a token one:

Wharton, the scorn and wonder of our days
Whose ruling Passion was the Lust of Praise
(180-1)

Pope seeks to expose and underline the uneasy mixture of

opposites which exists within the man. His 'lust of praise' causes him to court both 'women' and 'fools' (183); his oratory impressed 'wond'ring senates' yet also required the plaudits of the Hell Fire Club (184-5):

> Shall parts so various aim at nothing new?
> He'll shine a Tully and a Wilmot too.
> Then turns repentant, and his God adores
> With the same spirit that he drinks and whores.
>
> (186-9)

Tully (Marcus Tullius Cicero) was the most celebrated of Roman orators; Wilmot was a rake. Wharton wishes to emulate both, and he also worships his God with the same kind of indiscriminating fervour which he brings to the embracing of prostitutes. The headlong, accumulating, series of contradictions which form Wharton are very similar to those which produce the 'vile antithesis' of Pope's portrait of Sporus in the *Epistle to Dr Arbuthnot.* Both portraits – and it is difficult to know for certain which of them was written first – gain their bite from the cavorting inconsistencies of the characters they describe:

> A constant Bounty which no friend has made;
> An angel Tongue, which no man can persuade;
> A Fool, with more of Wit than half mankind,
> Too quick for Thought, for Action too refin'd;
> A Tyrant to the wife his heart approves;
> A Rebel to the very king he loves
>
> (198-203)

As in the Sporus portrait, Pope painstakingly dismembers the victim almost to the last fibre: no part of Wharton survives intact, he has been reduced to a heap of grotesque fragments.

The final section of the poem looks, as did the *Epistle to Bathurst*, at deaths, deathbeds and last words. In contemplating these things, Pope is inviting us, again, to consider the 'ends' of human life, showing us, through a series of judiciously curtailed vignettes, examples of human folly. The portrait gallery provides three main examples: one Greek and literary; one anecdotal; one contemporary and personal. Each one represents the natural terminus of a particular Ruling Passion: greed in the case of the ancient Greek poet Philoxenes, who, on realizing that he was dying of a surfeit, asked for more food in order to do the job properly:

> A salmon's belly, Helluo, was thy fate,
> The doctor call'd, declares all help too late,
> Mercy! cries Helluo, mercy on my soul!
> Is there no hope? Alas! – then bring the jowl.
>
> (234-7)

Miserliness rules the old lady of Paris, who, in trying to save her last candle, also extinguishes herself:

> The frugal Crone, whom praying priests attend,
> Still tries to save the hallow'd taper's end,
> Collects her breath, as ebbing life retires,
> For one puff more, and in that puff expires.
>
> (238-41)

The actress Anne Oldfield sees death as the final performance and clings tenaciously to her vanity:

> 'Odious! in woollen! 'twould a saint provoke,
> (Were the last words that poor Narcissa spoke)
> No, let a charming Chintz, and Brussels lace
> Wrap my cold limbs, and shade my lifeless face:
> One would not, sure, be frightful when one's dead –
> And – Betty – give this Cheek a little Red.'
>
> (242-47)

These and other portraits bring the epistle to an end. As the most theoretical of the four, it rests on ideas about human nature which Pope had developed elsewhere. What distinguishes this poem from *An Essay on Man* is its tendency to judge human character in action, and measure the lives of various men and women alongside the theoretical yardstick. If men are indeed 'Peculiar in each leaf and grain', the discovery of the peculiarity leads poet and reader into some strange recesses of human behaviour. If the poem does not have the wide-ranging earnestness of the *Epistle to . . . Bathurst* it equally offers no positive model of virtue as that poem does in *The Man of Ross*. Likewise it shuns the high spirits and optimism of the *Epistle to . . . Burlington*. This poem ends particularly abruptly:

> And you! brave COBHAM, to the latest breath
> Shall feel your ruling passion strong in death:
> Such in those moments as in all the past,
> 'Oh, save my Country, Heav'n!' shall be your last.
> (262-5)

Epistle to a Lady: Of the Characters of Women

This epistle is addressed to Martha Blount (1690-1763).[28] She was the younger of two sisters (the elder was called Teresa) to both of whom Pope had already addressed poems. He also indulged in a prolific correspondence with them. They belonged to a Catholic family, one of several resident in Berkshire at the time that Pope was living with his parents at Binfield in Windsor Forest. Teresa was the more attractive and sociable of the two, though, after some kind of disagreement with Pope, she left his orbit some time in the early 1720. His friendship with Martha, however, lasted for the rest of his life. She was a frequent visitor to Twickenham and, in later years, sometimes joined him on his summer 'rambles'.

It is not surprising given the gossip and scandal that surrounded Pope for so much of his life, that various rumours grew up about his relationship with Martha. The fact that Pope left her the use of his Twickenham estate after his death, was seized upon as proof that some kind of secret marriage had taken place between them. Another view simply put it about that Martha was Pope's mistress. No reliable evidence has been forthcoming to confirm either of these rumours, though Pope did on one occasion write a rather troubled letter to his old friend John Caryll (to whom *The Rape of the Lock* had been addressed) issuing strong denials of reports of intimacy between himself and Martha.

It is clear that Pope was sensitive to feminine beauty. His

letters to the Blount sisters and to Lady Mary Wortley Montagu are suggestive and flirtatious.[29] Contemporary conventions of letter writing to women might have been partly responsible for this tone, but it does seem likely that Pope had been susceptible to the Blount sisters' charms. The words which he addresses to Martha at the end of the poem are undoubtedly the warmest and most intimate to be found in any of the epistles. It is clear that Martha is a special and warmly regarded person, and it does no great harm to Pope to see him wearing, rather more than we customarily expect of him, his heart on his sleeve:

> Heaven when it strives to polish all it can
> Its last best work, but forms a softer Man;
> Picks from each sex, to make the Fav'rite blest,
> Your love of Pleasure, our desire of Rest,
> Blends, in exception to all gen'ral rules,
> Your Taste of Follies, with our Scorn of Fools,
> Reserve with Frankness, Art with Truth ally'd
> Courage with Softness, Modesty with Pride,
> Fix'd Principles, with Fancy ever new;
> Shakes all together, and produces – You.
>
> (271-80)

This passage placed as it is towards the end of the poem, seeks some kind of resolution and finality. In so doing it highlights the poem's problems. On the one hand these lines praise Martha Blount as something special, indeed transcendant. She is given the ultimate compliment (in eighteenth century terms at any rate) of being seen as 'a softer Man', an especially privileged result of the balance of the best male and female qualities. As such, Pope is placing her outside the criticisms which he has been making of women in general throughout the poem. On the other hand some of the concepts which have informed his criticism persist in this passage. 'Woman's at best a Contradiction still' (270). He writes of 'Your love of Pleasure, our desire of Rest'; 'Your Taste of Follies . . . our scorn of Fools'. These statements insist upon fundamental and discriminatory differences betwen men and women: women follow pleasures and are prone to folly, men are peaceful, constant, staid. Woman is 'at best' a contradiction.

To the modern reader these are not comfortable attitudes and they explain why the *Epistle to a Lady* can seem such a difficult and unpleasant text. It would be easy to dismiss it as outdated and valuable only as a period piece, charting the unsympathetic attitudes which men in the eighteenth century had towards women. Such a view is not unreasonable, especially as historically it is clear enough that in Pope's time very little was expected of, or desired from, women. A transgression from the role of submissive, powerless and uneducated servant of man could easily be seen as both unnatural and threatening. It is not surprising that Pope's sharpest barbs in the poem are directed at those women who threaten to transgress the normal bounds assigned to them.[30]

A critic of this poem is faced with an interpretative Hobson's choice. Either he can see the poem as reflecting a view of women which is essentially culturally conditioned, because commonly held in the eighteenth century, or he can see it as the result of a personal bitterness and animosity to the sex, emerging from Pope's own experience of them. This second approach to the poem would underline Pope's deformities and point out the extreme unlikelihood of his being able to enjoy the normal satisfactions of marriage. Consequently he vents his frustrations against the female sex, making them out as worth very little of a civilized man's respect.

This is a plausible enough theory, at least to a point. The more intimate areas of Pope's personal life are in all likelihood ultimately irrecoverable, though given his blatant physical disadvantages it is tempting to put two and two together. What better explanation for the torrent of misogynistic feeling which lies behind the poem, than a life of pent-up frustration with the 'crazy carcase' which denied him the pleasures of sexual intimacy?

To take either of these views, though, is to read the poem unsympathetically from the very beginning, and to refuse to take seriously what is serious in it, or comically what is comic. Anti-feminine satire in the late seventeeth and early eighteenth century was by no means uncommon; one need look no further than Swift for illustration.[31] The originating point for such satire, in a classically-minded age was the Roman poet Juvenal's Sixth Satire.[32] This work received the attention of more than one translator during Pope's lifetime. By the side of Juvenal and Swift, Pope emerges as rather restrained. Swift's poems are consciously indecent and the cynical worldliness of Juvenal makes Pope seem innocent in comparison. The misogynistic nature of Pope's poem might shock the modern reader, but there was little in the poem to shock his contemporaries.

It is also worth remembering the poem's place in Pope's 'Ethic Scheme'. There are clear attempts in *The Epistle to a Lady* to effect parallels with the *Epistle to Cobham.* In the latter poem, Pope's view of man's behaviour originates in the theory of the Ruling Passion. This theory is present in the *Epistle to a Lady* also.

> In Men we various Ruling Passions find,
> In Women, two almost divide the kind;
> Those only fix'd, they first or last obey,
> The Love of Pleasure; and the Love of Sway.
> (207-10)

It is noticeable that Pope's 'model' of a woman is instantly simpler than his model of a man. 'Various Ruling Passions' in men, have been reduced to two in women. The two 'Passions' are extremes, and are essentially contradictory. ('Love of Pleasure' . . . 'Love of Sway'.) The only way in which they can be seen as connected is that they both threaten or subvert an order of things in which male values are dominant. Pope, however, is insistent on the contradictions which the characters of women present, and he offers considerable encouragement to his readers in the notes which he published with the poem's second edition in 1735, to read the poem above all else with 'contrarieties' in mind.

Pope clearly views the representation of 'contrarieties' as a guiding structural principle of his poem.[33] The satirical portraits in the first half of it represent contrarieties: 'in the soft-natured' (29-40); 'in the cunning and Artful' (45-52); 'in the Whimsical' (53-68); 'in the Lewd and Vicious' (69-86) and 'in the Witty and Refin'd' (87-100). In each case types rather than individuals are presented to us. Although in a later passage, added in 1744, the portrait of Philomede represents 'the Lewd and Vicious':

> See Sin in State, majestically drunk,
> Proud as a Peeress, prouder as a Punk;
> Chaste to her Husband, frank to all beside,
> A teeming Mistress, but a barren Bride . . .
>
> (69-72)

Philomede, not unexpectedly, has a catalogue of sins to her credit. Her drunkenness is worthy of criticism, chiefly because it would be acceptable in a man. She infringes not only sexual but class barriers too. Only a Peeress could be drunk so 'majestically', but in so being her behaviour is reminiscent of a 'Punk' (prostitute). Likewise her sexual habits illustrate her 'contrariety', she is a 'teeming Mistress' but 'a barren Bride . . .'. The passage reaches its climax (or in a sense its anti-climax) when Pope writes:

> So Philomede, lec'tring all mankind
> On the soft Passion and the Taste refin'd,
> Th'Address, the Delicacy – stoops at once,
> And makes her hearty meal upon a Dunce.
>
> (83-6)

Men have always been less happy about finding rapacious sexual appetites amongst women than amongst themselves: once more it is a transgression of bounds. Here Philomede's desire is presented as an image of indiscriminating gluttony which is the more reprehensible for being hidden beneath pretensions of softness, refinement and delicacy.

Such a systematic portrayal of 'contrariety' is reminiscent of the sketch of '. . . the same man, in vigour, in the gout . . .' in the *Epistle . . . to Cobham* and the more extensive treatment expended on the Duke of Wharton who:

> . . . turns repentant, and his God adores,
> With the same spirit that he drinks and whores
>
> (*Epistle to Cobham,* 188-9)

There are similarities of emphasis and subject matter. Both

the Wharton and Philomede portraits emphasize hypocrisies: the way in which the characters mask their lusts beneath pretensions of virtue. These very protestations debase the characters further.

It would therefore be easy to think that the two epistles are drawing essentially the same conclusions about the characters of women and of men, but this is to miss an important distinction. The Wharton passage serves to illustrate the puzzling contradictoriness of man, but an explanation to the puzzle is found in Wharton's 'Lust of Praise',[34] his Ruling Passion. This explains the extremities of his behaviour. Pope cannot find a comparable explanation for the aberrancies of female behaviour. This is discernible in the poem from his opening proposition to Martha Blount:

> Nothing so true as what you once let fall,
> 'Most Women have no characters at all'
>
> (1-2)

to his final admission in the same ears that 'Woman's at best a Contradiction still' (270).

We feel that relatively little progress has been made. In men, patterns of contradictory behaviour are ultimately resolvable to 'various Ruling Passions', in women, the contradictions remain unresolved and are held against them. If Martha Blount is held up as a kind of ideal woman, it is in due recognition of her freakishness. ('Shakes all together and produces – You' (280).) The other women in the poem show no such satisfying reconciliation of opposites.

Great reliance throughout all the epistles is placed upon portraits of individuals or types. Wharton or Blunt or The Man of Ross are prime examples. It is notable, though, that the metaphor of painting portraits is insisted upon most explicitly in this particular epistle:

> How many Pictures of one Nymph we view,
> All how unlike each other, all how true!
> Arcadia's Countess, here, in ermin'd pride,
> Is there Pastora by a fountain side.
> Here Fannia, leering on her own good man,

And there, a naked Leda with a Swan.
(5-10)

Pope is drawing attention to the fashion for painting portraits of the same lady in a number of different attitudes or poses, as Countess and Shepherdess for example (notice the contradictoriness again) but he pursues the metaphor further:

Whether the Charmer sinner it or saint it,
If Folly grows romantic, I must paint it.
Come then, the colours and the ground prepare!
Dip in the Rainbow, trick her off in Air,
Chuse a firm Cloud, before it fall, and in it
Catch, ere she change, the Cynthia of this minute.
(17-20)

By suggesting that the characters in the poem are pictures rather than people, Pope distances himself from them. The impatience which he feels before women's irresolvable 'contrarieties' is supported by a desire to make objects rather than people out of them. This is also illustrated in the poem's tendency to transform individuals into types.

In later editions of the poem, however, certain specific portraits did appear. Posthumous versions of the text gave us Atossa, Cloe, and Queen Caroline. Pope had been keen to tell his editor, Warburton, of 'the author's Tenderness in using no living Examples or real Names',[35] and whilst no real names do appear in the poem, portraits of real people eventually do. Only one of them was still living at the time the revised version appeared, which suggests a certain caution on Pope's part, and one not normally extended to his male victims. His using pseudonyms for his 'living Examples' has inevitably led to some debate as to who, for example, the portrait of Atossa is meant to represent. Contemporary opinion favoured Sarah, Duchess of Marlborough, but this seems to misread the evidence, apart from the fact that Pope's relations with her were cordial in his later years. The Duchess of Buckingham seems to fit the facts a great deal more accurately.[36] Like so many of Pope's portraits in the epistle, his treatment of Atossa is very firmly rooted in topical and circumstantial detail. His description reveals (for all its apparent exaggerations) a great deal about the Duchess of Buckingham's life and death (she died in 1743, thus giving Pope an opportunity to 'update' the description the following year). Her eminence and her monstrousness are both emphasized:

> But what are these to great Atossa's mind?
> Scarce once herself, by turns all Womankind!
> Who with herself, or others, from her birth
> Finds all her life one warfare upon earth.
>
> (115-8)

Pope develops three contemporary ideas about the Duchess. Firstly, that her life was 'one warfare upon earth'. She had an enormous appetite for lawsuits, especially against members of her own family:

> From loveless youth to unrespected age,
> No passion gratify'd except her Rage.
>
> (125-6)

Her unpredictable bad temper was legendary

> Offend her, and she knows not to forgive
> Oblige her, and she'll hate you while you live.
>
> (137-8)

Pope goes on to show that this 'rage', comic as it may be to contemplate, was only one side of a frightening temperamental inconstancy:

> But die, and she'll adore you – Then the Bust
> And Temple rise – then fall again to dust.
> Last night, her Lord was all that's good and great,
> A Knave this morning, and his Will a Cheat.
>
> (139-42)

The Duchess was prone to building extravagant monuments to deceased relatives (including her husband) though this did not prevent her entering into prolonged litigation over his will.

All these violent emotional turns Pope attributes to a basic mental unbalance which led her to die insane:

> No Thought advances, but her Eddy Brain
> Whisks it about and down it goes again.
> (121-2)

At the end of her life, childless (all her issue had died), and isolated from the world as a result of her own aggressiveness towards it, the Duchess is a pitiful image of self-destruction:

> Strange! by the Means defeated of the Ends,
> By Spirit robb'd of Pow'r, by Warmth of Friends,
> By Wealth of Follow'rs! without one distress
> Sick of herself thro' very selfishness!
> Atossa curs'd with ev'ry granted pray'r
> Childless with all her children, wants an Heir.
> (143-8)

In the portrait of Cloe (which may refer to Mrs Howard, Countess of Suffolk),[37] we see exactly the opposite qualities. Where Atossa was ruled by rage against the world and against herself, Cloe is restrained, cold and calculating:

> 'With ev'ry pleasing, ev'ry prudent part,
> Say, what can Cloe want?' – she wants a Heart . . .
> (159-60)

> She, while her Lover pants upon her breast
> Can mark the figures on an Indian chest;
> And when she sees her Friend in deep despair,
> Observes how much a Chintz exceeds Mohair.
> (167-70)

Atossa and Cloe attain the same ends by different means. Both are shown to be loveless and unloved. Atossa makes enemies through an uncontrolled and unpredictable rage, whereas Cloe has not the capacity to form friendships in the first place:

> Of all her Dears she never slander'd one,

But cares not if a thousand are undone.
(175-6)

Consequently, she too is likely to die unmourned through her very insipidity:

Would Cloe know if you're alive or dead?
She bids her Footman put it in her head.
Cloe is prudent – would you too be wise?
Then never break your heart when Cloe dies.
(177-80)

Thus a character who is superficially the exact opposite of Atossa ends up likewise 'robb'd . . . of Friends . . . of Follow'rs'. Pope finds himself again showing forth contradictions. Apart from the clear opposition between the two characters, there is the contradiction within them. Atossa's dominance and egregious energies are self-destructive, just as Cloe's false charm and equability are.

The poem ends fulsomely, with a tribute, from which some quotation has already been made, to Martha Blount herself. The earlier part of it recalls Clarissa's speech from *The Rape of the Lock,*[38] where ladies are encouraged to look beyond the here and the now:

Ah Friend! to dazzle let the Vain design,
To raise the Thought and touch the Heart be thine!
That Charm shall grow, while what fatigues the Ring
Flaunts and goes down, an unregarded thing.
(249-52)

That women should look to greater and more enduring goals than youth, beauty and fashion, was the point of Clarissa's speech. Its essentially satiric force came from the fact that its words were ignored. The young ladies portrayed in *The Rape of the Lock* wanted to know nothing of Clarissa's good sense and wider view. There is a similar gap in this epistle between Martha Blount and the other women described in it. It is not difficult either to see in this poem echoes of *The Rape of the*

Lock's imagery where the ideal woman is described as one who:

> Let Fops or Fortune fly what way they will,
> Disdains all loss of Tickets, or Codille;
> Spleen, Vapours, of Small-pox, above them all,
> And Mistress of herself, tho' China fall.
>
> (265-8)

In both poems Pope seems to be suggesting that the female character can attain greatness only by rising above the petty concerns and distractions which are (he implies) inherent to it. Thus 'good sense', 'good humour', 'virtue' and 'merit' are recommended in *The Rape of the Lock*: tact, subtlety, composure and intelligent compromising with male power are praised here.

But a gap remains. Just as Clarissa's words are pointedly ignored in the earlier poem, so Pope's attribution of something like perfect female characteristics to Martha Blount, set her well aside of the deficient specimens of womankind which populate the rest of the epistle. It is not merely the perspective of a post-feminist age which causes the poem to seem problematic. Of the four epistles it is the one which deals with the least tractable subject. The epistles to Bathurst and Burlington deal directly and trenchantly with contemporary events, and, although on the surface they may seem circumscribed by their own contemporaneity, the moral concerns which they urge on the reader are recognizable enough and prevent them from seeming merely historical documents. They contain a good share of wit and spirited mischief too.

The epistles to Cobham and Martha Blount present something more in the nature of a search. Pope is less concerned with topical allusion (though it is to be found), than in trying to make definitions and explain theories. *The Epistle to . . . Cobham* is a part extension to Pope's quasi-philosophical interests in *An Essay on Man,* and its effect rests chiefly upon its having reached the same kind of conclusion to the complex question of what makes men behave as they do. Any reader is free to doubt or deny Pope's conclusions, and could well feel that Pope's whole direction is a misguided one, but the point, at least, seems to be proved to the poet's own satisfaction.

The Epistle . . . to a Lady is not so easily dealt with. We have already noted the rather provisional nature of the conclusion that 'Woman's at best a Contradiction still', as if more investigation were needed. In Pope's guiding metaphor of women as pictures, and its revealing lines at the end of the Queen Caroline passage:

> That Robe of Quality so struts and swells,
> None see what Parts of Nature it conceals
> (189-90)

the poem is less confident of having found out the complex truth about women. What its almost consistently destructive satire reveals is a distanced uncertainty. Pope can find many examples of the grotesque, the excessive or the gruesome in the female sex, and he had both classical and modern promptings to do so, but his case, ultimately, is partial and unproven, and the poem has just about enough honesty to say so.

From the South Sea Bubble and the financial revolution to 'Sappho at her toilet's greazy task . . .' (*Epistle to a Lady* (25)), is a considerable distance. The concerns of Pope's epistles are wide-ranging, and the reader is not instantly aware of their forming a single or coherent whole. Perhaps the most obvious unifying feature is their worldliness: they confront human character and action directly. There is no recourse to the powers of myth and fiction (as in *The Rape of the Lock* or *The Dunciad*). Pope speaks directly in his own voice ostensibly reporting what he sees to the sympathetic ears of a friend. Warburton's choice of the title *Moral Essays* for the four poems hints at something graver and more severe, and underlines the fact that each reader is faced with the question of how much to regard them as treatises on human behaviour, and how far as amused exposés of human folly. It is perfectly conceivable that Pope would see no distinction between the standpoints. The poet who was to speak of satire as the 'sacred Weapon left for Truth's defence' was underlining the serious purposes of his art, whilst sanctioning the continued employment of a poetic manner which took delight in mockery.

Chapter Four: Virtue's Friends

1. See Mack *Life,* p522.
2. The evolution of Pope's work during this period is detailed by Miriam Leranbaum *Alexander Pope's 'Opus Magnum'* (1977).
3. See Twickenham III i (1947) Introduction, p xiii.
4. Ibid p xi.
5. Pope's *Advertisement* Twickenham III ii (1951) p xviii.
6. Ibid, p xxxvii.
7. For a biography of Bathurst see James Lees-Milne *Earls of Creation* (1962 rev 1986) Chap 1.
8. Twickenham III ii p83.
9. Ibid Introduction, p xxxiii.
10. For the financial climate of Pope's time see Howard Erskine-Hill, *Pope and The Financial Revolution* in Peter Dixon (Ed) *Alexander Pope: Writers and their Background* (1972) pp200-229; also Peter Dixon *The World of Pope's Satires* (1968) Chap 7.
11. Pope's note Twickenham III ii p96.
12. Ibid p101.
13. Ibid p102.
14. Ibid p91.
15. Ibid p110; see also Howard Erskine-Hill, *The Social Milieu of Alexander Pope* (1975) p19.
16. Twickenham III ii, p114.
17. Ibid, p116. Earl R. Wasserman elaborates on this in *Pope's 'Epistle to Bathurst'* (1960) p12.
18. See Lees-Milne *Earls of Creation* Chap 3; also Pat Rogers *Pope and the Social Scene* in Dixon (Ed) *Alexander Pope* Chap 3.
19. See Pope's note Twickenham III ii p133.
20. Johnson *Lives of the Poets* World's Classics Edition Vol II p267.
21. Pope's note Twickenham III ii p148.
22. See M. Brownell *Pope and the Arts of Augustan England* (1978) pp89-99; also Dixon, *The World of Pope's Satires* Chap 4.
23. Pope's note Twickenham III ii p140.
24. See J.H. Plumb, *The Noble Houses of Eighteenth Century England* in *Men and Places* (1966) pp80-94.
25. To Arbuthnot see Twickenham III ii p xiv.
26. For Cobham's career see Mack *Life* pp596-599.
27. See Twickenham III ii pp28-29.
28. The relationship between Pope and Martha Blount is discussed at length by Valerie Rumbold in *Women's Place in Pope's World* (1989), passim.
29. See James A. Winn *A Window on the Bosom, The letters of Alexander Pope* (1977) pp101-124.

30. For a further discussion of this issue see Felicity Nussbaum, *The Brink of All We Hate: English Satires on Women, 1660-1750* (1984).
31. In particular, *The Lady's Dressing Room* and *A Beautiful Young Nymph Going to Bed.*
32. See Juvenal *Satires* (ed Green) pp127-152.
33. Pope's notes in Twickenham III ii pp49-53, passim.
34. *Epistle to Cobham,* line 181.
35. Quoted in Twickenham III ii p45.
36. Ibid Note to p57.
37. Ibid Note p61.
38. Canto V lines 11-34.
39. *Epilogue to the Satires, Dialogue II* line 212.

5

HIS OWN MASTER

The Imitations of Horace

It is never possible to talk about Pope for very long without talking about Horace. We have made several references to the Roman poet already and his influence can be felt in different ways in *An Essay on Criticism,* the *Epistles to Various Persons* and *An Epistle to Dr Arbuthnot.* In venerating him, and indeed using him as much as he did, Pope was reflecting the literary taste of the age in which he lived. Horace had been highly regarded in the seventeenth century, edited and translated with distinction, and, in the decades of Pope's maturity, imitated by other poets too.[1]

Quintus Horatius Flaccus lived from 65BC to 8BC. He was of humble rustic stock though his father took care to have him educated in Rome and later in Athens. As a young man Horace had fought in Brutus' army, returning from his campaigns only to find his father dead, and his father's lands confiscated. However, he embarked upon a career as a civil servant, began writing poetry, and along with Virgil came under the tutelage of the statesman and patron of the arts, Maecenas. Maecenas was the friend and confidant of Octavian (later the Emperor Augustus) and gave Horace a farm in the Sabine Hills. Despite the high society into which Maecenas's patronage gave him an entrée, Horace came to prefer the retired rustic life, to the urban bustle of Rome.

His literary career was long and varied. He began as a young man by writing Satires (of which Pope imitated four); his middle period was characterized by the composition of Odes, and in later life he wrote two books of verse Epistles. His early satires are explicitly moral poems, concerning themselves with human vices and follies, though in a fair-minded and tolerant way. He did not bristle with anger and outrage as Juvenal was later to do, and, especially by the side of Pope, Horace's satire seems restrained, being much less concerned with attacking individuals and naming names. Horace had no programme of reform for the human race, nor did he seek particularly to shock it.

It is from the Odes and the Epistles that Horace's modern reputation largely stems. The Odes show a friendly, reflective poet, satisfied with his lot and with the rural retreat of his Sabine Farm. The Epistles embody a discursive and dialectical way of talking about the public scene and Horace's reactions to it, and were much valued in Pope's time for their ease and urbanity. Horace was felt to be a poet both equable and durable, the ultimate embodiment of civilized good sense. He had been remarkably easily Christianized also.[2]

Pope's first attempt at imitating Horace is well documented as he gave an acount of it to his biographer Joseph Spence. Pope was confined to bed with a fever in January 1733. His friend Henry St John Bolingbroke, picking up a copy of Horace's poems lying nearby and turning to the first Satire of the second book remarked to Pope '. . . how well that would hit my case, if I were to imitate it in English. After he was gone I read it over; translated it in a morning or two, and sent it to the press in a week or fortnight after.'[3]

Pope's 'case', ostensibly, was the furore that had attended the publication of the *Epistle to Burlington* just over a year previously. With its alleged criticism of the Duke of Chandos and others, it is not difficult to see how Pope could relevantly update Horace and write:

> There are (I scarce can think about it, but am told)
> There are to whom my Satire seems too bold
>
> (Satire II i 1-2)

Horace's original poem was a defence of his writing satire, and had therefore an obvious topicality.

But Pope's identification with Horace goes deeper than this as the *Imitations* in places makes clear. Both poets came of humble stock, and were recognized by their parents as precocious. Both had had experience of political turmoil, and either the shadow or actuality of civil war. Both had experienced dispossession (Horace because he had fought on the wrong side in the civil war, Pope because his religion prevented him from owning property). Yet both had managed to acquire talented and influential friends ('Envy must own, I live among the Great' (Sat II i, 133)), and, from his Sabine farm or his riverside villa at Twickenham, each was able to sing the praises of rustic retirement.[4] One of the chief features of the *Imitations* is Pope's assumption of various personae, an identification with the Roman poet being the most pervasive of them.

Because it was a poem principally addressing itself to the Grub Street world, *An Epistle to Dr Arbuthnot* has already been discussed alongside the first versions of *The Dunciad,* but three of Pope's *Imitations of Horace* pre-date it. Indeed, when William Warburton produced his collected edition of the poet's works in 1751, *An Epistle to Dr Arbuthnot* was printed before the *Imitations of Horace* and sub-titled *Prologue to the Satires.* It is worth identifying some, at least, of the Horatian elements in this poem, before going on to look at the *Imitations* themselves.

An Epistle to Dr Arbuthnot reflects Horace at various levels. For a start, there is the implied dialogue-form in which it is presented. Some editions of the *Epistle* following Warburton have set it out as a dialogue with Pope and Arbuthnot shown to be speaking, as in a play. The caution of Pope's interlocutor ('Hold . . . you'll offend . . . learn Prudence' (101-2)) is an Horatian feature and there are also clear verbal echoes in places. The references to the raging Dog-star, to Bavius, Pitholeon and Fanny (Fannius) are directly from Horace, as is Pope's invocation of Horace's opinion that poets should keep their poems nine years before publishing them. From Horace, too, comes Pope's mocking of his own physical appearance (line 115-6), and his tribute in the closing lines of the poem to his father. Less superficially and more importantly, comes Pope's desire to 'Maintain a Poet's Dignity and Ease' (263), at some distance from the vices of the town, interrupted though this retirement is by the irritants of metropolitan literary life.

It could be argued though, that *An Epistle* . . . provides only a partial recovery of the Horatian tone. As we have already seen, the poem offers an ultimately unresolved conflict between a desire for 'Dignity and Ease', on the one hand and a frank aggressiveness on the other:

> A Lash like mine no honest man shall dread,
> But all such babling blockheads in his stead.
>
> (303-4)

One might well feel that in this poem the Horatian values of urbanity, detachment and good sense have been attempted rather than integrated. Pope recruits Horace to his side but finds it a struggle to actually become him.

In the *Imitations,* the balance is inevitably different, though constantly varying. The whole idea of imitation might well strike a modern reader as questionable. It has been widely, if unthinkingly, accepted since Wordsworth wrote his Preface to the *Lyrical Ballads* in 1800, stressing that poetry was a 'spontaneous overflow', that inspiration and originality have some essential part in the process of poetic creation. Pope is not alone in proving the inaccuracy of such dogmatisms, just as *The Imitations of Horace* would certainly refute any suggestion that to imitate is to indulge in something derivative and inhibiting. Pope's attitude to Horace is constructive rather than simply pious. As we have already seen, imitation was a common enough literary genre during Pope's time, and it proved to be an extremely fluid one. It should be distinguished from 'metaphrase' (which to Pope's age meant straight translation) or 'paraphrase' (which was the rendering of the sense or gist of an ancient poem), though it could, on occasion include both. Essentially, Pope was taking certain Horatian poems and applying them to modern circumstances. The objects of Horace's satire: corruption, excess, the abuse of wealth, the shortcomings of the metropolis, had strikingly contemporary, and political, applications. To point a critical finger at the public scene, with the authority of Horace behind him, added weight and importance to the satire against the times which Pope was writing. As Pope remarked in his 'Advertisement' to his first *Imitation:* '. . . An answer from Horace was both more full, and of more Dignity, than any I cou'd have made in my own person . . .[5] It also enabled certain political points to be made with varying degrees of directness for in these *Imitations* Pope does not shun difficult, or even dangerous ground.

The actual process of imitation involves Pope in a variety of strategies. His engagement with Horace's text is both a precise and a dynamic one. When the *Imitations* were first published, they appeared with Horace's Latin text (or at least a subtly adapted version of it) printed in parallel.[6] Certain words and phrases were identified by key numbers in each text so that their interrelatedness could be perceived by the reader. These were the places in which Pope was drawing attention to the minute and careful way in which he was adapting particularities of Horace's text. Equally though, there are areas of Pope's poems where the adaptation is free and expansive. Contemporary illustrations, examples and personalia are imported when appropriate, and entirely characteristically, Pope finds a great many more names to name than Horace does. Equally, some things in the original are abbreviated or excised: the strategy was never quite the same twice. Pope adapted as the original poem and his own concerns led.

The poems themselves appeared singly over a number of years (between February 1733 and the summer of 1738). Hence they should not be seen in any way as a planned sequence. They do not have the binding unity of the four epistles of *An Essay on Man,* for example, and the tone, structure and points of view of the poems change and develop. We noted of *An Epistle to Dr Arbuthnot* that Pope attained to the Horatian persona with some difficulty, and that this difficulty was what the poem had, in part, been dramatizing. The *Imitations of Horace* in a sense, engage with that same difficulty at greater length. In general the *Imitations* offer Pope's most sustained treatment of the public scene, and present his response to what he saw as the crisis in English politics and culture of the 1730s. As this crisis grew worse so Pope's poems became more urgent, critical and radical in viewpoint. Whilst such a poem as *Satire II* ii (1734) offers an elegant and attractive hymn to the pleasures of self-sufficiency and retirement, the *Epilogue to the Satires* (1738) is Pope's shrillest cry of all against corruption, and has no Horatian prototype. The art of imitation was not to Pope at all constricting. Indeed it could be argued that it leads to some of Pope's most assured and direct personal writing and that, in imitating Horace, Pope really was his own master.

The first *Imitation* to be written was of the First Satire of Horace's second book (henceforth *Satire II* i). Horace addressed his Satire to a prominent Roman lawyer, Gaius Trebatius. Pope likewise addresses a legal man, in the person of William Fortescue, who was one of his oldest friends.[7] Rather surprisingly, Fortescue was a supporter of Walpole, and was in time to be appointed Master of the Rolls. The presentation of a dialogue between Pope and his lawyer provides an admirable way for the poet to speak in his own defence. He seeks, at the beginning of the poem, Fortescue's advice about how he should proceed in the writing of satire. Fortescue throughout this poem is projected as a source of bluff, sensible, but ultimately inadequate advice. This dramatic fiction provides the framework in which Pope will defend the writing of satire, though the very opening of the poem is a fine illustration of the way in which Pope's satiric methods so frequently operate. On this particular occasion he takes the gist of Horace's opening remarks whilst craftily importing some modern victims of his own (the comparable passage in Horace names no names at all):[8]

> There are (I scarce can think it, but am told)
> There are to whom my Satire seems too bold,
> Scarce to wise *Peter* complaisant enough,
> And something said of *Chartres* much too rough.
> The lines are weak, another's pleas'd to say,
> Lord *Fanny* spins a thousand such a Day.
> Tim'rous by Nature, of the Rich in awe,
> I come to Council learned in the Law.
>
> (1-8)

As so often, Pope manipulates various tones of voice here. There is the slightly bemused mock-modesty of the opening lines, and the innocent and respectful petition to Fortescue at the end of the passage. Completely undercutting this assumed ingenuousness are the references to Peter Walter, Charters and Hervey: victims from the *Epistles to Several Persons*. Pope's innocence incorporates its share of irony, and instantly contrasts with Fortescue's bluntness:

> I'd write no more.
>
> (11)

Fortescue, as a lawyer, is predictably cautious, practical and pragmatic. To Pope's suggestion that writing satire is a kind of compulsive disease (lines 10-14), Fortescue suggests alternative cures:

> Why, if the Nights seem tedious – take a Wife;
> Or rather truly, if your Point be Rest,
> Lettuce and Cowslip Wine; *Probatum est.*
>
> (16-18)

Again one notices Fortescue's curt assurance that the problem is easily cured, but he goes on to prescribe another course of action. Perhaps Pope could become like Colley Cibber, this would keep him out of trouble and probably be quite profitable:

> Or if you needs must write, write CAESAR's Praise;
> You'll gain at least a *Knighthood* or the *Bays*
>
> (21-2)

Like Arbuthnot, Fortescue is worried about the animosities produced by Pope's directly or indirectly naming his victims:

> A hundred smart in *Timon* and in *Balaam*
> The fewer still you name, you wound the more:
> *Bond* is but one, but *Harpax* is a Score.
>
> (42-4)

Fortescue's ultimate lawyerly concern is that Pope's writings might run counter to the laws of libel:

> It stands on record that in *Richard's* Times
> A Man was hang'd for very honest Rhymes.

Consult the Statute

(145-7)

Pope's answer to this concludes the debate:

Libels and Satires! lawless Things indeed!
But grave *Epistles,* bringing Vice to light,
Such as a *King* might read, a *Bishop* write,
Such as Sir *Robert* would approve –
(Fortescue): Indeed?
The Case is alter'd – you may then proceed.

(150-5)

Pope has a number of responses to Fortescue's worry about the danger of libel. Firstly, he is keen to remind us that he is not dealing in cheap-jack 'Libels and Satires . . . But grave *Epistles* bringing Vice to light.' This is certainly an Horatian defence of writing satire, but it is a Popean one, too, as a letter to John Caryll the previous year had said of his satires:

> '. . . they are directed to a good end, the advancement of moral and religious virtue, and the disparagement of vicious and corrupt hearts.'[9]

Although Pope's closing comments to Fortescue may adopt a jocular tone, there is no reason to think that he is joking.

Less high-minded are the words which Pope puts by way of conclusion into Fortescue's mouth. So long as Sir Robert (Walpole) approves, Pope points out, the law can inevitably be rigged in your favour. Hence Fortescue is made to end his dialogue with Pope and one of the most serious satiric points of the whole poem.

Pope's dismissal of his friend's apparently irrelevant advice is done with great humour, but it is done also to show us that Pope is his own man with his own purposes and capable of manufacturing his own defence. He ignores Fortescue's advice not out of obstinacy but out of necessity. 'Council learned in the Law' cannot legislate against human folly:

Fools rush into my Head, and so I write.

(14)

This is one of Pope's pithiest statements about the business of writing satire, and it is very much his rather than Horace's.

To prove his point, Pope provides much by way of detailed contemporary illustration:

> Each Mortal has his Pleasure: None deny
> *Scarsdale* his Bottle, *Darty* his Ham-Pye;
> *Ridotta* sips and dances, till she see
> The doubling Lustres dance as fast as she;
> *F*[ox] loves the *Senate, Hockley-Hole* his Brother
> Like in all else, as one Egg to another.
>
> (45-50)

It is to these manifestations of human nature that the satirist is obliged to hold up the mirror:

> In this impartial Glass, my Muse intends
> Fair to expose myself, my Foes, my Friends;
> Publish the present Age . . .
>
> (57-9)

But this is only one image to describe the satirist's activity. Pope also tells us that 'Satire's my Weapon . . .' (69), however subtly he chooses to wield it. These two images of satire as mirror and weapon (and the contradiction which they go some way towards suggesting) are revealing ones in the context of this particular poem. The one suggests calm objectivity, the other arming for a cause. These two aspects of Pope's attitude to his satire are borne out in other issues which the poem raises.

The image of the satirist as the holder of a mirror had already been used by Swift: 'Satire is a glass wherein the beholder doth generally find every face but his own . . .'[10], and it supports very well the view that satire is a natural activity such as every truly objective gazer on the world might choose to indulge in. Pope is keen to stress this objectivity and to present himself as above the claims of sect or party:

> Papist or Protestant, or both between,
> Like good *Erasmus* in an honest Mean,
> In Moderation placing all my Glory,

While Tories call me Whig, and Whigs a Tory.
(65-8)

He also defends satire as an entirely rational activity and not as representing the consequence of gratuitous malice:

Peace is my dear Delight – not *Fleury's* more:
But touch me, and no Minister so sore.
Who-e'er offends. at some unlucky Time
Slides into Verse and hitches in a Rhyme
(75-8)

This is also the Horatian standpoint, but what follows next is quintessential Pope. Pope makes an eloquent and sustained case for his special and privileged position. Satirists, he points out, have often been tethered by their relationship with the powers they might otherwise wish to oppose. Boileau had been in receipt of a pension from Louis XIV, and even the revered Dryden was Charles II's Poet-Laureate (the first holder of that position) and 'Historiographer Royal'. Interestingly, Dryden in his time had criticized Horace himself for being sycophant to Augustus.

Could pension'd *Boileau* lash in honest Strain
Flatt'rers and Bigots ev'n in *Louis' Reign?*
Could Laureate *Dryden* Pimp and Fry'r engage,
Yet neither *Charles* nor *James* be in a Rage?
And I not strip the Gilding off a Knave,
Un-plac'd, un-pension'd, no man's Heir or Slave?
(111-16)

Pope was always keen to avoid accepting any kind of state pension. Clearly there were certain kinds of freedom he wished to retain for himself, and clearly he did not want to compromise himself with the government. As he was honest enough to point out elsewhere in the *Imitations,* he had some considerable reason to be grateful to the economic success of his translation of Homer. The mandarin stance which he can thus adopt enables him, at the climactic point in his poem, to draw capitalized attention to one particular line of Horace which obviously resonated strongly within his own mind:

Yes, while I live, no rich or noble knave
Shall walk the World, in credit, to his grave.
TO VIRTUE ONLY and HER FRIENDS, A FRIEND
The World beside may murmur or commend.
(118-121)

The word 'virtue' was to carry important connotations in the 1730s. Not only is it Horace's word, it is also a word much beloved by the increasingly large number of those who stood in opposition to the corrupt but durable Walpole ministry, about which Pope has made several remarks in his poem already. Again, it is seen as a quality which stands above, or apart from, the squalid realities of public life. Pope goes on to associate virtue with retirement, and with those very personal symbols of retirement with which he had surrounded himself in his own 'Sabine farm' at Twickenham:

Know all the distant Din that World can keep
Rolls o'er my *Grotto,* and but sooths my Sleep.
There, my Retreat the best Companions grace,
Chiefs out of War, and Statesmen, out of Place.
There *St John* mingles with my friendly Bowl,
The Feast of Reason and the Flow of Soul
(123-8)

Pope is keen to emphasize his retired position by reference to his Grotto: this is the place, like Yeats's tower, which defines him as a poet: in his case it is a symbol of withdrawal, privacy and contentment. However, whilst (Henry) St John (Bolingbroke) was perhaps Pope's dearest friend, his presence in the poem is not without political significance, prominent as he was as an opponent of Walpole, and of Jacobite sympathies. There is a little more provocation in these lines than there might at first seem.

Also, it is interesting that the Pope, who at the beginning of the poem had complained that the contemplation of folly had kept him awake at night, is here, at Twickenham sleeping the sleep of the just. Pope has, in fact, written an ambivalent poem which contains within itself on the one hand, the moderate Horatian view that the satirist has a duty to expose vice and recommend virtue. Pope links this point of view to an assertion of his own independence of party or sect, along with a belief that it is better to be removed from the fray in decent retirement.

Yet there is no way that a reader of this poem, either contemporary or modern, could see it as independent and moderate. *Satire II* i is an extremely partisan document, underlining a very clear political position. It opposes George II, his Queen, his court, his court poet, and his philistinism. It takes Sir Robert Walpole's corruption for granted, and it encompasses also a scarcely disguised compliment to a friend who was also a statesman 'out of place' (ie. in opposition). Equally, it is not easy to see Pope simply as the voice of moderation. The Papist was never taken for a protestant, nor, presumably, for a Whig. His assertion that he is detached from the public scene is undercut by the very political nature of his attitude to it.

Pope tells us that he was, in imitating Horace, seeking '. . . an Answer . . .' from the Roman satirist that would hold good against the times in which he lived. The poet in this particular poem emerges as a composite figure, part Pope, part Horace, using an Horatian argument against the times, and an Horatian persona to highlight his own points of view. Pope's defence of his own position is a sound one, even though his plea that he is objective and detached from what he is criticizing, is never quite borne out.

Pope's *Imitation* of the Second satire of the Second book of Horace (henceforth *Satire II* ii) was published in September 1734. It is addressed to Hugh Bethel, a Yorkshire squire.[11] Again Pope involves himself in some interesting adjustments to the personnel involved. In *Satire II* i, Gaius Trebatius had become Fortescue, and, ostensibly at least, Horace Pope, but there was one further adjustment. Pope's major statements about the role and function of the satirist were applied to himself: he was seen as the embodiment of the satiric poet. Horace, in defining what he saw as being the model for the satirist's stance, took for illustration not himself, but his Roman predecessor Lucilius. Pope's imitation becomes much more an examination of himself and his surroundings, where Horace's is essentially an examination of satire as an art.

A comparable adjustment takes place in *Satire II* ii. Horace puts most of the matter of his poem into the mouth of an old countryman called Ofellus. Horace himself is not a great deal more than an interlocutor. Pope presents his poem as a dialogue between Bethel and himself, with himself representing much of the point of view of Ofellus. The subject matter of this poem is perhaps less problematic than the first, though it is related to it. Horace's *Satire II* ii provides an exposition of the importance of moderation. Pope approaches this essentially moral argument with enthusiasm and subtlety. Bethel provides a 'sermon' on the subject of moderation and self-sufficiency, to which Pope responds by offering an account of his own life at Twickenham as the embodiment of these very virtues.

As in *Satire II* i, much of the general tone of what we hear, and even a number of the detailed examples, represent Horace very closely. (Pope can be amazingly close to the detail of Horace's text, even when sounding absolutely himself):

> Preach as I please, I doubt our curious men
> Will chuse a *Pheasant* still before a *Hen;*
> Yet Hens of *Guinea* full as good I hold,
> Except you eat the feathers, green and gold,
> Of *Carps* and *Mullets* why prefer the *great*,
> (Tho' cut in pieces e'er my Lord can eat)
>
> (17-22)

But Pope can seldom resist modernizing Horace by drawing attention to conveniently contemporary examples. As so often Lady Mary Wortley Montagu provides Pope with a topical illustration of a point he wishes to make. Lady Mary's husband was notoriously parsimonious, so he becomes Horace's Avidien, a type-cast figure of parsimony:[12]

> *Avidien* or his Wife (no matter which,
> For him you'll call a dog, and her a bitch)
> Sell their presented Partridges and Fruits,
> And humbly live on rabbits and on roots:
> One half-pint bottle serves them both to dine,
> And is at once their vinegar and wine.
>
> (49-54)

If this is gratuitously unpleasant to Lady Mary and her husband, it at least forwards the course of the argument relatively graphically. Excessive consumption on the one hand, and unreasonable parsimony on the other are both presented as types of social irresponsibility, much as they had been in *An Epistle to Bathurst.* Not only does excess have unfortunate effects on health:

> Where Bile, and wind, and phlegm, and acid jar,
> And all the Man is one intestine war
>
> (71-2)

but it causes the wealthy to forgo their obligations to the nation, both in terms of individual charity, and in the neglect of public works:

> Oh Impudence of wealth! with all thy store
> How dar'st thou let one worthy man be poor?
> Shall half the new-built Churches round thee fall?
> Make Keys, build Bridges, or repair White-hall!
>
> (117-120)

Grossness is also seen as very much a public, and establishment sin, it is associated with high offices of church and state:

> How pale, each Worshipful and rev'rend Guest
> Rise from a Clergy, or a City feast!
> What life in all that ample Body say,
> What heav'nly Particle inspires the clay?
> The Soul subsides; and wickedly inclines
> To seem but mortal, ev'n in sound Divines.
>
> (75-80)

Moderation is clearly a private and personal virtue, not institutionalized at all. This is why Pope's response to Bethel's 'sermon' takes the form of a hymn to the joys of retirement. This passage takes up only about a third of the poem, but does, in fact, provide the poem with most of its interest. The passage is more crucial than the comparable one in Horace's satire. There Ofellus talks of slightly more hearty and unpolished pursuits in his rustic haunts than Pope does, there are drinking contests, for example. Pope is more delicate and refined:

> Content with little, I can piddle here
> On Broccoli and mutton, round the year . . .
> 'Tis true, no Turbots dignify my boards,
> But gudgeons, flounders, what my Thames affords.
> To Hounslow-heath I point, and Bansted-down,
> Thence comes your mutton, and these chicks my own:
> From yon old walnut-tree a show'r shall fall;
> And grapes, long-lingring on my only wall
> (136-7; 141-6)

These lines extend and make more specific the picture of satisfied retirement which Pope had provided at the end of *Satire II* i. Both passages evoke the stock notion of contented Horatian rusticity. Additionally, both subtly politicize apparently innocent attitudes.

Horace's Ofellus draws attention to the fact that he, like his creator, had lost his patrimonial farm when lands had been commandeered and given as rewards to Octavian's soldiers after the civil war.We have already noted that Pope could be expected to feel some kinship with Horace in the light of experience of his own civil disabilities. Pope is surprisingly specific about his own situation. As a Catholic he was not allowed to own his own property (his Twickenham villa was leased, and his father had been forced to quit London). He also, because of his religion, was liable to double taxation:

> Fortune not much of humbling me can boast;
> Tho' double-tax'd, how little have I lost?
> My life's amusements have been just the same,
> Before, and after Standing Armies came.
> My lands are sold, my Father's house is gone;
> I'll hire another's is not that my own
> (151-6)

This passage sounds like Pope at his most bland, but an

experienced reader of him knows that blandness can often be one of Pope's weapons against his opponents, and so, to an extent, it is here. The pleasantly evoked life of retirement and self-sufficiency is also a complaint against the times: about those political and religious forces which expose a particular minority to double taxation, which in turn goes to support an unpopular and costly standing army (a particular Tory bugbear). The rustic seclusion which Pope is celebrating here is, for one who belongs to a distrusted minority, compulsory rather than chosen.

Once again Pope has identified yet not identified himself with Horace. He has taken on board the moral stance of the small but happy man, content with life on a limited scale, and well insulated from the world's grosser moral currents, whilst at the same time revealing a personal unease which is entirely his own.

> Let Lands and Houses have what Lords they will,
> Let Us be fix'd, and our own Masters still.
>
> (179-80)

'Un-plac'd, un-pensions'd, no Man's Heir or Slave': there are ways in which Pope is, indeed, his own master, free to think and write as he chooses, and enjoying as much financial independence as a literary man could reasonably expect. At the same time though, these closing lines of the poem indicate with remarkable precision just what the limitations to Pope's own personal liberties were.

The Epistles of Horace which Pope went on to imitate present a growing moral concern. We have already noted that the *Imitations* were poems written on sundry occasions, not part of a planned sequence, in consequence of which they become very much a map of Pope's mind as it developed during the 1730s. We will examine four more of them. His Imitation of the First Epistle of the First Book of Horace (*Epistle I* i), addressed to Henry St John Bolingbroke ponders the fickleness and inconstancy of the human race concerning itself not only with public vice and depravity but with the poet's own inner life. On the face of it these particular issues might seem completely separate ones, and the poem does little outwardly to link Pope's self-communings with his portraits of metropolitan life. Where the poem finds such unity as it has is in the person of Bolingbroke himself.

Henry St John Bolingbroke was arguably the most important man in Pope's life.[13] His influence on Pope had certainly been instrumental in the composition of *An Essay on Man.* Bolingbroke certainly had the philosopher's cast of mind, a great deal more so than Pope did, and Pope himself was the first one to own it. He provides some extremely fulsome praise at his conclusion to *An Essay on Man.*

> Come then, my Friend, my Genius, come along,
> Oh master of the poet, and the song!
> And while the Muse now stoops, or now ascends,
> To man's low passions, or their glorious ends,
> Teach me, like thee, in various nature wise,
> To fall with dignity, with temper rise;
> Form'd by thy converse, happily to steer
> From grave to gay, from lively to severe;
> Correct with spirit, eloquent with ease,
> Intent to reason, or polite to please.
>
> (373-382)

Pope's praise of Bolingbroke is no empty panegyric, but remarkably specific. In calling him his 'genius', he means, of course, his inspiration. Pope presents himself as a philosophic neophyte before Bolingbroke's mastery. 'Master of the poet, and the song' suggests considerable authority. But apart from Bolingbroke's intellectual gifts, Pope is keen to praise his personal ones: his equanimity, his constancy, his ability to be unperturbed by the problems which buffet lesser men.

It is this latter quality which Pope takes particular pains to praise in *Epistle I* i. All his Horatian poems are, in one way or another, shared with someone, whether by means of internal dialogue, or through the conventions of the epistle. No character dominates a poem so much as Bolingbroke does this one, and Pope is not simply engaging in fulsomeness for the sake of it. Bolingbroke's god-like stance at the end of the poem can almost be seen as the very *raison d'etre* of Pope's criticism of human folly and of his own personal shortcomings:

That Man divine whom Wisdom calls her own,
Great without Title, without Fortune bless'd,
Rich ev'n when plunder'd, honour'd while oppress'd,
Lov'd without youth, and follow'd without power,
At home tho' exiled, free, tho' in the Tower.
(180-4)

Granting Bolingbroke wisdom of a divine sort (much in the way that Tennyson was to do in his celebration of the dead Arthur Hallam in *In Memoriam*), Pope proceeds to illustrate Bolingbroke's constancy of soul by a series of paradoxes ('Rich ev'n when plunder'd, etc.) which confound our normal expectations of men. His greatness transcends the circumstances which normally keep men small: he doesn't seek love or power, he gains them; his wealth is of a kind which goes beyond that mere 'Lust of Gold' with which Pope deals elsewhere in the poem.

The passage immediately preceding this one describes Pope's view of himself by the side of Bolingbroke. Horace had a keen sense of his own ridiculousness, which Pope builds upon in this disconcertingly irrelevant picture of himself:

You laugh, half Beau half Sloven if I stand,
My Wig all powder, and all snuff my Band;
You laugh, if Coat and Breeches strangely vary,
White Gloves, and Linnen worthy Lady Mary!
But when no Prelate's Lawn with Hair-shirt lin'd,
Is half so incoherent as my Mind
(161-6)

This passage, in its almost embarrassing presentation of Pope's personal habits, affords a very sharp contrast with the Olympian stature which Pope grants Bolingbroke. By the side of his mind Pope's own, he tells us, seems incoherent. This incoherence is, of course, projected through the other images which occur in this passage. Pope descibes himself as 'half-Beau' and 'half-Sloven', manifesting cleaniliness and order in his white gloves, but in the rest of his attire being reminiscent of the slatternly Lady Mary Wortley Montagu.[14] This comically reductive treatment of himself, although it is a surprising and unexpected feature in the poem, is in fact of a piece with Pope's view of his intellectual position expressed earlier. As in *Satire II* i, Pope is keen to assert his eclecticism and independence, his movement from one position to another:

> Sworn to no Master, of no Sect am I:
> As drives the storm, at any door I knock,
> And house with Montagne now, or now with Lock.
> Sometimes a Patriot, active in debate,
> Mix with the World, and battle for the State,
> Free as young Littleton, her cause pursue,
> Still true to Virtue, and as warm as true:
> Sometimes with Aristippus, or St Paul,
> Indulge my Candor, and grow all to all
>
> (24-32)

In the earlier poem Pope had seen his intellectual independence as a sign of freedom from the narrow confines of sect and party, which he viewed as a desirable state in a satirist. Here his attitude is more quizzical. With its final picture of Bolingbroke as its apogee, and its concern (lines 3-15) with the approach of middle age, and the suggestion that the poet should be drawing in his horns, this is a more troubled poem than *Satire II* i. Pope is less happy about himself as he is less happy about humanity in general. He is aware of a need for guidance as his reference to consulting his medical advisers seems to show:

> Late as it is, I put my self to school,
> And feel some comfort, not to be a fool.
> Weak tho' I am of limb, and short of sight,
> Far from a Lynx, and not a Giant quite,
> I'll do what MEAD and CHESELDEN advise,
> To keep these limbs, and to preserve these eyes.
> Not to go back, is somewhat to advance,
> And men must walk at least before they dance.
>
> (47-54)

This is a Pope who is searching for the final good. We have already noted in discussing his *Epistle to Cobham,* Pope's perception of man as an inconstant creature whose mind is full of 'Quick whirls and shifting eddies.' This particular observation issued in Pope's treatment of the Duke of Wharton whose life embodied a tissue of reversals and inconsistencies.[15] The same kind of charge was offered against Lord Hervey '. . . one vile Antithesis . . .' in *An Epistle to Dr Arbuthnot.* It is applied to 'The People' in general in *Epistle I* i:

> Well, if a King's a Lion, at the least
> The People are a many-headed Beast:
> Can they direct what measures to pursue
> Who know themselves so little what to do?
> Alike in nothing but one lust of Gold
>
> (120-4)

Although Pope seems, in his identification of 'one Lust of Gold', to have identified the basic motivating principle in humanity, he is characteristically aware of the diverse and incongruous manifestations which this 'Lust' takes:

> . . . some farm the Poor-Box, some the Pews;
> Some keep Assemblies, and wou'd keep the Stews;
> Some with fat Bucks on childless Dotards fawn;
> Some win rich Widows by their Chine and Brawn,
> While with the silent growth of ten per Cent,
> In Dirt and darkness hundreds sink content.
>
> (128-133)

This is a disturbing treatment of the grosser aspects of human nature. It works by associating a number of things which are more commonly thought of as separate or opposite. For example, theft is associated with churches, and smart public gatherings (Assemblies) with well-tenanted brothels (Stews). The final lines present a disconcerting association of wealth, sex and meat, suggesting that rich widows have appetites of an exclusively (and literally) carnal sort. The investor of the final lines is made to sound like a product of the sewers, linking money (as authors have done since) with dirt.

That these sentiments are characteristically Pope's own, can be seen if we compare this passage with what Horace says in his original *Epistle to Maecenas.* We can see how Pope's passage was prompted by Horace, though it was a prompting only. There is nothing at all in Horace like Pope's desire to strip the surface from civilization, and examine the unglamorous network of beliefs and motivations which underline it.

> Some men are eager to secure public contracts, while others woo wealthy widows with fruit and dainty morsels, or catch childless dotards in a net to stock their fish-ponds. Many fortunes are fattened by the quiet growth of interest.
>
> (Horace, *Epistle I*, i, trans. Niall Rudd, 77-80)

Horace expresses a characteristic amusement at the quirks of human behaviour here. We do not feel that the characters whom he descibes are indulging in any particularly untoward activity, but it is an indication of Pope's strong feelings about the England of the late 1730s that he should write in so forceful a way.

> But show me one, who has it in his pow'r
> To act consistent with himself an hour.
>
> (136-7)

Pope's challenge cannot be met, as his portrait of Sir Job indicates. This is not quite as comprehensive a view of the man, as the portrait of Sir Balaam which closed the *Epistle to Bathurst,*[16] but there are similarities. Sir Job, having built '. . . a Palace . . .' on Greenwich Hill ('The silver Thames reflects its marble face.' (142)) is eventually moved by:

> . . . that Dev'l within
> Which guides all those who know not what they mean
>
> (143-4)

to pull the thing down, and return to London.

One of the chief effects that this poem has, is to make the reader aware of just how impossible Pope finds it to envisage any simple solution for the problems which he highlights. Although we can see that the theoretical basis for his presentation of human nature is familiar to us, and has been evolved elsewhere, Pope's sense of its endemic inconstancy means that he looks upon a world perpetually behaving in grotesque ways. As with all Pope's *Imitations of Horace,* this poem is laden with contemporary references, particularly to individual people, though the reader has to look harder in the text itself to find a specific and particular political motivation for it than in the two previous poems which we have discussed. The political standpoint is perhaps best underlined in the person of Bolingbroke. The Epistle of Horace which Pope was imitating was addressed to Maecenas, Horace's patron and benefactor, arguably the person to whom he owed the most. Comparably, Pope addresses the man in his own large circle of friends whom he admires the most, and the reverent tone of parts of the poem has been already discussed. What Pope was doing in this dedication was itself a politically provocative act. In his *Imitation to Epistle II* i *(To Augustus),* Pope's suggestion that Swift was the saviour of Ireland almost led to his imprisonment.[17] Bolingbroke had been prominent in trying to prevent a Hanoverian succession in 1714; his sympathies were avowedly Jacobite (he had been secretary of state to the Young Pretender in France, and had undertaken another period of exile there in the years immediately preceding the publication of this poem). Hence Bolingbroke was not simply a member of one political party opposed to another as we would expect today. He opposed the ruling dynasty from a position treasonous as well as treacherous.[18] Pope's explicitly political references at the end of the poem ('Great without Title . . .' '. . . honour'd while oppress'd . . .' 'follow'd without power') were making their own comment about the moral impoverishment of current leadership, and the tendency of that impoverishment to spread downwards. It, too, was a Bolingbrokian theme, and one to which Pope was to return more graphically at the end of the first part of his *Epilogue to the Satires.*

Pope's transformation of Horace's Maecenas into Henry St John Bolingbroke was not, perhaps, particularly difficult to accomplish. His transformation of George II into the Emperor Augustus was far less obvious, though much more original. The first Epistle of Horace's second book (*Epistle II* i) was addressed to the Emperor Augustus. On the face of it

Horace was a great deal more attuned to Augustus's greatness than Pope was to King George's. Horace had had employment under Augustus, rather than being associated with those in opposition to him. Horace had been seen as something of a toady, though others have found in Horace's praise of Augustus a hint of irony and complaint.[19] The poem which Horace addresses to him is a kind of protest about the position of the poet and of poetry in Augustus's empire.

The ostensible connection between George II and the Roman Emperor is the name: George's second name was Augustus. Thereafter multiple ironies take over. Horace was in a position to treat Augustus to at least some degree of flattery but in Pope's Epistle, the motions of flattery are gone through only to express the author's contempt:

> To Thee, the World its present homage pays,
> The Harvest early, but mature the Praise:
> Great Friend of LIBERTY! in *Kings* a Name
> Above all Greek, above all Roman Fame:
> Whose Word is Truth, as sacred and rever'd,
> As Heav'ns own Oracles from Altars heard.
> Wonder of Kings! like whom, to mortal eyes
> None e'er has risen, and none e'er shall rise.
> (23-30)

Extensive panegyric can become absurd. Pope exploits that tendency here. Whereas panegyric generally tends to the imprecise and the vacuous, each of the details which Pope includes here adds very specifically to the dimensions of the ridiculous figure he is creating. The thought that a blustering ill-educated German prince with limited fluency in the English language could receive tribute from the whole world is absurd. And to say that a man notoriously free in his sexual habits is a 'Great Friend of LIBERTY' is also stretching the resources of the language to comic extent.

But the irony of this section in the poem consists of more than merely stating the opposite of what is meant. A reader who knew the Horace poem would perceive the extra dimension inherent in the comparison between Pope's Augustus and Horace's. Also, there is the final point that George II, limited in his grasp of English and notably impervious to most forms of culture, would be completely incapable of appreciating that the irony was there. George did not really understand anything about what was going on in the literary scene, despite his possession of a copy of *The Dunciad.* A splendid example of the way in which he responded to Pope is quoted in the Twickenham edition of the *Imitations:*

> 'Who is this Pope that I hear so much about? I cannot discover what is his merit. Why will not my subjects write in prose?'[20]

Sustained irony is not a medium which one regularly associates with Pope. Swift in *A Modest Proposal* perhaps created the ultimate example of the kind, but Pope's ironies tend to be specific, local, and often parenthetic. Yet irony pervades most of this particular poem, going beyond merely the portraiture of the King. In a poem about the position of poets in society and of contemporary literature in general, Pope can be blithely deprecating about literary men:

> Yet Sir, reflect, the mischief is not great;
> These Madmen never hurt the Church or State:
> Sometimes the Folly benefits mankind;
> And rarely Av'rice taints the tuneful mind.
> Allow him but his Play-thing of a Pen,
> He ne'er rebels, or plots, like other men
> (189-194)

This kind of irony ends up embracing Pope too, as he presents himself, without naming names, as a typical case of what a poet is. An average poet, he informs us, embodies most of the features contained in his own favourite self-image:

> The good man heaps up nothing but mere metre,
> Enjoys his Garden and his Book in quiet;
> And then – a perfect Hermit in his Diet.
> (198-200)

Pope's suggestion that a poet may be '. . . useful to the State.' (203) also takes on ironic coloration as he points out to the uncomprehending monarch in nice simple language that poetry is really very pleasant stuff, eminently suitable for the retarded royal mind:

> What will a Child learn sooner than a song?
> What better teach a Foreigner the tongue?
> What's long or short, each accent where to place,
> And speak in publick with some sort of grace.
> I scarce can think him such a worthless thing.
> Unless he praise some monster of a King
>
> (205-210)

Irony can lead onto controversial if not plainly dangerous ground, too. The climax to the previous passage was a reference to a king who sounded a remarkably hypothetical figure in some ways but alarmingly close at hand in others. Likewise, Pope's illustrations of how poets have been useful to the state lead us to the example of Swift, where irony melts into something deadly serious. As we have already noted these lines nearly got Pope prosecuted:

> Let Ireland tell, how Wit upheld her cause,
> Her Trade supported, and supply'd her Laws;
> And leave on SWIFT this grateful verse ingrav'd,
> The Rights a Court attack'd, a Poet sav'd.
> Behold the hand that wrought a Nation's cure,
> Stretch'd to relieve the Idiot and the Poor
>
> (221-226)

In the unpredictable course which his argument frequently takes Pope upholds as supremely useful to the state two popular but untalented sixteenth-century versifiers of the psalms whose words have social value because orphans and foundlings are made to recite them:

> Not but there are, who merit other palms;
> Hopkins and Sternhold glad the heart with Psalms;
> The Boys and Girls whom Charity maintains,
> Implore your help with these pathetic strains
>
> (229-232)

In both these examples Pope has turned an apparently

innocent illustration of the uses of poetry into a portrait of human wretchedness.

Essentially though, the *Epistle to Augustus* is about the contemporary state of literature. This was Horace's subject, and despite deviations, it remains Pope's. It might seem that Pope has made his views on literary matters clear to us in several poems already. *An Essay in Criticism* provides us with a theoretical position which would be developed and mythologized in more directly satirical vein in *The New Dunciad.* The earlier *Dunciads* and *An Epistle to Dr Arbuthnot* provide abundant illustration of Pope's attitudes to many of his contemporaries and to the shortcomings of the literary culture in which he lived. On the face of it, Pope, in mounting a defence of contemporary literature, might, in this poem, be seen to be on contradictory ground. The poet who, at the end of *The Dunciad* could see the advent of universal darkness might not seem the obvious person to pen a defence of the contemporary scene.

We resolve this difficulty if we separate in meaning the 'contemporary' and the 'modern'. What the latter word connoted to Pope is discussed in Chapter Six. Pope's contempt for the 'modernist' position underlay completely all his cultural assumptions. But this contempt did not mean that Pope believed that there was no more literature to be written, rather that such literature was the preserve of a particular and important minority. Pope makes a case in this poem for the right kind of modern literature. As we shall see he has been adversely critical of much recent and contemporary writing, but he answers the charge that he is too hard to please:

> Yet lest you think I railly more than teach,
> Or praise malignly Arts I cannot reach,
> Let me for once presume t'instruct the times,
> To know the Poet from the Man of Rhymes:
> 'Tis He, who gives my breast a thousand pains,
> Can make me feel each Passion that he feigns,
> Inrage, compose, with more than magic Art,
> With Pity, and with Terror, tear my heart;
> And snatch me, o'er the earth, or thro' the air,
> To Thebes, to Athens, when he will, and where.
> (340-7)

Horace had made much the same point:

> You mustn't think I'm too mean to admit admiration for things which I would never try and others to excel at. Take the playwright who fills my heart with imaginary grief, illusory rage or fear, and then with peace; to me that's as hard as walking a tightrope; like a magician, he whisks me away – one day to Thebes, another to Athens.
>
> (*Horace, Epistle II* i, 203-213, translated Niall Rudd)

The verbal resemblances between these two passages will be clear, as will the fact that Pope makes Horace's tribute to the power of poetry the theoretical basis of his own. But Pope intensifies what Horace says, and appears to give it wider application. He provides an amazingly 'romantic' view of the effect of poetry on the reader, stressing the desirability of appreciating it through the heart, and equating the pleasure of that appreciation with the agony of '. . . a thousand pains'. Although the model poet at the end of the passage seems to be a Greek dramatist, Pope's appreciation of poetry here is explicitly emotional. It is unexpectedly so, particularly as the 'raillying' which he has been doing against recent and contemporary writers has taken place on different ground, focusing on their stylistic features, and especially their language. It is perhaps also significant that Pope's definition of what the true poet is, is defined only in terms of himself. He has been prepared to criticize many authors by name, but his own appreciation of what the good poet can give is neatly detached from any contemporary illustration. Pope is as much a mandarin in this Epistle as he was in the youthful *Essay on Criticism.*

An Essay on Criticism was a poem offering an approach to literature, of a traditional kind. Indeed many of its perspectives were themselves traceable to Horace's *Ars Poetica* (*Epistle II* iii – his own *Essay on Criticism* really). The concerns of *The Dunciad,* on the other hand were oppressively contemporary. The *Epistle to Augustus* treads something of a middle path. Like the latter poem it is keenly aware of mediocrity, of the proliferation of literature from unexpected and incongruous quarters:

> Now Times are chang'd, and one Poetick Itch
> Has seiz'd the Court and City, Poor and Rich:
> Sons, Sires, and Grandsires, all will wear the Bays,
> Our Wives read Milton, and our Daughters Plays,
> To Theatres and to Rehearsals throng,
> And all our Grace at Table is a Song.
>
> (169-174)

Likewise, we can hear the tones of Pope's satires against the Dunces when he concludes this section of the poem:

> But those who cannot write, and those who can,
> All ryme, and scrawl, and scribble, to a man.
>
> (187-8)

But to comment on the shortcomings of his contemporaries is not the principal feature of this poem. Other works of Pope have done that clearly enough. What Pope is offering ultimately in his *Epistle to Augustus* is a cultural overview of the native literary tradition. As such, the Epistle has been seen as representing a kind of manifesto of 'Augustan' literary values.

Obviously the poem foregrounds the concept of the 'Augustan'.[21] It is the term which has generally come to be used to describe the literature of the early eighteenth-century, in the way that 'romantic' is used for the later eighteenth and early nineteenth centuries. As such it is a convenient label, a kind of critical shorthand and the term is used simply to define a particular literary period, rather than with much regard to its precise meaning. Certainly the grounding of early eighteenth-century literature in the classical, and more particularly Roman tradition, causes it much more readily than the literature of other periods to acquire a critical tag which will point up its classical indebtedness. No more obvious an example of an Augustan practice exists than Pope's own activities in imitating Horace. The fact that in this poem Pope wished to make Horace's comments upon the contemporary literary scene in Rome relevant to his own age, indicates that he himself perceives some kind of relationship to exist between them. Much early eighteenth-century writing was related to classical forms, manipulation of which was second nature to a writer such as Pope. Early eighteenth-century poetry was conscious of itself as part of a tradition and it was, at least as far as Swift, Pope and later Dr Johnson were concerned, based on specific theories about the nature of poetic language and form. After Wordsworth's Preface to the *Lyrical Ballads* in which he claimed that his poetry sought to employ: '. . . a selection of the language really used by ordinary men . . .' there have been many and varied attempts by poets to relate the language of verse to the language of speech. Pope's literary conditioning was quite different. Of his youthful friendship with the critic William Walsh, Pope later told Spence:

> 'He encouraged me much, and used to tell me there was one way left of excelling, for though we had several great poets, we never had any one great poet that was correct – and he desired me to make that my study and aim.'[22]

Walsh would certainly appear to have been on hand when the young Pope was writing his *Pastorals,* to give him help and advice, perhaps of much the same kind as that of his father who used to 'correct' his son's verses. Recovering the precise meaning and connotations of the word 'correct' is important. Obviously, Pope throughout his entire poetic career was a supreme technician. Not only does just about all his work testify to technical accuracy, supreme fluency and unparalleled dexterity in the handling of rhyme, but there is also a stylistic homogeneity between early, middle and late work which is perhaps unique among English poets. Pope was certainly careful. As Warton said of the manuscript of the *Epilogue to the Satires*:

> (It was) '. . . more diligently laboured and more frequently corrected than any of our Author's compositions . . . Every line was . . . written twice over and . . . written twice over a second time'[23]

There can be no doubting Pope's finical self-criticism in the production of his own poetic texts, though 'correctness' means more than just a desire for technical accuracy and polish. It means also a concern for the purity of the poetic language, that it should be purged completely of 'low' or cant associations. Dr Johnson's criticism of one of Lady Macbeth's speeches (though he attributes it to Macbeth himself) illustrates a concern with correctness which might strike us as perverse in the extreme.[24] He quotes the lines:

> Come, thick night,
> And pall thee in the dunnest smoke of hell,
> That my keen knife see not the wound it makes,
> Nor heaven peep through the blanket of the dark,
> To cry 'Hold, hold'.
> (Shakespeare, *Macbeth,* Act i, Sc 5, 50-55)

Although accepting that 'In this passage is exerted all the force of poetry . . .', Johnson finds things to worry him, chiefly concerning what he sees as the inappropriateness of the words. To invoke the smoke of Hell strikes him as an awesome act, though he finds it subverted completely by Shakespeare's use of the word 'dunnest' which he reminds us is 'an epithet now seldom heard but in the stable . . . (which) . . . may come or go without any other notice than contempt.' The word 'knife' also bothers him: '. . . this sentiment is weakened by the name of an instrument used by butchers and cooks in the meanest of employments; we do not immediately conceive that any crime of importance is to be committed with a *knife* . . .' Shakespeare's poor knife threatens to become to Johnson, what Algernon's hand-bag was to Lady Bracknell.[25] And we may also be reminded by it of Pope's aversion from the word 'scissors' in *The Rape of the Lock*: put to admirably comic use, and entirely consistent with so much else in the poem, but transforming the humble object, upwards as it were into 'a two-edg'd Weapon' or 'little Engine'.

It is in the light of such poetic theory and practice that Pope mounts his discussion of the native tradition of English poetry. Contemporary poetry is to be valued and encouraged by the modern Augustus because it is superior to much of what was written before it. Pope, with Horace's guidance, is quick to expose the fallacy that 'classic' status is simply a function of time:

If Time improves our Wit as well as Wine,
Say at what age a Poet grows divine?
Shall we, or shall we not, account him so,
Who dy'd perhaps, an hundred years ago?
End all dispute; and fix the year precise
When British bards begin t'immortalise?
(49-54)

Pope is keen to point out that some British bards, even those who enjoy cultural respectability are ribald and debased:

Chaucer's worst ribaldry is learn'd by rote,
And beastly Skelton Heads of Houses quote
(37-8)

The poetic language of Spenser, Sidney and Milton can also be seen as deviating from correctness from time to time:

Spenser himself affects the obsolete,
And Sydney's verse halts ill on Roman feet:
Milton's strong pinion now not Heav'n can bound,
Now serpent-like, in prose he sweeps the ground
(97-100)

Stylistic sophistication, consistency and propriety, are, says Pope, recent inventions. Their appearance in England is the result of the efforts of Dryden and the effect of 'Exact' Racine, and 'noble' Corneille.

We conquer'd France, but felt our captive's charms;
Her Arts victorious triumph'd o'er our Arms:
Britain to soft refinements less a foe,
Wit grew polite, and Numbers learn'd to flow.
Waller was smooth; but Dryden taught to join
The varying verse, the full resounding line,
The long majestic march, and energy divine.
(263-9)

This is an important passage for an understanding of Pope's

aesthetic. Poetry is associated with manners, civilization, tact. Appropriate adjectives of approval are 'smooth', 'resounding', 'majestic', words quite alien to the style of later poets, Browning or Hopkins for example.

But Pope remains hard to please. Dryden's aesthetic is essentially fine, but we are reminded of his (in Pope's view at any rate) final carelessness:

> Ev'n copious Dryden, wanted, or forgot,
> The last and greatest Art, the Art to blot.
>
> (280-1)

Pope is consistently keen to relate 'culture' to 'society' in this poem. In particular, he discusses the seventeenth-century poets in the context of political happenings, reminding us again of the fundamentally provocative nature of this poem, given its addressee. This is particularly apparent where he talks about the culture of the Restoration court. He is responsive to its artistic abundance, but mindful also of its decadence:

> The Soldier breath'd the Gallantries of France,
> And ev'ry flow'ry Courtier writ Romance.
> Then Marble soften'd into life grew warm,
> And yielding Metal flow'd to human form:
> Lely on animated Canvas stole
> The sleepy Eye, that spoke the melting soul.
> No wonder then, when all was Love and Sport,
> The willing Muses were debauch'd at Court
>
> (145-152)

Pope is genuinely appreciative of the almost spontaneously abundant art of the Restoration period, yet its survival was fragile just as its content was essentially decorative and ultimately subsumed beneath political change:

> But Britain, changeful as a Child at play,
> Now calls in Princes, and now turns away.
> Now Whig, now Tory, what we lov'd we hate;
> Now for all Pleasure, now for Church and State;
> Now for Prerogative, and now for Laws;

Effects unhappy! from a Noble Cause.

(155-60)

The political dimension is never forgotten for long in this poem, nor, therefore, the conspicuously uncultured court over which George II ruled and which Walpole served. Pope has used contemporary habits of theatre-going elsewhere to symbolize contemporary habits of taste among the fashionable and wealthy and he does so again:

There still remains to mortify a Wit,
The many-headed Monster of the Pit:
A sense-less, worth-less, and unhonour'd crowd;
Who to disturb their betters mighty proud,
Clatt'ring their sticks, before ten lines are spoke,
Call for the Farce, the Bear, or the Black-joke.

(304-9)

It is the 'Wit' (ie. true poet) who remains mortified, and it is the work of wits whom Pope is seeking to commend before Augustus, despite his hesitation before the actual naming of their names. Pope, finally, calls on his Augustus to continue the best traditions of royal patronage. In so doing, he returns to his fully ironic mode:

Oh! could I mount on the Maeonian* wing,
Your Arms, your Actions, your Repose to sing!
What seas you travers'd! and what fields you fought!
Your Country's Peace, how oft, how dearly bought!
How barb'rous rage subsided at your word,
And nations wonder'd while they dropped the sword!

(394-9)

*(Maeonian=Homeric)

In conclusion Pope allows himself a Dunciad-like image. To illustrate his ironic assertion that he is telling the truth rather than flattering, he suggests that were he a flatterer his writings would be nothing other than so much waste-paper, hanging in public places waiting to be sold. In evoking such an image, he reminds us most graphically just what importance was *really* attached to literature in Georgian England:

> And when I flatter, let my dirty leaves
> (Like Journals, Odes, and such forgotten things
> As Eusden, Philips, Settle, writ of Kings)
> Cloath spice, line trunks, or flutt'ring in a row,
> Befringe the rails of Bedlam and Sohoe.
>
> (415-9)

The Epistle to Augustus is arguably the most fluent and sustained of Pope's *Imitations*. It does not, for example, feature any kind of debate between Pope and an adversary, and it allows him to elaborate at length a reading of recent literary and cultural history. It is a pertinent paradox that so substantial a poem is written to criticize the cultural vacuum that Pope found Hanoverian England to be. The constantly returning irony helps this, of course: it is only by making out George II to be the opposite of what he really is that the poem starts to function in the first place, but for all its objects of attack, and for all the coherence which its point of view acquires, it is a witty and spirited affair.

The chronologically last completed *Imitations* are those which we now know as the two dialogues comprising the *Epilogue To The Satires.* They date from May and July 1738, respectively. The first of them was printed as *One Thousand Seven Hundred and Thirty Eight. A Dialogue Something like Horace.* Pope's title was judicious, for after the first two lines of the poem, Horace ceases to be any influence at all. Indeed, it is possible to see the opening sections of the poem as marking a parting of company with Horace. The 'Friend' who is the other participant in Pope's dialogue is keen to illustrate the unHoratian features of Pope's verse here, in an analysis from which the poet does not demur.

> But *Horace,* Sir, was delicate, was nice;
> *Bubo* observes, he lash'd no sort of *Vice:*
> *Horace* would say, *Sir* Billy *serv'd the Crown,*
> Blunt *could do Bus'ness,* H-ggins *knew the Town,*
> In *Sappho* touch the *Failing of the Sex,*
> In rev'rend Bishops note some *small Neglects* . . .

His sly, polite, insinuating stile
Could please at Court, and make AUGUSTUS smile
(11-16; 19-20)

The 'Friend' in this poem is clearly conceptual rather than actual. He is, too, both a friend and an opponent: an opponent in that he argues consistently *against* what he considers to be Pope's position, but a friend in that he offers as many satirical contributions to the debate as Pope himself does. The argument is carried out almost entirely in terms of topical allusions and both parties (as the above-quoted extract amongst other things shows) have a great fecundity in the naming of names. Any difference between the points of view they seem to be expressing is ironic. Whilst the Friend's invocation of Bubo, Sappho and the others is couched in terms of an apparent plea for moderation, the plea is clearly arguing Pope's case for him.

There is a way, of course, in which all Pope's interlocutors in the *Imitations* had been hypothetical. Pope had put *his* words into their mouths. When the voice of Fortescue in *Satire II* i five years previously had said to Pope 'I'd write no more', he was saying something not very different from Pope's own note at the end of the Second Dialogue:

> 'This was the last poem of the kind printed by our author, with a resolution to publish no more . . . Could he have hoped to have amended any, he had continued those attacks; but bad men were grown so shameless and so powerful, that Ridicule was become as unsafe as it was ineffectual.'[26]

The addressees (particularly in the dialogues) of the *Imitations* can, arguably, be seen to represent Pope's own caution about his work. The frequent protestations of an unwillingness to write which occur in these poems underline Pope's inhibitions about running amuck and tilting at all he met. The statement that 'Fools rush into my Head, and so I write' (*Satire II* i, 14) is both an excuse for writing and a reason for not doing. ('. . . but bad men were grown so shameless and so powerful, that Ridicule was become as unsafe as it was ineffectual . . .')

One of the inevitable consequences of Pope's casting aside of Horatian moderation in this poem is its much more self-evident partisanship. Where the reference to Walpole, for example, at the end of *Satire II* i was teasing and oblique, in this poem the figure of Walpole is central to much of Pope's argument about the depravity of the times:

> Fr: Go see Sir ROBERT –
> P: See Sir ROBERT! – hum –
> And never laugh – for all my life to come?
> Seen him I have, but in his happier hour
> Of Social Pleasure, ill-exchang'd for Pow'r;
> Seen him, uncumber'd with the Venal tribe,
> Smile without Art, and win without a Bribe.
> Would he oblige me? let me only find,
> He does not think me what he thinks mankind.
> (27-34)

And, as we shall see, Walpole's presence covertly dominates the concluding section of the poem.

The political dimension of the poem is intensified through the sometimes very detailed and intricate topical allusions. When Pope's Friend has urged moderation yet again:

> Laugh then at any, but at Fools or Foes;
> These you but anger, and you mend not those
> (53-4)

the poet gives us one of his most intricate treatments of contemporary events by way of reply. Pope demonstrates that the rough tones of satire are what the times need as antidote to the vacuousness of the political yes-men:

> . . . *Henley's* Oratory, *Osborn's* Wit!
> The Honey dropping from *Favonio's* tongue,
> The Flow'rs of *Bubo,* and the Flow of *Y--ng!*
> (66-8)

To illustrate the way in which partisan flattery flourishes, Pope (and his own explanation serves as well as any):

> Alludes to some court sermons, and florid panegyrical speeches; particularly one very full of puerilities and flatteries; which afterwards got into an address in the same pretty style; and was lastly served up in an Epitaph, between Latin and English published by its author.[27]

Pope is concerned with the politics of literature in this poem just as much as he is the literature of politics. This passage serves very well to illustrate the way in which each has corrupted the other. Politics is reduced to '. . . florid panegyrical speeches . . .', and literature reduced to providing them:

> The gracious Dew of Pulpit Eloquence;
> And all the well-whipt Cream of Courtly Sense,
> That first was *H--vy's F-x's* next, and then
> The *S-te's,* and then *H--vy's* once agen.
> O come, that easy *Ciceronian* stile,
> So *Latin,* yet so *English* all the while
>
> (69-74)

> Or teach the melancholy Muse to mourn,
> Hang the sad Verse on CAROLINA's Urn
>
> (79-80)

The leaving behind of the more obvious Horatian echoes in this poem also causes the moral issues to be presented in a starker way. Pope offers most of his criticisms of the contemporary scene in terms of a contrast between virtue and vice. We have already noted that the anti-Walpole opposition (whose cause in 1738 seemed more desperate than ever) appropriated the word 'virtue' to themselves. Pope is particularly keen to present it in opposition to vice:

> *Virtue* may chuse the high or low Degree,
> 'Tis just alike to Virtue, and to me;
> Dwell in a Monk, or light upon a King,
> She's still the same, belov'd contented thing.
> *Vice* is undone, if she forgets her Birth,

And stoops from Angels to the Dregs of Earth
(137-142)

There then follows one of the most remarkable passages in late Pope. It shares something of the apocalyptic nature of the closing of *The Dunciad,* though its tone and methods are very different. Where *The Dunciad* presents a vision of cosmic dissolution, this poem takes on the dimension of a huge allegory. There is a visual precision about the details which give it the quality of an immense baroque painting. The fundamental idea is of the pernicious and corrupting power of vice when it is to be found in high places:

But 'tis the *Fall* degrades her to a Whore;
Let *Greatness* own her, and she's mean no more:
Her Birth, her Beauty, Crowds and Courts confess,
Chaste Matrons praise her, and grave Bishops bless
(143-6)

The passage goes on to exemplify the self-aggrandizing onward roll of Vice, encompassing more and more areas (just as in its own way, Dulness does):

Lo! at the Wheels of her Triumphal Car,
Old *England's* Genius, rough with many a Scar,
Dragg'd in the Dust! his Arms hang idly round,
His Flag inverted trails along the ground!
Our Youth, all liv'ry'd o'er with foreign Gold,
Before her dance; behind her crawl the Old!
(151-6)

Also like Dulness, Vice is followed by an essentially anarchic and insurrectionary force. It leads to noise, dissonance, and all the paraphernalia of civil disturbance:

All, all look up, with reverential Awe,
On Crimes that scape or triumph o'er the Law:
While Truth, Worth, Wisdom, daily they decry –
'Nothing is Sacred now but Villany'
(167-70)

But there is of course a determinedly contemporary dimension to this portrait. If its final effect is of some allegorical painting or tableau, the individual details which make up the picture are of specific people and events. Indeed, it would appear that the whole impetus for the personification of vice as a whore came from the marriage of Walpole, hard upon the death of his first wife, to his long-standing mistress Molly Skerrett.[28] The detail that Vice has a 'scarlet head' (line 149) is thus explained, as is the reference on the following line to seeing '. . . pale Virtue carted in her stead!' Prostitutes apparently, were wheeled through the streets in carts as punishment for their sins.[29] Hence Vice's 'Triumphal Car' is both impressive allegorical flourish and bathetic contemporary reference. The infamous venality of Walpole's regime is referred to in lines 154-5 as is the suspect alliance between state and church on line 146. The picture is highly coded, and we are reminded of Pope's method in his *Epistle to Augustus,* where part of the satire's ironic force comes from the fact that those who are being criticized might well be the last to notice.

Pope ends with a quite and unexpectedly self-deprecating couplet which punctures the large allegorical balloon he has just sent up:

> Yet may this Verse (if such a verse remain)
> Show there was one who held it in disdain.
>
> (171-2)

The question 'Why write satire?' persists to inform the whole of the Second Dialogue. It is one of the fundamental questions which lies beneath practically everything Pope wrote during the 'Horatian' 1730s. In *An Epistle to Dr Arbuthnot* the issue centres on the question of tact: should the satirist name names or should he deal with matters generally? Various of the *Imitations* seek to define the poet's relationship with the world of public events in order to explain what the satirist has to satirize. This Dialogue is perhaps the most searching of Pope's attempts to defend himself. It deals not merely with the question of whether the satirist should write in this or that way: it is an exploration of the power and importance of satire in corrupt times. Pope urges upon his interlocutor that he writes not merely out of personal spite, but that as a poet he has an important, almost divinely inspired job to do:

> Truth guards the Poet, sanctifies the line,
> And makes Immortal, Verse as mean as mine.
>
> (246-7)

The rhetoric of Dialogue II is undoubtedly Pope's most assertive and challenging. The poem is a hymn to satire's power. It emphasizes the position of poet as satirist, and as such may well be seen as Pope's most egocentric poem, proclaiming, defending, explaining the importance of his position:

> Yes, I am proud; I must be proud to see
> Men not afraid of God, afraid of me;
> Safe from the Bar, the Pulpit, and the Throne,
> Yet touch'd and sham'd by *Ridicule* alone.
>
> (208-211)

The urgency of Pope's satire in this poem is increased by the introduction the previous year of a censorship act which required all new publications to be read in case their contents were libellous to the government. Pope starts from the Juvenalian position that it is difficult *not* to write satire:

> Vice with such Giant-strides comes on amain,
> Invention strives to be before in vain;
> Feign what I will, and paint it e'er so strong,
> Some rising Genius sins up to my Song.
>
> (6-9)

This is no mere repetition, though. Vice is personified as a large, almost irresistable force, human yet inhuman, challenging almost any alternative form of earthly energy. Vice likewise seems to be able to rise and fly. The poem is much concerned with the delineation of various kinds of power, one of which is satire itself which acquires new dimensions. It, too, can fly and swoop like a hawk (to 'sowze' means to swoop):

Come on then Satire! gen'ral, unconfin'd,
Spread thy broad wing, and sowze on all the Kind.
(14-15)

Likewise, satire is, in several places in the poem granted supernatural powers. The satirist is one and the same thing as the very Muse of poetry itself:

No Pow'r the Muse's Friendship can command;
No pow'r when Virtue claims it, can withstand
(118-9)

Satire is being defined in much more potent, and grandiloquent terms than Pope has used before. The final tribute to satire's force comes at the end of the poem:

O sacred Weapon! left for Truth's defence,
Sole Dread of Folly, Vice and Insolence!
To all but Heav'n-directed hands deny'd
The Muse may give thee, but the Gods must guide.
(212-5)

The vocabulary is that of holy warfare. Satire comes close to being the voice of God. It is both sacred and a weapon. As the reference to men not afraid of God being afraid of the satirist as already suggested, the satirist lays claim to an almost divine authority. His power is expended effortlessly but it is deadly:

Spin all your Cobwebs o'er the Eye of Day!
The Muse's wing shall brush you all away
(222-3)

These statements emerge in response to provocative questioning from Pope's interlocutor. In this poem, the 'Friend' is much more of an inquisitor, as a result of which the poet is often forced into almost casuistical strategies of self-defence. Urbanity of tone is kept at a distance and the dialectical atmosphere is significantly more tense. Pope and Friend argue each other into a series of tight corners:

(P): Ye Statemen, Priests, of one Religion all!
Ye Tradesmen vile, in Army, Court or Hall!
Ye Rev'rend Atheists – *F:* Scandal! name them,
Who?
P. Why that's the thing you bid me not to do.
Who starv'd a Sister, who foreswore a Debt,
I never nam'd – the Town's enquiring yet.
The pois'ning Dame – *F.* You mean – *P.* I don't. –
F. You do
P. See! now I keep the Secret, and not you.
(16-23)

One senses a mixture of patience and exasperation in his replies to his Friend. The ground has indeed been gone over before, but the present continues to give it proof:

I fain wou'd please you, if I knew with what:
Tell me, which Knave is lawful Game, which not?
Must great Offenders, once escap'd the Crown
Like Royal Harts, be never more run down?
(26-29)

Likewise Pope is not happy with the accusation that he indulges in gratuitous malice, or that his criticism of people is grounded in nothing other than partisanship:

Do I wrong the Man?
God knows, I praise a Courtier where I can.
(62-3)

Pope is perhaps more than ever in this poem on oath to say something appreciative of human behaviour, to expose, in fact, the ideological position from which his satire emerges. In *An Epistle to Dr Arbuthnot,* Pope had looked back appreciatively to the literary figures ('great Dryden's friends before') who had surrounded him in his youth, before the sacred art had fallen into inferior hands.[30] Similarly, in this poem, Pope is able to provide a portrait gallery of men whose virtue he can commend. As in the comparable passage in *An Epistle* . . ., Pope finds himself looking backwards to a previous generation, or at least to a previous political regime, for his examples:

Thus SOMMERS once, and HALIFAX were mine.
Oft in the clear, still Mirrour or Retreat,
I study'd SHREWSBURY, the wise and great:
CARLETON's calm Sense, and STANHOPE's noble Flame,
Compar'd, and knew their gen'rous End the same:
How pleasing ATTERBURY's softer hour!
How shin'd the Soul, unconquer'd in the Tow'r!
(77-83)

Pope again takes a rather casuistical tone on the question of his own friendships. His interlocutor wants to suggest a simple solution to Pope's choice of victims: he is simply jealous of them because his own friends are not receiving preferment:

Yet think not Friendship only prompts my Lays;
I follow *Virtue,* where she shines, I praise,
Point she to Priest or Elder, Whig or Tory,
Or round a Quaker's Beaver cast a Glory . . .
To find an honest man, I beat about,
And love him, court him, praise him, in or out . . .
Find you the Virtue, and I'll find the Verse.
(94-7, 102-3, 105)

In what is perhaps the most inquisitorial passage of all, Pope neatly side-steps the accusation that he is merely the opposition's spokesman:

Fr. Faith, the thought's no Sin,
I think your friends are out, and would be in.
P. If merely to come in, Sir, they go out,
The way they take is strangely round about.
Fr. They too may be corrupted, you'll allow?
P. I only call those Knaves who are so now.
(122-127)

Pope's objections to the various kinds of turpitude before him on the public scene reach their climax in the image of the Westphalian hogs. Pope's Friend reminds him of the passage in the First Dialogue (lines 69-75) where he talks about the way in which meaningless panegyric passes for literature among courtiers, and the way in which empty tributes and praise, whether in English or Latin, are passed around. Pope's describing these pigs as German ones is clearly significant: for Westphalian hogs, read Hanoverian Kings. The image of an idea passing from one pig to another suggests not simply the debasement of the processes of communication, but it implicates courtiers with dark hints of bestiality and other forms of sexual perversion:

> Let Courtly Wits to Wits afford supply,
> As Hog to Hog in Huts of *Westphaly;*
> If one, thro' Nature's Bounty or his Lord's,
> Has what the frugal, dirty soil affords,
> From him the next receives it, thick or thin,
> As pure a Mess almost as it came in;
> The blessed Benefit, not there confin'd,
> Drops to the third, who nuzzles close behind;
> From tail to mouth, they feed, and they carouse;
> The last, full fairly gives it to the *House.*
>
> (171-80)

It is because the highest activities of state are susceptible to discussion in these terms, that the business of satire attains to an importance of an ultimately God-given kind. The climax of this section of the poem is one of Pope's best-known, if misunderstood couplets:

> Ask you what Provocation I have had?
> The strong Antipathy of Good to Bad.
>
> (197-8)

By this question and answer Pope does not simply mean that he is right and the rest of the world is wrong. Pope, rather than asserting his own superiority, is asserting a classical humanist position, as he makes clear not only in the lines which immediately follow, but in the note to them which he himself provided. He cited the well-known statement from Terence: *Homo sum: humani nihil a me alienum puto* (I am a man, and I believe nothing human to be separate from me).[31] It is Pope's agony as a member of the human race before the corruption he sees which causes him to raise his voice in the way he does here:

When Truth or Virtue an Affront endures,
Th'Affront is mine, my Friend, and should be yours.
Mine, as a Foe profess'd to false Pretence,
Who think a Coxcomb's Honour like his Sense;
Mine as a Friend to ev'ry worthy mind;
And mine as Man, who feel for all mankind.
(200-204)

The satirist is thus presented as compassionate altruist rather than scourge or trouble-maker. What will prove Pope's ultimate statement about satire is a humane and indeed almost self-denying one. Satire itself remains an agent of the divine will, it is both holy and aggressive:

O sacred Weapon! left for Truth's defence,
Sole Dread of Folly, Vice and Insolence! . . .
Rev'rent I touch thee! but with honest zeal;
To rowze the Watchmen of the Publick Weal,
To Virtue's Work provoke the tardy Hall,
And goad the Prelate slumb'ring in his Stall.
(212-3; 216-9)

The rhetoric takes on an other-worldliness. The concerns of the satirist are, in these final paragraphs of the poem, associated less with the here and the now than with ultimate questions of right and wrong. We feel the apocalyptic strain entering the discourse again, just as it does in its different ways at the end of the First Dialogue, and at the end of *The Dunciad.* If the car of Vice was triumphant at the end of the First Dialogue, there are suggestions here about the solving power of Virtue:

. . . when diadem'd, with Rays divine,
Touch'd with the Flame that breaks from Virtue's Shrine,
Her Priestess Muse forbids the Good to dye,

And ope's the Temple of Eternity

(232-5)

Truth guards the Poet, sanctifies the line,
And makes Immortal, Verse as mean as mine

(246-7)

Pope is keen to make the largest of claims for the importance of his art whilst asking little for himself. His friend's final remarks are neatly self-deflating:

Alas! alas! pray end what you began,
And write next winter more *Essays on Man.*

(254-5)

The ending of the poem contains ambiguities, though. If it is Pope's most determined, most rhetorical, defence of his position as poet, it also masks despair. If satire is the tool of Virtue, and Virtue is the instrument of God, an age in which politicians and courtiers are no better than Westphalian hogs could hardly be expected to take much notice of the fact. The conclusion to which Pope is forced to come is that his warnings against the age, his siding with good against bad are an irrelevance. '. . . Ridicule was become as unsafe as it was ineffectual . . . but [our author] had reason to be satisfied with the approbation of good men and the testimony of his own conscience.'[32]

Apart from the *New Dunciad* which is, in any case, very much a turning back to earlier preoccupations, Pope had no further completed satire against the age to offer. The *Imitations of Horace* chart a lengthy yet determined movement in Pope's mind. They chart, in fact, both engagement and disengagement with the Roman poet: from believing that Horace 'would hit my case' to believing that he was far too delicate in tone to face contemporary vice. Pope had in various ways and in various poems endeavoured to acquire an Horatian urbanity and detachment. The tone was there sometimes, but the ambivalences which underpin *An Epistle to Dr Arbuthnot* were there too. The poems in which Pope imitates Horace most closely are perpetually ingenious and inventive. The relating of Horatian details to contemporary incidents is judicious and elegantly done. At the same time, though, Pope was never more his own master than he is in these poems. If Horace was a critic of the human race, an observer of the species of man in general, Pope's imagination was much more spontaneously in love with the specific and the particular. For more than two decades he had been the butt of insult and satire himself. It is not too surprising that he knew where and how some old scores could be settled. He lived in an age of partisan politics, where the concept of an opposition to parliamentary government was emerging. Although he never made any direct and public statement of political allegiance (and was, as we have seen, positively keen to deny it), his emotional loyalties through friendship and through background were clear. Biographers have been able to credit Sir Robert Walpole with considerable political gifts: Pope's reading of his age is significantly different. The amalgam of Pope and Horace is a potent and refreshingly unpredictable one, but there is no way in which Pope could ever identify with the Roman wholly and completely. The most potent interplay of all in the *Imitations* is between Pope and his own experience of life.

Chapter Five: His Own Master

1. See Frank Stack *Pope and Horace* (1985) pp18-23.
2. For Horace and Christianity see Stack p10. For the Horatian influence on Pope see also Reuben A. Brower: *Alexander Pope. The Poetry of Allusion* (1959) Chap 6.
3. See Twickenham Edition Vol IV (1939) p xiii.
4. The question of Pope's emulation of Horace in his own life is dealt with at length by Maynard Mack in *The Garden and the City. Politics and Retirement in the Later Poetry of Pope* (1969). For a succinct account of Horace's life, see Niall Rudd (Ed) *The Satires of Horace and Persius* (Penguin Classics, 1987) pp15-26.
5. Pope's *Advertisement* Twickenham IV p3.
6. See Stack pp18-20.
7. For details of Fortescue's career and of Pope's friendship with him see Mack *Life* pp189-91.
8. See Rudd (Ed) p85.
9. 27 September, 1732 see Twickenham Vol IV p xiv.
10. *Author's Preface* to *The Battle of the Books* (Ed. Ross and Woolley) (1984) p104.
11. See Twickenham Vol IV, Biographical Appendix pp346-347.
12. For Lady Mary and her husband see Mack *Life* pp293-295.
13. The fullest treatment of Pope and Bolingbroke is Brean S. Hammond *Pope and Bolingbroke: A Study of Friendship and Influence* (1984).
14. See *Epistle to A Lady* lines 25-26.
15. See *Epistle to Cobham* lines 180-209.
16. *Epistle to Bathurst* lines 339-402.
17. See Mack *Life* pp683-684.
18. See Hammond (above); for a brief outline of Bolingbroke's career, see Mack *Life* pp505-512.
19. See Rudd, Introduction p18.
20. Quoted in Twickenham IV p362, which gives its original source as Prior's *Life of Malone* (1860).
21. Howard Erskine-Hill, *The Augustan Idea in English Literature* (1983) has two chapters (XI and XII) on Pope.
22. For the young Pope's relationship with Walsh see Mack *Life* pp110-117. The particular quotation can be found on p111.
23. Twickenham IV, Introduction p xxxix.
24. From an essay by Johnson in *The Rambler,* No 168, 26th October 1751. It can be found in W.K. Wimsatt *Dr Johnson on Shakespeare* (Penguin Edition, 1969) pp44-45.
25. See Oscar Wilde *The Importance of Being Earnest* Act 1.
26. Pope's note Twickenham IV p327.

27. Pope's note Twickenham IV p303.
28. See Mack *Life* p717.
29. See Twickenham IV p309.
30. *An Epistle to Dr Arbuthnot* lines 135-146.
31. Acknowledged in Twickenham IV p324.
32. See above Note 26.

6

MAKING A MIGHTY DUNCIAD

The 'Dunciads' of 1742-3

The end of *The Dunciad* of 1728-9 was abrupt and provisional. The ghost of Elkanah Settle afforded the Dunce Theobald '. . . a glimpse or Pisgah – sight of the promised Fulness . . .' of Dulness's glory.[1] Examples of this fullness were provided: the fashion for opera; the growing gimmickry of the theatre; the influence of Dulness on arts and learning:

> 'Enough! enough!' the raptur'd Monarch cries;
> And thro' the Ivory Gate the Vision flies.
>
> (Book III, 357-8)

Pope reminded us in his Preface that the subject matter introduced in these closing lines '. . . will, in all probability, hereafter be the Theme of many other and greater Dunciads',[2] and it has been noted previously that, inherent in the scheme of *The Dunciad,* is an almost infinite extendability. For this reason alone, it is not surprising that Pope found appropriate additions to make to the poem, though it is quite possible that he had had material in hand with which to do so from the very outset.[3] Equally, whilst Pope was stung by immediate events into revising all of the poem in 1743 with Colley Cibber as hero, it is not impossible that Cibber's place in the poem had been under contemplation for some time.[4]

The *New Dunciad* (that which we now know as Book IV) appeared in March, 1742. In origin it presents an enlargement of Settle's prophecies from the old Book III, extended in both detail and range. It also involves some use of material concerning education from an immense didactic poem which Pope had planned as a sequel to *An Essay on Man.* Critics have always been quick to point out the more general conspectus which this additional Book presents. It has a wider cultural and political dimension which takes the reader some way beyond the Grub Street provenance of the earlier Books. It ceases to be the densely allusive Scriblerian text of 1728-9. Although certain individuals are satirized in it the 1742 addition is more concerned with types, and there is undoubtedly less scoring of points over particular personal adversaries than there was in the earlier version.

Scriblerian in one sense though, *The New Dunciad* remains. The original Martinus Scriblerus was a pedant. Pope's letter to Swift in which he first planned the activities of the Scriblerus Club said that he hoped that '. . . follies in learning and criticism would be satirized . . .',[5] and it is the mixture of 'learned lumber' and Grub Street hacking in the person of Lewis Theobald which made him such an appropriate hero for the original *Dunciad.* Literary scholarship is a degraded and degrading activity, Pope seems to be telling us. It is a catchpenny trade, plied by mediocrities.

For an author as clearly interested in the state of literary culture as Pope was, this might seem an odd view. It would seem more likely that Pope would respect scholarship, and insist on its importance. He himself had written *An Essay on Criticism* as one of his earliest published works. But he had also pointed out in *An Epistle to Dr Arbuthnot,* that there was criticism and criticism:

> Pains, reading, study, are their just pretence,
> And all they want is spirit, taste, and sense.
> Comma's and points they set exactly right,
> And 'twere a sin to rob them of their Mite.
> Yet ne'er one sprig of Laurel grac'd these ribalds,
> From slashing Bentley down to pidling Tibalds.
> (158-164)

The passage makes several accusations. It would firstly seem to say that there is little to be gained from 'Pains, reading, study . . .'. These things are merely 'pretence'. The consequence of them is trivial: the textual critic is concerned only with minutiae, not with the spirit or meaning of the work at all. The last line regards the likes of Bentley and Theobald as worthy of nothing better than a scatological dismissal.

Pope's point of view in *An Essay on Criticism* was rather different. By the side of what he says there, modern critics do indeed seem to be little more than meddlers. Modern critics, concerned for the establishment of correct texts, for precision, and for attention to particular words are, Pope believes, turning their backs on the traditional qualities of taste and culture which discriminating readers of literature have always possessed. *An Essay on Criticism* is both a conservative and an aggressive poem. Its thesis is that literature proceeds by rules, rules which were evolved in classical times. A judicious study of the ancients gives a critic all the skills he needs, and classical literature is sacred and established:

> Still green with Bays each ancient Altar stands,
> Above the reach of sacriligious Hands
>
> (181-2)

Much of what Pope has to say about the critic's art is neatly epigrammatic (*An Essay on Criticism* is probably Pope's most quoted poem).

> A perfect judge will read each Work of Wit
> With that same spirit that its author writ
>
> (233-4)

or:

> True Wit is Nature to advantage drest,
> What oft was Thought, but ne'er so well Exprest
> Something whose Truth convinc'd at Sight we find,
> That gives us back the image of our Mind.
>
> (297-300)

Despite the nimbleness and elegance of the verse, we might feel that Pope's assumptions about criticism are flimsy, or at least too glib. He shows little tendency to define or examine his terms, seeming to assume that such ideas as 'wit', 'nature', 'spirit', or 'truth' are self-explanatory, just as works of classical literature are self-evidently valuable.

It is against such traditional and mandarin views that the modern critics were working, and Pope's *Essay on Criticism* is a valuable document in the debate between the 'ancients' and the 'moderns' which had been going on since the late seventeenth century. It was an important debate, closely linked to wider intellectual developments of the day.[6] The 'ancients' believed not only in the supremacy of classical culture, they believed that classical culture existed to edify and inspire. They also believed that it could best be appreciated by those who possessed 'spirit, taste and sense', in short, polished amateurs whose insight was as much as anything a function of manners and breeding. The 'moderns' took a more scientific line altogether, believing that truth about the ancient world was discernible only by close study of literary manuscripts and by examination of archaeological remains, and so forth. It is easy to see that Pope was on the losing side here, though he did not fight alone. One of the most combative spirits in the ancients versus the moderns debate had been Sir William Temple, Swift's early patron. Swift remained pervasively convinced of the strength of the ancients' case, which influenced his own work considerably, from *The Battle of the Books* in 1704 to the *Laputan* section of *Gulliver's Travels* over twenty years later. Swift's input into the collectively devised Martinus Scriblerus is thus clear enough.

It must have been particularly galling for Pope to discover that, judged by 'modern' standards, Lewis Theobald was a better Shakespearean scholar that he was. Pope had been worsted by the very kind of figure which the Scriblerus club had been set up to ridicule. He gained his revenge by pulling poetic rather than scholarly rank over him, but the battle needed to be fought on, and *The New Dunciad* became the place to do it. The rather more wide-ranging nature of this poem and its less surrealistic atmosphere have often caused critics to see it as imposing an unfortunate disunity on *The Dunciad* as a whole. On the purely textual level this is, of course, true. *The Dunciad* can never be accurately seen as one poem, it is the product of too many diverse components. What Book IV does do, though, is to extend *The Dunciad*'s authority as a contribution to the ancients versus moderns debate.

Perhaps the most fundamental revelation of Book IV's satirical axis is to be found in Pope's own note to line 501:

> '. . . the whole Course of Modern Education . . . confines Youth to the study of Words only in Schools, subjects them to the authority of Systems in the Universities and deludes them with the names of Party-distinctions in the world. All equally concurring to narrow the Understanding, and establish Slavery and Error in Literature, Philosophy and Politics.[7]

The New Dunciad is much concerned with the study of words. Indeed Pope's most fundamental premise in the sections dealing with education, is the idea that the word has been corrupted. It is also the 'uncreating word' of Chaos (line 653) which leads to the final dissolution of all civilization at the end of the poem.

The textual critics clearly contribute to this dissolution, Their effect on the authors ('wits') whom they study is violent and brutal:

> When Dulness smiling – 'Thus revive the Wits!
> But murder first, and mince them all to bits . . .
>
> Let standard-Authors, thus, like trophies born,
> Appear more glorious as more hack'd and torn,
> And you, my Critics! in the chequer'd shade,
> Admire new light thro' holes yourselves have made.
> (119-120; 123-126)

The two individual characters whom Pope satirizes at some length, Dr Busby and Richard Bentley, are both seen as arch-propagators of academic mincing and tearing. Dr Richard Busby was Headmaster of Westminster School which he ruled with the rod. On the face of it his is an unexpected presence in *The Dunciad,* being himself well outside Pope's own orbit. He is seen very much as Dulness's representative in schools, debarring pupils from genuine enlightenment by heavy pedantry:

We ply the Memory, we load the brain,
Bind rebel Wit and double chain on chain,
Confine the thought, to exercise the breath;
And keep them in the pale Words till death.
What'er the talents, or how'er design'd,
We hang one jingling padlock on the mind.
(157-162)

Here, instead of words being a means to knowledge, they are built into a barrier against it, from which Busby's pupils are unable to escape. The idea of Dulness binding, confining and imprisoning has been presented earlier:

Beneath her foot-stool Science groans in Chains,
And Wit dreads Exile, Penalties and Pains.
There foam'd rebellious Logic, gagg'd and bound,
There, stript, fair Rhet'ric languish'd on the ground
(21-24)

Richard Bentley, Master of Trinity College, Cambridge, was probably the foremost classical scholar of the age. He became very much a bête noire for the 'ancients' after he had mangled the text of Milton's *Paradise Lost* which he believed owing to Milton's blindness to have been inaccurately transcribed.[8] He easily made himself a hostage to his opponents on this particular issue, though he was in other respects a powerful figure in the academic establishment. He, too, is a corrupter of words:

Turn what they will to Verse, their toil is vain,
Critics like me shall make it Prose again
(213-214)

Bentley's textual attentions are seen as superficial, trivial, and irrelevant:

'Tis true on Words is still our whole debate,
Disputes of ME or TE, of AUT or AT,
To sound or sink in CANO, O or A

Or give up Cicero to C or K
(219-222)

Just as the scholars fragment literature to a series of meaningless words and disjointed letters which cease therefore to signify, so the archaeologists, numismatists and naturalists deal in incongruous fragments from the physical world. Pope presents two fictional collectors, Annius and Mummius.

Annius whose major interest is coins, Pope cannot take at all seriously. Annius's collection represents little more than the fraudulent relics of a medieval pardoner:

But Annius, crafty Seer, with ebon wand,
And well-dissembl'd em'rald on his hand,
False as his Gems, and canker'd as his Coins,
Came, cramm'd with capon, from where Pollio dines.
(347-350)

He asks Dulness for power to continue with his 'deceit': the fact that his coins are anything other than forgery, Pope is not prepared to countenance. Likewise Mummius (the pun in the name is a guideline) is proud of even more exotic and rather grosser 'finds':

Mummius o'erheard him; Mummius, Fool-renown'd,
Who like his Cheops stinks above the ground,
Fierce as a startled Adder, swell'd and said,
Rattling an ancient Sistrum at his head . . .
(371-374)

Pope is keen to exploit the quarrelsome nature of these collectors, too. Annius and Mummius are soon at loggerheads with the same inspired triviality that characterizes Bentley's textual criticism.

Naturalists fare no better. They, too, are seen as grotesque in their obsession with unimportant, indeed unbecoming objects:

Each with some wond'rous gift approach'd the Pow'r,
A Nest, a Toad, a Fungus or a Flow'r.
(399-400)

Pope was interested in the incongruity of things in *The Rape of the Lock.* In that poem the way in which characters attached immoderate importance to particular objects, was one of his chief sources of social and cultural comment. In that poem there is a tendency always for routine objects to be invested with almost religious significance, and to be registered as precious or attractive. In *The Dunciad* the method is the same, but the transitions which the objects experience are different. Where in *The Rape of the Lock* the trivial was made significant, in *The Dunciad* the potentially significant is trivialized in order to present a view of culture and learning which has become fatally fragmented and concerned with mere shards rather than with real objects. What started with words has moved to things. The whole superficiality of learning and apprehension is summed up in Pope's treatment of the young man undertaking his grand tour. Pope offers a criticism of tourists which has become with time commonplace enough: that they like to visit places simply for the joy of having been there, rather than because they are particularly well-equipped to get anything out of what they see.

Pope's 'young Aeneas' makes a breezy whistle-stop tour of Europe.

Intrepid then, o'er seas and lands he flew,
Europe he saw, and Europe saw him too . . .
(293-4)

Not only are Europe's cultural monuments cheapened by the young man's indiscriminating avidity before them ('The Stews and Palace equally explor'd/Intrig'd with glory, and with spirit whor'd' (315-316), some are degraded by time anyway. For example in Venice the once great city is now merely effete and vicious:

Where, eas'd of Fleets, the Adriatic main,
Wafts the smooth Eunuch and enamour'd swain.

Led by my hand he saunter'd Europe round,
And gather'd every Vice on Christian ground
(309-312)

Pope's presentation of contemporary fashions such as the Grand Tour or the Italian Opera ('a Harlot form' (45), both female and effiminate) underline the deeply conservative critique of intellectual developments which the poem provides. The court of Dulness is ultimately transformed into a kind of university graduation ceremony:

The Queen confers her Titles and Degrees.
Her children first of more distinguish'd sort,
Who study Shakespeare at the Inns of Court,
Impale a Glow-worm or vertu profess,
Shine in the dignity of F.R.S.
(566-70)

The Royal Society, with which this passage climaxes, was one of the most substantial and enduring monuments to the intellectual expansion of late seventeenth century England. Along with such institutions as the Bank of England or the Greenwich Royal Observatory, it was formed in a spirit of hope and patriotism. It was a sign to Europe of England's intellectual vitality. Many of the leading scientists and thinkers of the day were Fellows of the Royal Society but Pope and Swift both found the institution impossible to take seriously. It was to them simply a place where trivial experiments were performed, and traditional academic pursuits devalued. Swift was to provide a graphic example in *Gulliver's Travels* of the apparent idiocy of the institution when he showed his Laputans busily working on a scheme to extract sunbeams from cucumbers.[9] Effective though this image is as a piece of satire, it cannot ultimately mask the fact that Pope, Swift and their friends, were, intellectually on the losing side, as in his own way, Lewis Theobald had shown. Whilst it is quite easy to sympathize with the growing political revulsion which Pope felt from the materialistic and corrupt practices of Sir Robert Walpole's Whigs, his steadfast adherence to the intellectual practices of the 'ancients' manifests a blindness, and renders the satire of *The New Dunciad* uncomfortably tendentious and uncompromising, witty and agile though it undoubtedly is.

There are developments in the presentation of Dulness itself in the 1742 *Dunciad.* In the earlier text the effects of Dulness were often perceived at work within individuals. There was a tendency for Pope to work through vignettes. *The New Dunciad* makes the force of Dulness larger and more difficult to resist. As a 'Force inertly strong' (7), it becomes cosmic and we can feel the effects of its force throughout the book. Essentially these effects are soporific. There is an emphasis on the power of sleep, just as there was at the end of the Dunces' games in Book II. In the earlier book the sleep came as a consequence of a hard and energetic day's work. At the end of Book IV it is a much more omnipresent, not to say involuntary business. Even Bentley, for all his malign influence on the world of learning 'now sleeps in Port' (202), and the grand tourist encounters:

> . . . happy Convents, bosom'd deep in vines,
> Where slumber Abbots, purple as their wines.
> (301-2)

The *vis inertiae* of Dulness has overtaken the Church as well as the arts and academe, so that it is not surprising that as a result of Queen Dulness's final exhortations to her subjects '. . . All Nature nods' (605). From church this contagious somnolence spreads to state:

> Wide and more wide, it spread o'er all the realm;
> Ev'n Palinurus nodded at the Helm:
> The Vapour mild o'er each Committee crept;
> Unfinish'd Treaties in each Office slept;
> And Chiefless Armies doz'd out the Campaign;
> And Navies yawn'd for Orders on the Main.
> (613-8)

Dulness's desire 'TO MAKE ONE MIGHTY DUNCIAD OF THE LAND!' (604) has been well fulfilled. From a purely technical point of view Pope has led up to the apocalyptic final section of the poem in a much steadier and more logical way than he did in the original version. As we have noted already Pope intensifies the vision of final dissolution in the 1742 text, and he delivers the lines himself, rather than through a fictional mouthpiece. Spence reported that Pope could not read these lines without a quiver in the voice, and they have often been quoted as, effectively, Pope's last words. He is remarkably comprehensive in his treatment of those areas of thought which have become buried by the universal darkness:

> Philosophy, that lean'd on Heav'n before,
> Shrinks to her second cause, and is no more.
> Physic of Metaphysic begs defence,
> And Metaphysic calls for aid on Sense!
> See Mystery to Mathematics fly!
> In vain! they gaze, turn giddy, rave and die.
> Religion blushing veils her sacred fires,
> And unawares Morality expires.
>
> (634-650)

The totality of Pope's closing visions has often been commented upon, though as we have seen it is a vision which Pope had first compassed fifteen years previously. Equally we have to bear in mind that *The Dunciad* had yet to undergo another major modification. The poem to which the final lines of the new Book IV were to be a conclusion was poised for one final change.

Pope's best-known and most direct satirical reference to Colley Cibber[10] was in *An Epistle to Dr Arbuthnot*. ('And hath not Colly still his Lord and Whore?' (97), referring to Cibber's sycophancy and easy sexual habits.) Another fleeting reference to him in the same poem had been removed by Pope in the second edition. The earlier *Dunciads* had also contained fleeting references in the footnotes as well as the text, though there had been little by way of open hostility, and the most recent reference which Pope had made to Cibber (in *The New Dunciad*) had not mentioned him by name at all. ('Soft on her [ie. Dulnes'] lap her Laureat son reclines' (20)). In comparison with the treatment which some of Pope's contemporaries received from him, this all seems rather mild. Also, like Addison, Cibber was someone with whom Pope had been professionally associated and whose stage works he had been known to praise, so there was a certain ambiguity in their relationship which had kept satirical thrusts restrained.

It would be misleading, though, to press comparisons with Addison any further. It is difficult to think of two men more opposite than Addison and Cibber. Where the former was grave, censorious and superior, Cibber was licentious, self-advertising, lightweight, and perfectly happy to describe himself as a 'comedian'. He had spent most of his working life in the theatre, first as a comic actor (being unsuited in voice or stature for tragedy), later as a manager and impressario. He was very much a low-brow popular commercial figure, as his autobiography, *An Apology for the Life of Colley Cibber*, published in 1740, had made clear. He has not received a good press from modern scholars. The Editor of the Twickenham edition of *The Dunciad* calls him '. . . a kind of popular buffoon.'[11] Maynard Mack in his biography of Pope describes him as '. . . considerably an ass and perpetually in the public eye.'[12]

What rendered Cibber particularly harmful was that, at some surprise to himself, he had been made Poet Laureate in 1730, in succession to Laurence Eusden. His friends in high places had clearly proved useful and had brought about yet another perfect Duncely succession. He was of no stature as a poet and the victory of sycophancy over talent hardly pleased Pope. Additionally there had been some difficulty between the two men over twenty years earlier. The mixture of fact and fantasy surrounding this particular matter is hard to separate, but it is certainly true that in 1717 Cibber had acted in a farce jointly composed by Pope, Arbuthnot and Gay, called *Three Hours After Marriage.* The play had been a dismal failure.[13] Shortly afterwards Cibber played the part of Bays in Buckingham's *The Rehearsal,* which afforded him the opportunity of directing a few ad-libbed comments against Pope and his friends. At this point the pamphlet war takes over the story,[14] and reports are made of a furious Pope or Gay, storming backstage after the performance and threatening violence. These kind of scenes, of course, were the stock in trade of Grub Street lampoonery, and, it might be thought, best forgotten. Unfortunately, Pope and Cibber were preparing to square up to each other. It is possible that Pope had been contemplating replacing Theobald with Cibber as the hero of *The Dunciad* for some time, and almost certain that Cibber suspected it. Whatever the truth of the matter may have been, Cibber brought things to a head by publishing a pamphlet in July, 1742, four months after *The New Dunciad* had appeared, entitled *A Letter from Mr Cibber to Mr Pope, Inquiring into the Motives that Might Induce Him in His Satyrical Works to be so Frequently Fond of Mr Cibber's Name.*[15] A study of the evidence suggests that Pope, in fact, had not been unduly keen to mention Cibber's name (after all, his most recent reference to Cibber had been oblique), but the pamphlet cares little for truth or caution. It is, from the hand of a reputedly easy-going man, a surprisingly immoderate production. Apart from providing a perhaps over-graphic account of the *Three Hours After Marriage* fiasco, it tells a story of how Cibber persuaded Pope to visit a brothel, and how he had to extricate the poet '. . . like a terrible Tom Tit, pertly perching upon the Mount of Love . . .' from the clasps of a large prostitute. We have no means of establishing the truth of this narrative, other then by noting that we are in a literary world in which respect for accuracy of detail is not inherently strong. It is not surprising that Pope felt moved to reply.

Cibber is really a much more natural and logical hero for *The Dunciad* than Theobald. Theobald had done Pope little personal wrong, enjoyed a quite prestigious literary position anyway, and had published an edition of Shakespeare in 1734 which proved him a better scholar than Pope. Cibber was the living proof of literary mediocrity, and of the cultural impoverishment of Walpolean England, where influence and connections were the chief components of literary eminence, and where a figure essentially from the world of 'pop' culture occupied the titular position of the nation's chief poet. He could thence be turned into the King of the Dunces very easily, just as the names Theobald (pronounced 'Tibbalds') and Cibber are easily interchangeable.

The version of *The Dunciad* which appeared in 1743 was, in terms of the purely poetic text, the largest of the four. It has thus come to be for most readers and critics of Pope, the definitive version. The 1728 text receives its most obvious modification and extension in Book One. Books Two and Three are revised in places, mainly on the level of personalia, but with little effect on their tone. Book Two is slightly lengthened, Book Three shortened, especially as its original prophecy of universal darkness is now re-worked as the climax to the *New Dunciad* of Book Four. It is Book One which most clearly feels the presence of Colley Cibber. Indeed it feels the presence of the new hero more abundantly than it felt the presence of Theobald who was more symbolic or representative of Duncehood whereas Cibber's character and antics were much more widely known, and thus provided much more precise material for the poem.

By happy coincidence Cibber's father, an artist and sculptor, was the creator of two statues which adorned the gates of the Bethlehem (Bedlam) hospital for lunatics in London. Consequently Pope is able to intensify the links between poetry and madness ('All Bedlam or Parnassus is let out' (4)) which he had made in *An Epistle to Dr Arbuthnot,* by locating 'The Cave of Poverty and Poetry' within the walls of the hospital. Indeed, with a powerfully surreal touch Pope images this obscure lunatic's cell as the origin of all the town's Dulness:

> Hence Bards, like Proteus long in vain ty'd down,
> Escape in Monsters, and amaze the town.
> Hence Miscellanies spring, the weekly boast
> Of Curl's chaste press, and Lintot's rubric post:
> Hence hymning Tyburn's elegiac lines,
> Hence Journals, Medleys, Merc'ries, Magazines:
> Sepulchral Lyes, our holy walls to grace,
> And New-year Odes, and all the Grub-street race.
> (37-44)

Cibber is introduced, not by his own name, but by the name of Bays. This was the name of the role he played in the production of *The Rehearsal* which had been critical of Pope in 1717. Also, of course, the Bays is the traditional 'laureate' symbol, so Pope is able to exploit the incongruity of exalting to the most prominent poetical position a popular comedian. Pope emphasizes the extrovert and skittish nature of Cibber. Where Theobald had been associated with 'learned lumber' and groaning shelves, Cibber is 'the lively Dunce', trivial and lightweight.

> Bays, form'd by nature Stage and Town to bless,
> And act, and be, a Coxcomb with success.

Dulness with transport eyes the lively Dunce,
Remembering she herself was Pertness once.
(109-12)

Could the reference to 'Pertness' possibly be a return gibe for what Cibber had said about Pope 'pertly perching' in a brothel? Most certainly Pope's own charges against Cibber are more detailed than they were against Theobald:

Swearing and supperless the hero sate,
Blasphem'd his Gods, the Dice, and damn'd his Fate.
Then gnaw'd his pen, then dash'd it on the ground,
Sinking from thought to thought, a vast profound!
Plung'd for his sense, but found no bottom there,
Yet wrote and flounder'd on, in mere despair.
(115-120)

The passage obviously reiterates Pope's associations of Dulness with weight and with sinking, but there is a new dimension, too. There is something pitifully child-like about the laureate chewing his pen, and casting it petulantly away when inspiration won't come. Likewise, the poet's appeal to the gods and to fate is caused by no more than his having lost money at games of dice.

What follows, the description of 'future Ode and abdicated Play' (122) has been already discussed. Pope emphasizes the sheer derivativeness of what Cibber composes:

Next, o'er his Books his eyes began to roll,
In pleasing memory of all he stole,
How here he sipp'd, how there he plunder'd snug
And suck'd all o'er, like an industrious Bug.
(127-130)

Cibber's capacity for self-advertisement is underlined by the modifications which Pope makes to the closing sections of the Book. The 1728-9 *Dunciad* satisfied itself with a brief:

'God save King Tibbald!' Grubstreet alleys roar.
(256)

Whereas rather more ado is made with Cibber:

> . . . Then swells the Chapel-royal throat:
> 'God save king Cibber!' mounts in ev'ry note.
> Familiar White's, 'God save king Colley!' cries;
> 'God save king Colley!' Drury-lane replies:
> To Needham's quick the voice triumphant rode,
> But pious Needham dropt the name of God;
> Back to the Devil the last echoes roll,
> And 'Coll!' each Butcher roars at Hockley-hole.
> (319-326)

Thus Cibber's fame: trumpeted about the town from the court, by way of Drury Lane (which bore certain 'red light' connotations in the eighteenth century) to the bear-pit at Hockley Hole. Pope enjoys here, as always, the exploitation of topographical detail for satiric effect. He is sensitive to both the evocations and the incongruities of place names. He is sensitive, too, to the cultural phenomenon which Colley Cibber was: friend of ministers, protégé of the King, but essentially a commonplace popular entertainer of no particular creative talent at all. He was a heaven-sent hero for Pope's last major poetic undertaking, representing economically within himself all those cultural ills which had been *The Dunciad's* original prompting.

Pope did no more major work after his final modifications of *The Dunciad.* His health was beginning to deteriorate, and as we have already seen, the shrillness of voice which characterized the 1739 Satires had been keen to declare that there was little point in continuing to write satire when vice stalked the world unabated. It is noteworthy that Pope's final effort was backward-looking, not simply to the poem which he had originally published fifteen years previously, but to the Scriblerian origins of it. The final *Dunciad* is also firmly placed in the tissue of personal animosities which had characterized so much of Pope's public and professional life. Pope's tendency to refine and tinker are well-known, but his sustained interest in his *Dunciad* was perhaps an indication that the poet knew where his most substantial literary achievement lay.

Chapter Six: Making a Mighty Dunciad

1. Pope's *Argument* of Book III (1729). Twickenham V line 27 p56.
2. Ibid line 29.
3. See Howard Erskine-Hill *Pope: The Dunciad* (1972) p15.
4. Twickenham V, Introduction p xxxiii.
5. See above Chapter 3 Note 2.
6. The issue is discussed in Mack *Life* pp479-488; also by Brean S. Hammond in *Pope (Harvester New Readings)* 1986 pp100-107.
7. Twickenham V p391.
8. Bentley's edition of *Paradise Lost* is discussed by Mack *Life* pp624-626.
9. *Gulliver's Travels* Part III *A Voyage to Laputa* . . .
10. Cibber's autobiography *An Apology for the Life of Colley Cibber* is mentioned below. For a brief biography see Kenneth Hopkins *The Poets Laureate* (1973) Chap 7.
11. Twickenham V, Introduction p xxxv.
12. Mack *Life* p775.
13. See Hopkins pp71-2.
14. The quite considerable amount of pamphlet material provoked by *Three Hours After Marriage* is assembled by J.V. Guerinot in *Pamphlet Attacks on Alexander Pope* pp47-51; 59-70, 73.
15. See Guerinot pp288-294.

BIBLIOGRAPHY

(a) Editions

As previously stated, all quotations in this book have been taken from the one volume Twickenham text, edited by John Butt (1963) which is an abridgement of seven original volumes. All of these volumes contain copious explanatory notes, reproductions of Pope's own comments about his poems, and a wealth of information about the genesis and backgrounds of the works concerned. Specifically relevant to the poems discussed here are: Volume II, *The Rape of the Lock* (1940); Volume III (part ii), *Epistles to Several Persons (Moral Essays)* (1951); Volume IV, *Imitations of Horace, An Epistle to Dr Arbuthnot and the Epilogue to the Satires* (1939); Volume V, *The Dunciad* (1943). The standard edition of Pope's Correspondence is by George Sherburn, five volumes (1956). Unfortunately there is no substantial or easily available selection from this. The *Prose Works* are collected in two volumes. Volume I edited by Norman Ault (1936) and Volume II by Rosemary Cowler (1986), though all the prose works referred to in the present book can be found in Paul Hammond (Ed) *Selected Prose of Alexander Pope* (1987), with the exception of *The Memoirs of Martinus Scriblerus* which is edited by Charles Kerby-Miller (1950). J.V. Guerinot's *Pamphlet Attacks on Alexander Pope* (1969) is a descriptive catalogue rather than a discursive account, but its documentation is invaluable, and it contains a most useful introduction.

(b) Biography

George Sherburn's *The Early Career of Alexander Pope* (1934), although covering Pope's life only up to the mid-1720s remains indispensable and has not been entirely superseded by the encyclopaedic though highly readable Maynard Mack: *Alexander Pope: A Life* (1985). A recent briefer yet still comprehensive treatment can be found in Felicity Rosslyn's *Alexander Pope: A Literary Life* (1990). Specific aspects of Pope's biography are addressed in Dustin Griffin: *Alexander Pope, the Poet in the Poems* (1978); Valerie Rumbold: *Women's Place in Pope's World* (1989), and James A. Winn: *A Window on the Bosom: The Letters of Alexander Pope* (1977). Pope's medical history is considered by Marjorie Nicholson and G.S. Rousseau: *This Long Disease, My Life: Pope and the Sciences* (1968).

(c) General Works

There are a number of one-volume treatments of Pope's life and work in more or less general terms. Venerable and durable is *Pope: The Poetry of Allusion,* by Reuben A. Brower (1959). Two other valuable general discussions are Pat Rogers: *An Introduction to Pope* (1975) and Brean S. Hammond *Pope (Harvester New Readings)* (1986). Peter Dixon's *The World of Pope's Satires* (1968) is particularly useful on the *Moral Essays* and the *Imitations of Horace.* Two books which deal with Pope's critical reputation amongst contemporaries and in later times are John Barnard (Ed): *Pope: The Critical Heritage* (1973) and James Reeves: *The Reputation and Writings of Alexander Pope* (1976), though the latter is largely vitiated by the degree of its hostility to its subject. A.D. Nuttall's *Pope's Essay on Man* (1984), whilst concerning itself principally with matters of only oblique relevance to the present survey contains an important and substantial introductory essay on Pope in general, and a most comprehensive bibliography.

(d) Works dealing with specific poems

There is a short though comprehensive survey of *The Rape of the Lock* by J.S. Cunningham published as a small volume in 1961. John Dixon Hunt (Ed) *The Rape of the Lock: A Casebook* (1968) assembles both modern and older criticism, and also contains Pope's own *Receit to make an Epic Poem* and *A Key to the Lock.* A useful selection of sources and analogues is contained in William Kinsley (Ed) *The Rape of the Lock: Contexts* (1979). Different perspectives on the poem are provided by Robert Halsband: *The Rape of the Lock and its Illustrators 1714-1896* (1980). The foundation of modern scholarship on *The Dunciad* is Aubrey Williams' *Pope's Dunciad: A Study of its Meaning* (1955). Howard Erskine-Hill's *Pope: The Dunciad* (1972) is an important treatment, as is Emrys Jones's essay *Pope and Dulness*, which is contained in *Proceedings of the British Academy* (1968). A recent and challenging book-length reading of the poem is Douglas Brooks Davies: *Pope's Dunciad and The Queen of Night* (1985). The origin and development of the *Moral Essays* are discussed by Miriam Leranbaum in *Alexander Pope's 'Opus Magnum'* (1977). Earl R. Wasserman deals in depth with the relevant poem in *Pope's Epistle to Bathurst* (1960), and Morris Brownell in *Pope and the Arts of Augustan England* (1978) has much to say about gardening and architecture as they figure in the *Epistle to Burlington.* For Pope's treatment of women in the *Epistle to a Lady,* see Felicity Nussbaum: *The Brink of All we Hate: English Satires on Women, 1660-1750* (1984). For Pope as an imitator of Horace Frank Stack's *Pope and Horace* (1985) is immensely informative, as is, in a completely different way Maynard Mack's *The Garden and the City: Politics and Retirement in the Later Poetry of Pope* (1969).

(e) Background

Two books which deal with eighteenth-century satire in general are Ian Jack's perennial *Augustan Satire* (1952) and David Nokes' *Raillery and Rage: A Study of Eighteenth Century Satire* (1987). Pat Rogers surveys the literary underworld in

Grub Street: Studies in a Subculture (1972), revised as *Hacks and Dunces: Pope, Swift and Grub Street* (1975). Kenneth Hopkins: *The Poets Laureate* (1954, revised 1973) says much about the literary mediocrities of the period, whilst Howard Erskine-Hill: *The Social Milieu of Alexander Pope* (1975) looks at some important and influential contemporaries. Peter Dixon (Ed) *Alexander Pope: Writers and their Background* (1972) contains some useful essays on the social, aesthetic and financial background to Pope's poems. Two useful books by J.H. Plumb sketch in the history of the period: *England in the Eighteenth Century* (1950) and *The First Four Georges* (1956).

INDEX